Dec 6, 1974

For Mel + Sylvia,
The very best of people.
Ralph

260 But he [Niebuhr] never succeeded in making clear precisely how it is that the agape of Christ which is "beyond history" affords a way of concretely taking into account of all the quandaries which men face in ~~dealing~~ attempting to build systems of reciprocity that are just and
261 humane . . . which is to say that there is no systematic specification of how it is, in the perspective of Christian faith, that God actually renews and transforms human life.

THE MINNESOTA

LIBRARY

ON AMERICAN WRITERS

LEONARD UNGER

AND GEORGE T. WRIGHT,

EDITORS

THE SEVEN *essays which appear in this book were first published separately in the series of University of Minnesota Pamphlets on American Writers and, together with the other pamphlets in the series, are intended as introductions to authors who have helped to shape American culture over the years of our colonial and national existence. The editors of the pamphlet series have been Richard Foster, William Van O'Connor, Allen Tate, Leonard Unger, Robert Penn Warren, and George T. Wright. Many pamphlets, in addition to the seven represented here, are available from the University of Minnesota Press.*

MAKERS OF AMERICAN THOUGHT

An Introduction to Seven American Writers

edited by Ralph Ross

UNIVERSITY OF MINNESOTA PRESS
MINNEAPOLIS

Printed in the United States of America
at North Central Publishing Company, St. Paul.
Published in the United Kingdom and India by the Oxford
University Press, London and Delhi.

Library of Congress Catalog Card Number: 74-78993

ISBN 0-8166-0712-5

The verses from Henry Adams's "Prayer to the Virgin of Chartres" are quoted from *Letters to a Niece and Prayer to the Virgin of Chartres* by permission of the publisher, Houghton Mifflin Company.

The author acknowledges permission to reprint passages from the following works by H. L. Mencken: *Notes on Democracy*, copyright 1926 by Alfred A. Knopf, Inc.; *Happy Days*, copyright 1940 by Alfred A. Knopf, Inc.; *Newspaper Days*, copyright 1941 by Alfred A. Knopf, Inc.; *A Vintage Mencken*, © copyright 1955 by Alfred A. Knopf; *Minority Report*, copyright 1956 by Alfred A. Knopf, Inc.; *Prejudices: A Selection*, © copyright 1958 by Alfred A. Knopf, Inc.; *Letters of H. L. Mencken*, © copyright 1961 by Alfred A. Knopf; *H. L. Mencken on Music*, © copyright 1961 by Alfred A. Knopf. He also wishes to acknowledge permission to use excerpts from William Manchester's biography, *Disturber of the Peace*, copyright 1950 by the author, on which he has also leaned for names and chronological details.

Excerpts from the letters and manuscripts of Randolph Bourne are quoted with the permission of Columbia University Libraries, which owns the materials.

In the chapter on Niebuhr the lines from Yeats's "The Second Coming," which appears in *The Collected Poems of W. B. Yeats*, are quoted with the permission of Mrs. W. B. Yeats, Messrs. Macmillan and Company Limited of London and Basingstoke, The Macmillan Company of Canada, and The Macmillan Company of New York.

CONTENTS

MAKERS OF

AMERICAN THOUGHT

RALPH ROSS

INTRODUCTION

REVOLUTIONS may occur in idea as well as action. If we consider the Copernican Revolution and the French Revolution, it is easy to tell which was bloodier but hard to tell which was more revolutionary, which brought the greater change in idea, attitude, and conduct. Theory may precede practice in revolutions of action, but that theory is not always full-blown, as Marxism was before the Bolshevik Revolution: sometimes it is fragmented, as it was in the American Civil War, and its coherence and development may depend on whether the revolution was successful. Further, the theory that precedes practice may itself be the result of a still earlier practice and is often in opposition to it.

America has been fortunate up till now and may continue to be fortunate: American revolutions tend to return to the ideals of the first American Revolution or to the practice of those who made the Republic. The change our revolutions bring about is not based on a new principle but is a new application of the principles of 1776 and 1789, and occasionally of their English precursor in 1688. Sometimes the nation has grown away from ideals which need restatement. Sometimes the ideals were never applied ("All men are created equal" was affirmed by slaveholders, for example) and we move an inch or more toward their realization. At other times a living practice was simply taken for granted until it was at last formulated and became a revolutionary principle.

The United States is, of course, a very young nation, although it has a claim to having the oldest democratic government on earth. The Bicentennial of the United States is 1976, counting from its birth on July 4, 1776, with the Declaration of Independence. The essential author of that extraordinary document, Thomas Jefferson, was then not quite thirty-three years of age. When he died, Emerson was already twenty-three, and when Emerson died Henry Adams was forty-four and William James forty. At the time of James's death, an important contemporary of ours, Reinhold Niebuhr, was eighteen.

Three lifetimes, at the standard threescore and ten years, exceed the life of the nation from the Declaration to its Bicentennial, and four overlapping lifetimes, four awarenesses, run from colonial America to the 1970s. In that time a fledgling nation became a giant, an agrarian society became urban, and "the last great hope of earth" turned to empire and self-doubt. The men whose lives and achievements are described in this book were witnesses to our changes and growing pains. The oldest were young men during the Civil War; the others include our contemporaries. Those men were not actors but thinkers and critics, except that they were concerned and public thinkers, not solitary spirits like Emily Dickinson. As public figures, they struggled to capture the minds of men. Although their own time weighed on them and concentrated their energies, they knew the American past very well and drew on it for contrast, for strength, and for continuity. America's revolutions were the background of their interests, not just 1776 but its successors as well, and they used them in different ways to bring the nation to maturity.

Jefferson's Revolution of 1800 had been in principle a return to the Founding Fathers. The Federalist monopoly of power was ended by the election of 1800, yet Jefferson did not intend to destroy the Federalists and replace them by his Democratic-Republicans. He sought conciliation and wholeness, declaring that we are all Federalists and all Republicans. But we were still ruled by gentlemen and scholars, and our presidents were both, at least through the administration of John Quincy Adams. The Jacksonian Revolution, which did end that domination, reminded us that all men (if they were not black) were created equal and should have equal chances at the instruments of power.

The Civil War again unified a country that had become divided (although Reconstruction undid some of that unity) and proclaimed that "all men" meant *all* men. The result was a still greater move to equality that brought both rejoicing and denunciation. There was buoyancy, energy, and optimism in some Americans, and pessimism in others. The superiority of America to "decadent Europe" with her feudal, divisive background was perfectly clear to Jefferson and, for all his qualifications, it was also clear to Tocqueville. But the new America looked increasingly callow to others who vastly preferred the maturity, culture, and ancient traditions of Europe to the awkwardness of the adolescent Republic. Equality seemed a lack of standards to them, the majority meant the unlettered and unwashed, and democratic statesmanship appeared to be, and often was, political corruption. Who could forget the carpetbaggers in the aftermath of the Civil War, and the Tweed Ring, and the scandals in Washington? Mark Twain was attracted by the American West, but Whistler and Henry James went to England to live, as a later generation of American writers and painters went to Paris and then again to London. A return to Europe was a living option. Emerson had proclaimed the necessity of an American culture, but America seemed increasingly unfriendly to the artist, who felt himself the bearer of culture. Van Wyck Brooks chose grimly not to be an expatriate, but the allure of Europe made his soul ache.

The buoyant and energetic Americans were building for a future. Even if they were thinkers, not men of action, action was a vital part of their thought, and their rightful places are with the pioneers, explorers, and engineers who charted and tamed the wilderness. William James is the ideal type of intellectual pioneer, combative but loving, nervously delicate but daring, a young artist turned physician and then psychologist and philosopher. The pessimist looked back, not forward, and not back to ideals and principles to be actualized in the future, but back to a time of aristocrats, scholars, and gentlemen, perhaps above all to a time of settled faith. Henry Adams is the American type of the pessimist. Born into the great American family in which he was preceded by two presidents of the United States, initiated into politics but a writer and scholar by choice (at least he said so), historian of early America, biographer and novelist, he became most famous for his remarkable autobiography, *The Edu-*

cation of Henry Adams, and his penetration into the European faith of the late Middle Ages, *Mont-Saint-Michel and Chartres*.

William James and Henry Adams are perhaps more central to the directions of American thought after them than is usually observed. The similarity of their backgrounds obscures the enormous difference between them. Both were members of very talented families, both were Massachusetts men educated at Harvard (although James, who was born in the city of New York, was first educated in Europe, and later went back to Europe for further study), masters of prose, concerned to be scientific, with very much the same circle of old friends. Oliver Wendell Holmes, Jr., was a friend to both, but, typically, only to the young James was he "Wendy Boy."

The differences are guideposts in American thought. Even titles sometimes reflect them. James, for example, wrote "The Will to Believe," and Adams wrote *The Degradation of the Democratic Dogma*. Adams yearned for the unity and shared faith of the European thirteenth century, while James wanted a universe that was uncertain and unfinished to which, somehow, we could contribute. Adams felt helpless; James believed in the strenuous life. As he grew older, Adams, according to Holmes, "would spend his energy in pointing out that everything was dust and ashes." As James grew older, he happily denounced monism and a static universe, and proclaimed pluralism and a changing universe.

What Adams and James said explicitly about the future and the past, the nation and its destiny, and democracy (in James's case, for he said little) is not so important as the implications and images of their prose. There is some ambivalence about social and political belief in them, which is also a dichotomy of faith and reason. Often the faith was steadfast, though the reason wavered. Perhaps Holmes betrayed the same ambivalence best in his asides. One of them is very revealing: he had written the "clear and present danger" limitation on free speech, and then, in a letter to the famous English jurist Sir Frederick Pollock, he wrote: "It is one of the ironies that I, who probably take the extremist view in favor of free speech (in which, in the abstract, I have no very enthusiastic belief, though I hope I would die for it), that I should have been selected for blowing it up."

In James's pragmatism the very meaning of an idea consists in its particular consequences. The pragmatic question, which can be asked of any idea, is "What practical — or concrete — difference will it make if this is true?" The emphasis is on the future. The same emphasis is found in pragmatic writings on truth, which consists ultimately in the verification of an idea, and of good and evil, which are judged by the consequences of action. There is also a sense in which, for James, *we* make ideas true or false by submitting them to a process of verification. Throughout, we enter a transaction with the rest of nature, the fruits of which are in the future.

Adams, as I said, looked backwards for the ideal. When he surveyed the future he found it ever worse than the past, and he saw no possibility of man helping it. The second law of thermodynamics taught him there was a constant loss of energy in the physical world, that the universe was running down, and he decided that what was true of the physical world was true also of the moral world, of history, of the whole realm of human affairs. This doctrine he wrote in *A Letter to American Teachers of History*, later incorporated in *The Degradation of the Democratic Dogma*. Apparently he gave William James a copy of the former, and thus provoked a response, dated June 17, 1910.

James started his comment on the *Letter* by writing: "To tell the truth, it doesn't impress me at all, save by its wit and erudition; and I ask you whether an old man soon about to meet his Maker can hope to save himself from the consequences of his life by pointing to the wit and learning he has shown in treating a tragic subject." He went on to say that the second law was scientific orthodoxy at the moment, although it might be overthrown tomorrow, but that it is irrelevant to history (which we *make*) and to what we regard as precious. Things at the same energy level are nonetheless superior and inferior from the standpoint of man. As for human institutions, "their value has in strict theory nothing whatever to do with their energy-budget — being wholly a question of the form the energy flows through." Finally: "Though the *ultimate* state of the universe may be its vital and psychical extinction, there is nothing in physics to interfere with the hypothesis that the penultimate state might be the millennium — in other words a state in which a minimum of difference in energy-level might have its exchanges so skillfully *canalisés* that a maximum of happy and virtuous consciousness would be the only result. In short, the last expiring pulsation of the universe's life might be, 'I am so happy and perfect that I can stand it no longer.' " A marvelous echo and reversal of *Faust*.

This final confrontation between two aging thinkers who were almost polar opposites within the American context sounds again and again in their successors. One cannot place all those successors squarely with James or Adams, but one usually finds them very much more on one side than the other. Most of the crusading reformers are chiefly with James, repeating his anger at what he called "the bitch-goddess, Success." Most of the world-weary, the cynical, and the Europeanized are chiefly with Adams, although America has not bred many men of stature so truly disenchanted that they see no hope at all in the human condition. The later Eugene O'Neill sounds like such a man, and perhaps we are breeding more of them now. (Especially in the theater?)

John Dewey, of course, stood squarely with James in most things and wrote at length about matters James barely touched, art, morals, logic, education, society, and politics. He brought James's influence to new generations and was responsible for much thought consonant with his beliefs and much thought that deliberately turned against them. Reinhold Niebuhr and Randolph Bourne were attracted by Dewey and learned from him, Bourne being an active disciple for a time, and then criticizing him sharply. In Niebuhr's case, the move away from Dewey was impelled by a feeling for the darker and more tragic qualities of life, emphasizing original sin; in politics he emerged as a spokesman for democracy without illusions about human goodness, neither optimistic nor pessimistic, but struggling to reconcile personal interest with community welfare.

Randolph Bourne was another matter. A cripple, doomed to a short life, immensely talented, he did not attend college until he was twenty-three. There, in 1909, at the Columbia of Dewey, Charles Beard, Franz Boas, and James Harvey Robinson, he came to sudden intellectual life. In 1911 Bourne was first published, in the *Atlantic Monthly*, because of the good offices of the remarkable Frederick Woodbridge, a philosopher who had come to Columbia from his post at the University of Minnesota and was about to become a graduate dean. From then on, Bourne made a career as a writer and journalist, at first as an avowed disciple of Dewey, with James and Whitman as background, even concentrating for a time on Dewey's special interest, the theory and practice of education.

A period in Europe brought Bourne to great admiration for Germany, especially because of her planned cities, to an appreciation of the importance of non-English immigration to America, and to an acceptance of Horace Kallen's "cultural pluralism," resulting in annoyance with those who emphasized Anglo-Saxon tradition. These attitudes intensified his pacifism in World War I and he broke sharply with Dewey, a supporter of the war, criticizing pragmatism as a philosophy helpless to deal with the narrowed alternatives of crisis. This brought him no closer to Adams, especially the snobbish, anti-Semitic, Anglo-Saxon aspect of Adams, and for all his attack on pragmatism, it did not move him away from the spirit of James. Bourne opposed the idea that the war had been inevitable, insisting that it came because of the choices we made, and he remained a believer in "moral freedom" and "abounding vitality," terms with a Jamesian cast.

The war was a watershed, too, in the career of H. L. Mencken. In his case it threatened his livelihood, although he had some private income, because he was openly pro-German. For some years he lost all access to the publications that had supported him, and a new Mencken emerged, the scholar of *The American Language*. Yet he had another chance to be the old Mencken when the publisher Alfred Knopf, his steadfast friend, backed him in the publication of the *American Mercury* in 1924, a new and more Mencken-like version of the *Smart Set*, which he had edited with George Jean Nathan. Mencken had dedicated himself to an attack on American mediocrity, and that as he understood it included the Puritan tradition, the "booboisie," and finally democracy and religion. He felt strongly about cant, hypocrisy, and humbug, and made himself a scourge of the second-rate and pretentious. His prose and wit made him not only famous, but feared, a man no one wanted for an enemy. But there was a crackpot, village atheist side to him that was continuous with his cleansing of the American stables. Like Bourne, he turned against the Anglo-Saxon American. But he went much farther than

Bourne, and he extended his feeling to the English as well. In condemnation of both, he said: "The Anglo-Saxon of the great herd is, in many important respects, the least civilized of white men and the least capable of true civilization." Then he pushed his Anglophobia to denunciation of national traits. The Anglo-Saxon race, he insisted, is cowardly, and "a fair-minded examination of its history" would bear that out. "Both empires," Mencken added, meaning the English and American, "were built up primarily by swindling and butchering unarmed savages, and after that by robbing weak and friendless nations." And further, "The British won most of their vast dominions without having to stand up in a single battle against a civilized and formidable foe, and the Americans won their continent at the expense of a few dozen puerile skirmishes with savages." Imagine the "fair-minded examination" of history that found the British facing an uncivilized, weak foe at sea when they met the Armada, and on land at Agincourt and Waterloo, and the Americans facing savages (led by Wellington's brother-in-law) at New Orleans. As Benjamin De Casseres, a friend who admired Mencken greatly, said: "He has raised Prejudice to a metaphysic."

Mencken's scorn for the common man, his reverence for the great (he compared Bach to Genesis 1:1), and his fear of the leveling effect of democracy, would be like Adams's except that it lacked Adams's fastidiousness and reached out to Nietzsche's thunder, without Nietzsche's poetry. The enormous gusto in Mencken was somewhat like James's, but more strident, with the tone on occasion of Whitman. But although by no means a democrat, he was a dedicated libertarian who found even Holmes's judicial opinions repressive, defending the right to say or print almost anything, no matter how scurrilous.

Even those American thinkers whose concerns are essentially literary and rhetorical are likely to reveal the social or philosophical attitude of James or Adams in their choice of words. Especially when one chooses a category, a key term under which other terms are grouped, the word that stands for the category is important. Kenneth Burke is a kind of systematizer whose world is explained by categories, and he prefers *act* to all his other categories. *Act* has been a term favored by Americans, especially those in the pragmatic tradition. *Act*, *action*, and for Dewey *conduct*, too, vie with the psychologists' and social scientists' *behavior* for preeminence in describing and explaining human beings. Talcott Parsons, the most eminent of our contemporary sociologists, makes *act* and *actor* his basic categories.

It was not always thus. In the secular European tradition, man was a thinker rather than an actor. For Aristotle that was true of the highest type of man; for Descartes it was man's very essence. But America moved to *act* and *behavior*, and if there is a turning point, it is probably the thought of William James. Even *consequences*, so crucial to pragmatism, embraces and to some extent is made up of action.

In the Europe of the eighteenth and nineteenth centuries, *act*, like *feeling*, had a romantic flavor. It went beyond thought and sometimes replaced it. In the twentieth century *act* is sometimes used in Europe to mean thoughtless and without reasons of any kind, as in the *acte gratuit*, or gratuitous act, of Gide and the existentialists, an approved act whose virtue is its spontaneity, not its wisdom, for there is no reason to perform it. Perhaps the most famous use of *act* in the romantic tradition occurs in the first part of *Faust*, when the medieval scholar is translating the Gospel According to John into German. The opening line, "In the beginning was the Word," puzzles Faust, who tries Mind (*Sinn*) and Force (*Kraft*) as substitutes for Word, but then rejects them. At last he is satisfied by "Act" (*Im Anfang war die Tat* is his line), replacing the logos with the deed.

In the American vein, *act* has not been, typically, mindless. Idea, instead, issues in act and is to some extent judged by it. There is a continuity between thought and action, theory and practice, when they are rightly understood (i.e. as Americans understand them), and there is a tendency in America to condemn those whose ideas have no consequences in behavior.

Burke does not regard *act* as a pragmatic word, although I think it is, but treats it as fundamental to realism, while *agent*, he thinks, is the operative term in pragmatism. Yet George Herbert Mead, one of the three most eminent American pragmatists (if one leaves out Peirce, who influenced James, but would not call himself a pragmatist), is the author of *The Philosophy of the Act*. James, Dewey, and

Mead were psychologists as well as philosophers, and all three affected the development of social science, especially in America, but it is Mead, perhaps, who had the most direct influence on social psychology and sociology. Agency is an important idea in pragmatism, but act is vital to it. If one wants to use *act* as a category of realism, it is useful to know that American realism was developed out of the thought of William James, in part by his disciples (e.g., Ralph Barton Perry).

The continuity of thought and action in America is found in our practice, if not at once stated as a principle, going back to the Founding Fathers. The philosophers of the Republic were also its statesmen. *The Federalist* papers, which contained a political philosophy, were written by three statesmen, Hamilton, Madison, and Jay, who dealt in ideas they were prepared to translate into action. And Jefferson came as close as anyone, perhaps, to the ideal of the philosopher-king. The pragmatic revolution of Peirce and James was like other American revolutions in returning to our origins in order to influence our future.

LOUIS AUCHINCLOSS

HENRY ADAMS

ON DECEMBER 6, 1885, fate almost, in Henry Adams's words, "smashed the life" out of him. His wife, Marian Hooper Adams, on that day took a fatal dose of potassium cyanide. Suicide makes a clean sweep of the past and present; worst of all, it repudiates love. Adams was a man of few intimacies. "One friendship in a lifetime is much," he wrote; "two are many; three are hardly possible." Certainly his two were Clarence King, the geologist, and John Hay, the biographer of Lincoln. And there were others like the painter John La Farge with whom he had warm and pleasant associations. But it is doubtful if Adams, who used a sharp wit and a gruff, kindly cynicism as a barrier to and possibly a substitute for the closest human communion, ever revealed his deepest emotions or thoughts to any but Marian. She was quick, even caustic, but blessed with gaiety and an exquisite sensitivity. She adored her husband, and their childlessness was only a further bond. But nothing could pull her out of the black depression into which she sank after her father died.

Until that day of tragedy Henry Adams might have reasonably considered that his life was successful. He had not, to be sure, been president of the United States, like his grandfather, John Quincy Adams, or like his great-grandfather, John Adams, or minister to England, like his father, Charles Francis Adams, but he had been a brilliant and popular teacher of medieval history at Harvard, a successful editor of the *North American Review*, a noted biographer and essayist, and he was in the process of completing his nine-volume history of the Jefferson and Madison administrations which even such a self-deprecator as he must have suspected would one day be a classic. But above all this, far above, he had believed that he and his wife were happy.

Recovering from the first shock, he took a trip to Japan with John La Farge. Then he went back to Washington and worked for three laborious years to finish his history and prepare it for the press. After that, at last, he was free. He had neither child nor job, and his means were ample. In August of 1890 he and La Farge sailed again from San Francisco for a voyage of indefinite duration to the South Seas. His life, at fifty-two, seemed over. Like a worn-out racehorse, he had quit the course and was seeking pasture. "Education had ended in 1871, life was complete in 1890; the rest mattered so little!" And yet that rest was to contain the two great books for which Adams is chiefly remembered today: *Mont-Saint-Michel and Chartres* and *The Education of Henry Adams*.

The Pacific opened up a new dimension of color. La Farge taught Adams to observe the exquisite clearness of the butterfly blue of the sky, laid on between clouds and shading down to a white faintness in the distance where the haze of ocean covered up the turquoise. He made him peer down into the water, framed in the opening of a ship's gangway, and see how the sapphire blue seemed to pour from it. He pointed out the varieties of pink and lilac and purple and rose in the clouds at sunset. Adams never learned to be more than an amateur painter, but his vision was immensely sharpened. For the first time he began to allow the long-repressed aesthete, the author of two anonymous novels, to predominate over the intellectual, the historian.

In Samoa the natives, grave and courteous, greeted the travelers benevolently and made them feel at home. They drank the ceremonial *kawa* and watched the *siva*, a dance performed by girls seated cross-legged, naked to the waist, their dark skins shining with coconut oil, with garlands of green leaves around their heads and loins. The girls chanted as they swayed and stretched out their arms in all directions; they might have come out of the nearby sea. It was a world where instinct was everything.

After Samoa came the disillusionment of Tahiti. Adams described it as a successful cemetery. The atmosphere was one of hopelessness and premature decay. The natives were not the gay, big animal creatures of Samoa; they were still, silent, sad in expression, and fearfully few in number. The population had been decimated by bacteria brought in by Westerners. Rum was the only amusement which civilization and religion had left the people. Tahiti was a halfway house between Hawaii and Samoa. Adams complained that a pervasive half-castitude permeated everything, a sickly whitey-brown or dirty white complexion that suggested weakness and disease.

He was bored, bored as he had never been in the worst wilds of Beacon Street or at the dreariest dinner tables of Belgravia. While waiting for a boat to take them elsewhere, anywhere, he amused himself by returning to his role of historian and interviewing members of the deposed royal family, the Tevas. Next to Mataafa in Samoa, he found the old ex-queen of Tahiti, Hinari, or Grandmother, the most interesting native figure in the Pacific. She showed none of the secrecy of the Samoan chiefs, but took a motherly interest in Adams and La Farge and, sitting on the floor, told them freely all her clan's oldest legends and traditions. Adams was even adopted into the Teva clan and given the hereditary family name of Taura-Atua with the lands, rights, and privileges attached to it — though these consisted of only a few hundred square feet.

But later when he attempted to recapture Hinari's tale in a book which he had privately printed, it was little more than an interesting failure. Tahiti had no history, in the Western sense of the word, until the arrival of the white man. Of the thousands of years that had preceded Captain Cook, when generation had succeeded generation without distinguishable change, there was nothing left but genealogy and legend. The genealogy, which makes up a large part of Adams's book, is boring, and, as for the legend, he admitted himself that he needed the lighter hand of Robert Louis Stevenson, whom he had met in Tahiti.

Yet *The Memoirs of Arii Taimai* (1901) nonetheless marks an important step in Adams's career. He had gone, by 1890, as far as he could go as a historian in the conventional sense. His great work on Jefferson and Madison was history at its most intellectually pure. The author stands aside and lets the documents tell the story, from which a few precious rules may be deduced. In the South Seas he had tried to abandon intellect for the sake of simplicity and instinct. He had sought peace and found ennui. Even the unspoiled natives, in the long run, palled. He had to return, in Papeete, to his profession, but he had to try it with a new twist, for how else could Tahitian history be done? And if *The Memoirs* was a bore, was it altogether his fault? Might it not be in the subject? Suppose he were to happen upon a subject that required not only the imagination of the man who had sat on the floor with the old queen of Tahiti as she intoned the poems of her family tradition but also the industry of the devoted scholar who had pored through the archives of European foreign offices? Suppose he were to find a subject, in short, that required an artist as well as a historian? A subject like the Gothic age of faith?

To go back to his origin (as he himself so often did), Adams was born in Boston in 1838, in Mount Vernon Street under the shadow of the State House. He always loved to dramatize the irony of the seemingly fortunate circumstances of his birth. According to his claim, he had been less equipped for life in America in the nineteenth century than had he been born a Polish Jew or "a furtive Yacoob and Ysaac still reeking of the Ghetto, snarling a weird Yiddish to the officers of the customs." The notion is not to be taken too seriously. If Adams was aloof from the political and economic competition of his day it was not because he was the grandson of a president and, on his mother's side, of the richest merchant in Boston. It was quite of his own volition. Had he been born obscure the idea would never have occurred to him, as an old and respected seer, that he was a failure.

From earliest childhood he was close to the great. When he refused to go to school, it was old John Quincy Adams himself who took him by the hand and led him there. When he went to church, it was to sleep through the sermons of his uncle, Nathaniel Frothingham. Studying his Latin grammar in a corner of his father's library in Mount Vernon Street he heard Charles Sumner hold forth on the politics of antislavery, and at the age of twelve he was taken to Washington to call on President Zachary Taylor and the leaders of Congress. The pattern of receiving his impressions of current history from the very apex of the political pyramid was to continue for the rest of a long life.

He grew up in a large and happy family of six children, two girls and four boys, with devoted parents who were always close to them. He attended the Dixwell School in Boston and entered Harvard College in 1854. When he graduated, four years later, he was elected class orator. Although he always maintained that he learned nothing at Cambridge, this was part of an affectation that covered every stage of his life. In fact, he seems to have read widely, obtained good grades, and made friends with classmates who were also to make their mark in life. One was Henry Hobson Richardson, the Romanesque architect who later built Adams's house in Washington; another was Oliver Wendell Holmes, Jr., of the Supreme Court. Adams's class oration contained none of the pessimism for which he was afterwards noted, and his Class Book has this entry under his signature: "My immediate object is to become a scholar, and master of more languages than I pretend to know now. Ultimately it is most probable that I shall study and practise law, but where and to what extent is as yet undecided. My wishes are for a quiet literary life, as I believe that to be the happiest and in this country not the least useful." This should rebut those who claim that Adams abandoned public life in later years because he disliked the rough and tumble of competition. At twenty he had already elected to be a writer.

After graduation he spent two years in Europe. His original purpose had been to study German civil law in Berlin, but he found it hopelessly boring and decided to learn only the language. Ultimately his trip turned, more profitably, into a sort of grand tour. In Sicily he had an interview with Garibaldi, and in Rome he sat, like Gibbon, on the top of the steps to Santa Maria di Ara Coeli and mused over the great work of history that that historian had visualized on the same spot. When he returned to Boston, he was still determined to read for the bar, but he was interrupted again — this time by his father's election to Congress and the latter's proposal that he accompany him to Washington as private secretary.

Adams remained his father's secretary for nine years, from 1860 to 1868. It was the nearest he ever came to public office. After a brief time in a capital seething with secession, Charles Francis Adams was sent to London as minister. He occupied this position brilliantly and successfully throughout the Civil War and during the difficult period of the adjustment of war claims that followed. There is little reason to believe that his son felt estranged from his generation — as did his friend Henry James — by not having seen combat. Adams knew that his father, supported by a tiny staff, was fighting a battle against British Confederate sympathies that was quite as vital as any in the field, and his older brother warned him sternly from his army camp that if Henry left his post to enlist he would be derelict in his duty to both family and nation. There was no feeling on anyone's part that the little isolated Union group in London was having an easy time. Adams was perfectly sincere in his belief that combat, under the circumstances, would have come as a relief.

But whatever the pressures during crises, there must have been periods, in the more leisurely diplomatic life of that era, when there was not enough to do, for Adams in these years traveled all over England and began to write. He gave considerable attention to a piece on John Smith and Pocahontas, ultimately published in the *North American Review*, in which he was able to disprove some of the foundations on which that flimsy legend rested. Why he took this article, then and later, so seriously is hard to see. He seemed to think, a bit naively, that it might upset those British aristocrats who claimed descent from the Indian princess. At any rate, it is only interesting today as his first serious historical work and because it shows his method, developed more skillfully later, of letting the quoted documents tell most of the story.

When the war ended, he continued to write solid, scholarly articles, such as "The Declaration of Paris" and "The Bank of England Restriction," but it was not until his return to live in Washington as a free-lance correspondent that his distinctive style and point of view began to appear. It took anger and disgust to bring this out: the anger and disgust that was felt by thousands of idealistic young men who saw what they had hoped would be the brave new world of an emancipated and now indissoluble union turned over to a gang of ward politicians and economic pirates. Abraham Lincoln was dead, and Jay Gould seemed to reign at the White House.

"The New York Gold Conspiracy," dealing with the attempt of Gould and Fisk to corner the gold market with the aid of President Grant's brother-in-law, is a fine, taut narrative that crackles with the author's contempt for the crooks and dupes of the sordid adventure. Adams had by now completed his mastery of finance, and his exposition is as clear as it is eloquent. "The Legal Tender Act," about the sorry federal financing of 1862, and "The Session," about the congressional session of 1869-70, are in much the same vein. But the world was not interested in the lucid diagnoses of this brilliant thirty-two-year-old reformer. The world cared about votes and dollars, and Adams lacked the temperament needed to acquire the first and the greed for the second. Besides, he was well enough off, not rich, by the standards of Wall Street, but able to make himself completely comfortable. Adams was always to live rather exquisitely; he was at heart a bit of a sybarite. In his old age this was to make his pretenses of being an anarchist seem an occasionally tiresome parlor joke to younger observers.

In 1870 his life changed again when Charles W. Eliot offered him the post of assistant professor of medieval history at Harvard. Characteristically, Adams told Eliot that he knew nothing about medieval history. Characteristically, Eliot responded by offering to appoint anyone who, in Adams's opinion, knew more. He held the job for seven years during which he also held the editorship of the *North American Review*. His classes were small and select, and his students were turned loose to forage for themselves in original source material. Adams worked with them, rather than over them. He called the experiment a failure in *The Education*, but his students remembered the course as an inspiring one. One class even wrote and published a book under his direction, *Essays in Anglo-Saxon Law*. One may doubt that Adams, at the time, really believed that this was failure.

At any rate, he gave up both teaching and editing before he was forty. He and his wife, Marian Hooper of Boston, whom he had married in 1872, settled in Washington, and he began at last a full-time career as a historian. The next eight years were the happiest of his life. The young Adamses were the center of the brightest, gayest group in the capital. Henry James was to describe them at this period with good-natured sharpness in the guise of the Alfred Bonnycastles in "Pandora." Mrs. Bonnycastle in that tale has a fund of good humor that is apt to come uppermost with the April blossoms; her husband is "not in politics, though politics were much in him." They solve their social problems simply by not knowing any of the people they do not want to know, although here Mr. Bonnycastle sometimes finds his wife a bit too choosy. He remarks toward the end of the season: "Hang it, there's only a month left, let us be vulgar and have some fun — let us invite the President!"

But with all the fun and the parties Adams was still hard at work. He had acquired the Albert Gallatin papers which he edited in three large volumes, with a fourth for his own biography of Jefferson's secretary of the treasury (1879). As history the life is admirable; as entertainment it is very dry. One doubts if even such a literary magician as Lytton Strachey could have made Gallatin's personality interesting. However high-minded, judicious, industrious, patriotic, conscientious, Gallatin was dull and his correspondence is dull, and dullness permeates his biography. Adams demonstrates all of his subject's best qualities in his own careful, clear rendition of the important facts, and there they remain for students, and for students only.

Just the opposite is true of Adams's biography of John Randolph of Roanoke (1882). Here he is dealing with an absolutely reprehensible man who was the scourge of the House of Representatives for two decades and who ultimately came to symbolize everything that was violent, recalcitrant, and irrational in the point of view of the southern slaveholder. Randolph's importance in history is that he became the prophet around whom the forces of secession could ultimately rally. It is certain that he was alcoholic; it is probable that he was partially insane. No more different character from Gallatin could possibly be conceived, and they face each other a little bit like Milton's God and Milton's Satan, with the balance of interest falling in Satan's favor. Fortunately, the book on Randolph is short, for about halfway through one begins to lose interest. The character is too absurd to hold the stage except as a grisly historical fact, and once that historical fact has been set forth there is little to be gained by summaries of his irrational speeches. The work ultimately fails, like *Gallatin*, because of its subject. It could have only been strengthened if Adams had had the material and the inclination to delve into the psychological reasons for Randolph's behavior. He would have done better to have made it the topic of one of his masterly essays in the *North American Review*. As he said himself, Randolph's biographer had the impossible job of taking a "lunatic monkey" seriously.

Gallatin and Randolph were both to play major roles in the great historical work on which Adams now embarked: *The History of the United States of America during the Administrations of Thomas Jefferson and James Madison*. When completed it ran to nine volumes, the last of which was not published until 1891. Before the appearance of Dumas Malone's study of Jefferson's first term, Adams's *History* was considered by many the definitive work on the first years of the American nineteenth century.

The short chapters, the straightforward, vigorous, masculine prose, the geographical and political sweep of the narrative, and the sharp, pungent assessments of motives and failings, conceal the enormous and laborious research in American, French, English, and Spanish state papers that underlay them. Adams was to say in *The Education* that he had published a dozen volumes of American history for no other purpose than to satisfy himself whether, by the severest process of stating, with the least possible comment, such facts as seemed sure, in such order as seemed rigorously consequent, he could fix for a familiar moment a necessary sequence of human movement. He selected his period (1801 to 1817) because it represented a natural semicolon in American history. By the turn of the century the United States had established itself as an independent nation that was bound, one way or another, to survive, and by 1815 that nation had accepted the fact, whether all of its statesmen did so or not, that it was going to survive more or less as other nations survived. It was not, in other words, to be an Arcadia — set apart.

The two double terms of Jefferson and Madison represent, therefore, the historical hiatus in which Americans gave up their dream that they were different from other human beings. Adams's central theme is the disillusionment of two presidents who found that their governments were ineluctably controlled by facts and not ideals.

Both presidents were to find themselves in the position of Napoleon in Tolstoi's *War and Peace*, pulling at tassels inside a carriage under the illusion that it was they, rather than the charging horses, who made it go. Adams demonstrates that when history offered Jefferson the chance to purchase Louisiana, he discovered that he could not turn it down — that he did not even want to. So he doubled the size of the union by means of a treaty for which there was no shadow of authority in the Constitution whose strict construction he had so passionately urged. And Madison, in his turn, according to Adams, found himself obliged to build up the armed forces that he had wished to abolish and to engage in warfare which he had believed fatal to liberty. And both he and Jefferson found themselves caught up in the job of enforcing an embargo as despotically as any tyrant abroad.

This conception of Jefferson as an idealist philosopher-president, imbued with the fatuous faith that there were no international difficulties that could not be solved by negotiation, has been subject to the criticism that Adams was prejudiced against the third president, who, after spurning the political ideas of John Adams, ended by adopting them. There may be some truth in this. Why should Adams attack Jefferson for inconsistency, which can be a very great virtue in a statesman, unless he believed that the latter had preempted a credit in history that more properly belonged to his great-grandfather? Then, too, Adams, with the down-to-earth thinking of the scholar who has never been tempted to compromise, may have found it difficult to appreciate the enormous range and flexibility of Jefferson's political mind. Adams admired diplomats and rarely politicians. Jefferson was rarely a diplomat and always a politician. One is reminded at times of Lord Morley's statement that if Adams had ever surveyed himself naked in a mirror, he might have been more tolerant of human deficiencies.

Adams's predilection for diplomacy is the source of the best and weakest parts of the *History*. The more brilliant passages are those that take place outside the United States: in London, Paris, and Madrid; in St. Domingo and on the high seas. The chapters that deal with Napoleon have a particular fascination, not only because they put the naive, serious-minded American statesmen in dramatic contrast with this monster of Old World cynicism and champion of brute force, but because they show Adams, the historian, struggling desperately in his quest for sequence, for cause and effect, against the tide of chaos, against the appalling evidence that a single individual was turning history into whim. Napoleon plays in the *History* just the reverse of the role that he plays in *War and Peace*. It is ironical that Adams, who largely agreed with Tolstoi's concept of political leaders being carried along in the flood of events which they try vainly to control, should take exception to Tolstoi's primary illustration of his theory. Yet so it is. Napoleon seems to strike Adams as the one human being of the period who contains in himself an energy equivalent to a nation's energy and who is thus able to deflect history from its normal course. When one sees the emperor lolling in his hot bath and shouting at his brothers about the Louisiana Purchase, one feels that Adams is here dealing with a different kind of force from that generated by Jefferson, by Burr, by Canning, or even by Andrew Jackson. The mere fact that Napoleon is the only man in nine volumes whom we see in a bathtub underlines his individuality. Eventually, the processes of history would right themselves, and Napoleon's empire would disintegrate, even more quickly than it was put together, but it still remains a phenomenon unique in European history.

One can see why Adams was ultimately disappointed in his sequences. For despite all his labors and all his perceptions, the true cause of the War of 1812 is never made clear. Through several volumes of lucidly described diplomatic negotiations between England and the United States we see the government first of Jefferson and then of Madison submit tamely to every humiliation imposed upon it by a British crown determined not only to keep its former colony a small power but to seize by any means, legal or illegal, its growing trade. Adams pursues skillfully, if at times tediously, the endless negotiations in the seven years preceding the war: in Paris,

Washington, and London, over the American embargo, the American Act of Non-Intercourse, the British Orders in Council, and Napoleon's Berlin and Milan decrees. Fixed in the policy of isolation, hallucinated by the vision that the new democracy, left to itself, would develop powerfully and peacefully, Jefferson and his successor are seen deliberately blinding themselves to the fact that neither Canning nor Napoleon will give the slightest consideration to any diplomatic protest that is not backed up by force.

But why then the war? Why did the United States, having suffered every diplomatic rebuff, finally elect to throw away the price of its shameful submission? So far as the reader can make out, the country was hounded unprepared into a war which its administration did not seek by a group of young hotheads in Congress led by Henry Clay and John C. Calhoun. But Adams did not know why: "The war fever of 1811 swept far and wide over the country, but even at its height seemed somewhat intermittent and imaginary. A passion that needed to be nursed for five years before it acquired strength to break into act, could not seem genuine to men who did not share it. A nation which had submitted to robbery and violence in 1805, in 1807, in 1809, could not readily lash itself into rage in 1811 when it had no new grievance to allege; nor could the public feel earnest in maintaining national honor, for every one admitted that the nation had sacrificed its honor, and must fight to regain it. Yet what honor was to be hoped from a war which required continued submission to one robber as the price of resistance to another? President Madison submitted to Napoleon in order to resist England; the New England Federalists preferred submitting to England in order to resist Napoleon; but not one American expected the United States to uphold their national rights against the world."

It is difficult for the reader at this point not to ask why, if a war is going to be created simply by an unreasonable war fever, such an inordinate amount of space has been devoted to the unraveling of the diplomatic skein that is not directly related to it. Of course, it might be answered that the unraveling of the diplomatic skein is part of a historian's task simply because it is there to unravel, but even conceding this, one cannot escape the conclusion that the diplomatic chapters could be summarized without losing much of their importance. One suspects here that Adams, being a pioneer in the British, French, and Spanish archives, fell a little bit in love with material so far virgin to the historian and indulged in overquotation. There is also the fact that, having himself spent eight years as secretary to the United States minister in London, he had a natural fascination in peering under the formal cover of diplomatic interchange to the reality beneath.

Adams believed that a historian should first detach himself and his personal enthusiasms and disapprovals from the field of human events that he has selected to study. He should then develop his own general ideas of causes and effects by observing the mass of phenomena in the selected period. After the formation of such ideas, he should exclude all facts irrelevant to them. In Adams's *History*, his most important general idea is that the energy of the American people ultimately seized control of a chain of events which was initiated by energies in Europe. He attempted to trace this American energy in finance, science, politics, and diplomacy. Individuals were not of primary importance to him, which explains why even Jefferson is never presented in a full portrait and why Madison remains a more shadowy character than any of the British statesmen described. Adams believed that in a democratic nation individuals were important chiefly as types. In the end, his *History*, like most great histories, is a failure, if a splendid one, because we are never brought to a full comprehension of what this all-important energy consists. It seems possible that Adams might have approached its nature more closely had he widened his field of study, had he spent more time observing the commercial society of American cities, the farms of the North and the plantations in the South, and less of the day-to-day negotiations of the Treaty of Ghent.

During the years of heavy work on his *History*, Adams relaxed from one discipline, characteristically, by subjecting himself to another. He wrote and published two novels, *Democracy*, which appeared anonymously in 1880, and *Esther*, which he brought out under the pseudonym of Frances Snow Compton in 1884. The identity of the author was for years a carefully guarded secret. These novels have aroused an interest in our time incommensurate with their merit. They are in the class of Winston Churchill's paintings —

of primary interest to the biographer. That is not to say that they are bad. Indeed, competently organized and agreeably written, they cause no squirms of embarrassment even to the most critical reader. But compared to Adams's other work they are pale stuff, and commentators are reduced to the scholar's game of spotting the origins of the *Education* in *Democracy* and that of *Mont-Saint-Michel and Chartres* in *Esther*. Mrs. Lightfoot Lee's disenchantment with her corrupt senator, exposed by Adams's alter ego, John Carrington, reflects the author's own disgust with post-Civil War Washington, and Esther Dudley's rejection of the Episcopal Church contains the seed of Adams's nostalgia for a church that she might not have rejected. Yet neither novel significantly illuminates the later works. They remain in the end footnotes for Adams enthusiasts.

Democracy attained considerable popularity in its day as a political roman à clef. Certainly, the characters are more subtle than the issues. Mrs. Lightfoot Lee, like a Jamesian heroine, has money and social position and a bright, fresh spirit full of ideals. She has come to Washington in quest of some great and enlightened statesman whose humble and helping consort she may become. Her cousin John Carrington falls in love with her, but he is not at all what she wants. He is a Confederate veteran who has lost all and accepted defeat, but only because he has grimly accepted the verdict of history. Despising the victors, he concentrates on making a lonely living as a lawyer in the conquerors' land, a cynical, trenchant, attractive figure, the only real man in the book, so much like Basil Ransom in Henry James's novel *The Bostonians* of the same period that one wonders if he and Adams might not have used the same model.

Madeleine Lee wants something much more effervescent than Carrington; he is cold tea to the champagne that she visualizes. At last she thinks that she has found her ideal in Senator Ratcliffe, the colossus of Illinois who is able to gain control of the administration of the new president before the latter has even taken office. It is Carrington's distasteful duty to disillusion Madeleine, and he resolutely goes about putting together the necessary proof that the senator's career has been founded on a bribe. Madeleine, convinced, flees both senator and Washington. That is the whole story.

It is flat. One might have hoped that Madeleine would at least fall in love with the villain — if only to make her decision harder — but her creator, who detested senators, could not allow this. One might also have hoped that the senator would devise an interesting defense to her charge. But he tells Madeleine that the end justifies the means, and his end is nothing but the tired old rhetorical goal used by every contemporary statesman who ever waved the bloody shirt: preservation of the union. Adams might have answered this criticism of his plot by pointing out that he was telling the simple truth. Statesmen like Senator Ratcliffe in the reconstruction era *did* dominate the scene, and men like Carrington *were* helpless to do more than record their own indignant dissent. Madeleine Lee, in flying off to Europe, has only expressed the despair of her creator at the prospect of Washington. Living a century later in not dissimilar times, should we not appreciate her position? Perhaps. But we are dealing with a novel, and novels must be concerned less with truth than the appearance of it.

Esther Dudley's choice in *Esther* is a good deal harder than Madeleine's, for she is very much in love. The story again involves a renunciation, her renunciation of a deeply religious young minister whose faith she finds she cannot share. The novel is full of their arguments and finally bogs down in the reader's inability to see why an agnostic, with a little bit of tact, could not be a perfectly good minister's wife. One is almost surprised, in the end, that the subject has not been more interesting. It cannot be only that we care less about the question of faith today. Our interest in *Anna Karenina* is not diminished by our knowing that today the heroine could have divorced her husband and married Vronski with no loss of social position. No, it is rather that Adams himself has so little sympathy for the Reverend Stephen Hazard. He makes his evangelicism ridiculous, so that one suspects that Esther may be well out of her engagement. If the man of political power in the 1870s and 1880s was a pirate, the man of God was an anachronism. As husbands went, there was not much to choose between them. Esther would have to wait twenty years and visit Chartres Cathedral, as one of Adams's adopted nieces, before she would encounter a religion that could move the hearts of men. And even then it would only be the memory of one.

There is a distinct similarity between Adams's two heroines and the heroines of Henry James's early and middle periods. Madeleine and Esther each have the impulsiveness, the charm, and the strict integrity of Isabel Archer in *The Portrait of a Lady*. It is probable that this freshness and ebullience, this happy idealism united with a stubborn, at times gooselike, refusal to compromise, was a characteristic of American girls of the period and perhaps of Marian Adams herself. It was what made them ultimately pathetic, at times even tragic. One can find analogies in the American girls of Anthony Trollope's later novels. But certainly with Adams himself, this concept reflects a deep preoccupation. All his life he was more at ease with women than men, and after Marian's death he transferred some of his dependence to Elizabeth Cameron, the brilliant wife of Senator Don Cameron of Pennsylvania. When he wrote Mrs. Cameron that he valued any dozen pages of *Esther* more than the whole of his *History*, he may have been only half serious, but he may also have been expressing an intuitive conviction that the charm of Esther Dudley was precisely what was missing from the historical work.

Esther was Adams's last publication before his wife's suicide, and the years that followed, as we have seen, were occupied with the laborious completion of the *History*. His winters were now spent in the house designed for him by Henry Hobson Richardson on Lafayette Square directly opposite the White House. The adjoining larger mansion, also designed by Richardson, belonged to the John Hays. Adams had given up going out socially, but he continued to entertain a select number of friends for lunch, or what he called breakfast. In the other seasons he traveled: in the Pacific, in the Caribbean, in Europe, in the Middle East. He had ceased to consider himself a historian. He was simply a student of the universe, an asker of questions, a humble seeker after knowledge who hoped to have a peek into the essential nature of man and matter before he died. This picture of a small, gruff gentleman, poking about the planet and asking questions of every sphinx, is the character, of course, that he himself was to make the subject of *The Education of Henry Adams*.

Among Adams's intimates was Senator Henry Cabot Lodge of Massachusetts who had been one of his students at Harvard. The friendship at times was a rather prickly one, since Adams tended to distrust senators in general and Lodge in particular, but with Mrs. Lodge, a woman of large sympathy and intellect, the relationship was always good. It was she who invited him on the tour of northern France in the summer of 1895 which first aroused his interest in Norman and Gothic cathedrals. In the Cathedral of Coutances he suddenly saw his ideal image of outward austerity and inward refinement and felt a consequent release from the era in which he had been condemned to live. From this point on he began to play a mental game in which he identified himself with his Norman ancestors.

It did not matter whether these had been peasants or princes. All classes, in the eleventh century, must have felt the same motives. It had been, as Adams saw it, a natural, reasonable, complete century in which to live. Its cathedrals showed neither extravagance nor want of practical sense. He could almost remember the faith that had given his ancestors the energy to build them and the sacred boldness that had made their towers seem so daring. Within these citadels of faith no doubts existed. There was not a stone in the whole interior of Coutances that did not treat him as if he were its own child. Going back eight hundred years, he mused: "I was simple-minded, somewhat stiff and cold, almost repellent to the warmer natures of the south, and I had lived always where one fought handily and needed to defend ones wives and children; but I was at my best." The fatal mistake had been ever to conquer England and its "dull, beer-swilling people." From 1066 to the Boston of Adams's own childhood, there had been nothing but a long decline in religion, in art, in military taste, until now, in the summer of 1895, the Back Bay descendants of Caen and Coutances had pretty nearly reached bottom.

In Mont-Saint-Michel the party encountered large numbers of tourists. Adams described them petulantly as pigs and the meals that he had to eat as hogpens. He does not seem to have run into many tourists in the other places, and one shudders to think what his reaction would have been had he traveled today. What struck him most in the Mount was that its character was more military than religious. He was fascinated by Senator Lodge's enthusiasm for it.

Adams had not anticipated much from his friend as a sightseer. Lodge, he had been afraid, would visit the dreary old capitals of Europe as though he was still twenty and as though Napoleon III was still reigning. Now, however, Lodge returned to the enthusiasm that he had manifested as a student under Adams at Harvard, and lectured the party brilliantly on the construction and fortifications of the monastery.

The climax of the trip came with Chartres. After "thirty-five years of postponed intentions," Adams worshiped at last before the splendor of "the great glass gods." For the first time he encountered something that even his critical mind could regard as perfection. It was an experience that he was never to get over. He divined in the cathedral the intention of twelfth-century man to unite all arts and sciences in the service of God. It was an architectural exhibit, a museum of painting, glass staining, wood and stone carving, music (vocal and instrumental), embroidery, jewelry, gem setting, tapestry weaving. It was the greatest single creation of man, to whom it gave a dignity which he was in no other instances entitled to claim. Adams likened himself to a monkey looking through a telescope at the stars.

Chartres was a beautiful gate by which to leave his Norman paradise, but he could hardly bear to leave it. The chateaux of the Loire seemed now as vulgar as Newport. Valois art was a "Jewish kind of gold-bug style" best fitted to express the coarseness and sensuality of Francis I and Henry VIII and their unspeakable Field of the Cloth of Gold. And when Adams returned to Paris, it was even worse. He was sickened by the "dreadful twang of his dear country people" on the Rue de la Paix. But people did not so much matter so long as one had the Gothic cathedrals.

After his trip with the Lodges Adams returned every summer to Paris. He rented an apartment as a base for his excursions and always invited a niece or nieces to visit him. Friends of nieces were also welcome, and "Uncle Henry" became a cult, the adored center of a group of attractive and intelligent young women. He would usually take one or more with him on his motor trips in search of the twelfth and thirteenth centuries. By the summer of 1904 he wrote to John Hay that these expeditions had become a craze and that he had fallen a victim to his Mercedes. He spent the warm months running "madly through the centuries" hunting "windows like hairs," covering sixty miles in a morning and ninety in an afternoon. Traveling down a straight French road through the countryside hypnotized him "as a chalk line does a hen." He gathered the fruit of these excursions into the volume which he entitled *Mont-Saint-Michel and Chartres*.

It has always been a difficult book for librarians to classify. Should it be catalogued under travel or history or even fiction? Certainly, it purports to pass in the first category. The narrator claims that he is writing a guidebook for a niece, adoptive or actual, on a long, leisurely summer tourist trip from Brittany to Paris to Chartres. The point of view from which we take the story is the uncle's. He, of course, is Adams himself, a first-class traveler, as selective in his scholarship as he undoubtedly is in his foods and wines, with nothing to interrupt him in a happy season of poking about in Gothic cathedrals. The atmosphere of the golden age of tourism pervades the story. A generation before, and travel was all dusty roads, jolting carriages, and pot luck inns. A few years later it would be the sharing of treasures with a million seekers and a thousand buses. But just at the turn of the century, with the advent of the automobile, for a brief delectable time, the past belonged to a few happy exquisites, who wrote big illustrated volumes such as Henry James's *Italian Hours* and Edith Wharton's *A Motor Flight through France*. The "pigs" whom Adams had seen in Brittany were easily avoided.

The reader of *Mont-Saint-Michel* soon learns that he is in the hands of no ordinary guide. The uncle disclaims any pretensions of being an architect, a historian, or a theologian; he insists on only one virtue, an indispensable one in any honest tourist: he is "seriously interested in putting the feeling back into the dead architecture where it belongs." That he succeeds in this I think no reader will dispute. Whether it is always the appropriate feeling may sometimes be in question. When it is, Adams is a great historian. When it is not, he is a great romantic.

We start in the eleventh century at Mont-Saint-Michel in Brittany just before the Norman Conquest of England. Adams's architectural plot begins with the Romanesque, the rounded arch, the age of the conquering soldier and militant priest, of the Chanson de Roland, an age of simple, serious, silent dignity and tremendous energy. We move through Caen to Paris and at last to Chartres and the year 1200, the time of the Gothic arch and the cult of the Virgin. This Adams sees as the finest and most intense moment of the Christian story. The chapters on the Cathedral of Chartres, on its statuary, its apses, its incomparable glass, are a remarkable lyrical achievement. Adams sees Mary as superior to the Trinity. She is what equity is to law. There is no hope for sinful men in the rigid, logical justice of Christ. He is law, unity, perfection, a closed system. But the Virgin is a woman, loving, capricious, kind, infinitely merciful. She is nature, love, chaos. The cathedral is her palace, and the most beautiful art in history is displayed there to please her. Adams makes us feel at one with the crushed crowd of kneeling twelfth-century worshipers as we lift our eyes after the miracle of the Mass to see, far above the high altar, "high over all the agitation of prayer, the passion of politics, the anguish of suffering, the terrors of sin, only the figure of the Virgin in majesty." But the chapter ends on a dry note. Moving suddenly back to his own day the uncle leaves the Virgin "looking down from a deserted heaven, into an empty church, on a dead faith."

That is the end of the architectural trip, yet the book is only half finished. Adams now traces the influence of the Virgin in literature, in contemporary history, and in theology. He offers translations of some of the versifications of her miracles; he describes the great royal ladies of the period; he conveys the sense of Mary's ambience in the world of court poems and courteous love. The emotion in these chapters begins to approach that of the naive and passionate chroniclers whom he quotes. He sternly warns us that if we do not appreciate the charm of this or that, we may as well give up trying to understand the age. Our guide has become a priest and one of Mary's own. The feeling conveyed is a unique aesthetic effect.

He does not, however, leave us in the days of Mariolatry. The priest now turns professor. In the last chapters he explains how the church was taken away from the Virgin. She was a heretic, in essence, for she denied the authority of God and asserted the greater force of woman. The theologians had to put her back in her place and build a religious philosophy that would stand up to the most unsettling questions of the logicians. In the final chapter on St. Thomas Aquinas Adams sees him building his theology as men built cathedrals: "Knowing by an enormous experience precisely where the strains were to come, they enlarged their scale to the utmost point of material endurance, lightening the load and distributing the burden until the gutters and gargoyles that seem mere ornament, and the grotesques that seem rude absurdities, all do work either for the arch or for the eye; and every inch of material, up and down, from crypt to vault, from man to God, from the universe to the atom, had its task, giving support where support was needed, or weight where concentration was felt, but always with the condition of showing conspicuously to the eye the great lines which led to unity and the curves which controlled divergence; so that, from the cross on the flèche and the keystone of the vault, down through the ribbed nervures, the columns, the windows, to the foundation of the flying buttresses far beyond the walls, one idea controlled every line; and this is true of Saint Thomas's Church as it is of Amiens Cathedral. The method was the same for both, and the result was an art marked by singular unity, which endured and served its purpose until man changed his attitude toward the universe. . . . Granted a Church, Saint Thomas's Church was the most expressive that man has made, and the great Gothic cathedrals were its most complete expression."

Is it true? Was France like that in the twelfth and thirteenth centuries? It has often been pointed out that Adams's idyllic era of true faith was actually a period of lawless strife and brigandage in which a few ambitious and secular-minded priests raised cathedrals to their own glory. Undoubtedly he oversimplified, exaggerated. His Chartres may be to cathedrals as Moby Dick is to whales. But if the religious spirit that he so brilliantly evokes in his strong sinuous prose did in fact exist, he may, by isolating it from the turmoil in which it was embedded, have come closer to the essence of his era than some more comprehensive historians.

How far Adams has traveled in his experiments with historical method may be measured by contrasting his *Gallatin* with *Mont-Saint-Michel*. The former shows the historian at his most restrained. The documents speak for the author, while in the latter the historian (or guide) propels us despotically by the elbow, allowing us to see only what appeals to his own taste (at times almost his whim), and colors the whole panorama with his violent personal distaste for his own times. But the guide is always entertaining, and the reader, one submits, may know Eleanor of Guienne and Abélard better than, in the earlier works, he knows any member of Jefferson's cabinet.

At this period of Adams's life he was close to political power for the first time. He had always been close enough to observe it, but now he was in a position, if not to exercise it, at least to influence its exercise. John Hay, his most intimate friend, his soul's brother, was Theodore Roosevelt's secretary of state. Might Adams not be a Gray Eminence? He had always maintained that a friend in power was a friend lost, but this cynical observation had to be modified to except the case of Hay whose gentle, affectionate, and loyal disposition was proof against all strains of high political life. Also, Hay was an ill man who held on to the office which finally killed him only at the promptings of duty. A necessary relaxation was his daily walk with Adams, after which Mrs. Hay would give them tea. If Adams, according to Hay, could "growl and tease" in "hours of ease," he could also be a "ministering angel" in times of anguish. When Hay died, still in office, in the summer of 1905, Adams wrote to his widow: "As for me, it is time to bid good-bye. I am tired. My last hold on the world is lost with him. I can no longer look a month ahead, or be sure of my hand or mind. I have hung on to his activities till now because they were his, but except as his they have no concern for me and I have no more strength for them . . . He and I began life together. We will stop together."

The exaggeration was characteristic. Adams had another thirteen years to live, and he was already at work on his most famous book. He had planned the *Education* as a companion piece to *Mont-Saint-Michel*. It would present the twentieth century in contrast to the twelfth: the chaos of infinite multiplicity as opposed to Saint Thomas Aquinas's divine order. Adams had been fascinated at the Paris Exposition of 1900 by the Gallery of Machines of the Champ de Mars. This he had visited day after day to watch in entrancement the silent whirring of the great dynamos. He wrote to Hay that they ran as noiselessly and as smoothly as the planets and that he wanted to ask them, with infinite courtesy, where the hell they were going. He saw in them the tremendous, ineluctable force of science in the new century. Surely, it was the very opposite of the warm concept of the overwatching Virgin of Chartres. As his new book came to mind, it may have occurred to him in that very gallery that the narrator who would constitute the most dramatic contrast to the dynamo would be the one who was then watching it: Henry Adams himself.

He may also have been induced to put the book in the form of a memoir (in the third person) by two other factors: first, his dislike of biographies in general, coupled with the fear that he himself might one day be the victim of a hack, and, second, by his enthusiasm for Henry James's life of William Wetmore Story, a complimentary memoir, written at the request of the family, in which the author avoided the embarrassment of facing up to his subject's bad sculpture and poetry by a colorful evocation of his background, including the Boston of his origin. Adams saw much more in this than James had ever intended. He professed to find in the picture of Boston all the ignorance and innocence of a small, closed, parochial society that had been blind enough to believe that a Story could sculpt or a Sumner legislate. It gave him the point from which to start his own *Education*.

It is less the story of an education than the story of the purported failure of one. Adams contends that his family background, his schooling, even his experiences in political and diplomatic circles, in no way prepared him for life in the second half of the nineteenth century. When he and his parents returned to the United States from London in 1868, they were as much strangers in their native land, he claimed, as if they had been Tyrian traders from Gibraltar in the year 1000 B.C. But this, he should in fairness have conceded, was not so much the fault of Harvard or of Boston society, or even of the Adams family, as it was the fault of the raging speed of change in his century. Grant, the new president in 1869, was not, according to Adams, a thinking man, but a simple energy. To achieve worldly success in his era, very little in the way of education was needed. But was worldly success the only kind of success? Because a tycoon had not been educated, was education useless? Adams never convinces us that he would have been willing to scrap the least part of his own maligned education.

Having made his basic point that he was not educated by any of his supposedly educating experiences, Adams proceeds to outline the kind of quasi education that he received through a series of disillusionments. As a boy he had regarded Senator Charles Sumner as a great statesman and friend; in later years he found him a vain and malicious old peacock. In the early London days he had been convinced that Lord Palmerston was bent on the destruction of the American union and that Gladstone favored the North; later he discovered that just the opposite was true. Friends turned out to be enemies; enemies, friends. Even in the world of art there was no certainty. No expert could tell him whether or not the supposed Raphael sketch that he had bought in London was genuine.

Adams tells the story of each disillusionment entertainingly enough, but in the illusionless world in which we live, we may find his surprise a bit naive. It does not seem to us in the least astonishing that a statesman should say one thing, intend another, and desire a third. Self-interest is so taken for granted that we require our most eminent citizens to sell their stocks before serving in the president's cabinet, and, as for art, we should simply shrug in amusement if it turned out that the roof of the Sistine Chapel had been painted by Boldini.

Finally, in the *Education*, the "uneducated" author, on the threshold of old age, amalgamates his own laws of the sequence of human events with those of the physical sciences to deduce a "dynamic theory" of history that is not taken seriously by either scientists or historians today.

If, then, Adams's claim that he was never educated is simply a paradox for the sake of argument, if his disillusionments strike us as naive, and if his dynamic theory is without validity, wherein lies the greatness of the book? It lies, I submit, in the extraordinarily vivid sense conveyed to the reader of history being formed under his eyes, in the crystallization of the myriad shapes of the twentieth century out of the simple substance of the eighteenth. I know of no other autobiography (as I shall impenitently insist on calling it) which conveys anything like the same effect. And in no other of his writings does Adams more luminously demonstrate what Henry James called "his rich and ingenious mind, his great resources of contemplation, resignation, speculation."

The first chapter introduces us immediately to the philosophic distinction between unity and multiplicity on which the whole work rests. The ordered world of the Federalist era is exemplified by the Adamses and their spare, dignified house in Quincy with its Stuart portraits, family Bibles, and silver mugs, its mementos of Bunker Hill and air of republican simplicity. Surely, this is unity which must have emanated from a single substance, which must radiate a supreme being's will. And the opulent, plush, crowded world of the Brookses in Boston, on the distaff side, with all its tassels and bric-a-brac, its State Street commercialism, must be multiplicity. Is it not town against country, the mad many against the wholesome one? But Adams can spin this wheel so it stops where he wants, and he can make us see each world in terms of the other even at the expense of contradicting himself: "The double exterior nature gave life its relative values. Winter and summer, cold and heat, town and country, force and freedom, marked two modes of life and thought, balanced like lobes of the brain. Town was winter confinement, school, rule, discipline; straight, gloomy streets, piled with six feet of snow in the middle; frosts that made the snow sing under wheels or runners; thaws when the streets became dangerous to cross; society of uncles, aunts, and cousins who expected children to behave themselves, and who were not always gratified; above all else, winter represented the desire to escape and go free. Town was restraint, law, unity. Country, only seven miles away, was liberty, diversity, outlawry, the endless delight of mere sense impressions given by nature for nothing, and breathed by boys without knowing it."

Now follows the unforgettable picture of John Quincy Adams taking his grandson to school. Adams, at six, on a visit to Quincy, had refused to go, and his mother, embarrassed to exercise discipline in her father-in-law's house, was giving in to him when suddenly the door to the ex-president's library opened, and the old man came slowly down the stairs. "Putting on his hat, he took the boy's hand without a word and walked with him, paralyzed by awe, up the road to the town." Not till they had traversed almost a mile on the hot morning did the grandfather release his hand. But Adams did not resent this treatment. "With a certain maturity of mind, the child must have recognized that the President, though a tool of tyranny, had done his disreputable work with a certain intelligence. He had shown no temper, no irritation, no personal feeling, and had made no display of force. Above all, he had held his tongue. During their long walk he had said nothing; he had uttered no syllable of revolting cant about the duty of obedience and the wickedness of resistance to law; he had shown no concern in the matter; hardly even a consciousness of the boy's existence. Probably his mind at that moment was actually troubling itself little about his grandson's iniquities, and much about the iniquities of President Polk, but the boy could scarcely at that age feel the whole satisfaction of thinking that President Polk was to be the vicarious victim of his own sins, and he gave his grandfather credit for intelligent silence. For this forbearance he felt instinctive respect. He admitted force as a form of right; he admitted even temper, under protest; but the seeds of a moral education would at that moment have fallen on the stoniest soil in Quincy, which is, as every one knows, the stoniest glacial and tidal drift known in any Puritan land."

This quotation gives the flavor of the book. We travel through the nineteenth century with a guide who is a good deal less detached than he claims, who is almost at times romantic, almost at times passionate. It is a unique fusion of history and memoir. We see the century growing more diverse and chaotic until it becomes terrifying, but always in the foreground, shrugging, gesticulating, chuckling, at times scolding, is the neat, bustling figure of our impatient but illuminating observer. He can stretch his imagination to any limit, but not his tolerance or his personality. He ends where he began, an aristocrat, a gentleman, a bit of a voyeur. The fixed referent of Henry Adams holds the book together even more than the constant pairing off of unity with multiplicity. At times it almost seems as if Adams himself, cool, rational, skeptical, were the one, and observed mankind, moving at a giddy rate of acceleration toward nothingness, the many. Only in the very end, when the observer disappears into the theorist and the memoir into a theory, does multiplicity at last prevail. One's trouble in reading the *Education* is that as one moves from unity to multiplicity, the story inevitably loses its character and vividness. Most of the memorable passages are from the earlier chapters.

One remembers particularly, after the walk with the grandfather, the desperate snow fight on the Common between the Latin School and the Boston roughs and blackguards, the charm, ignorance, and mindlessness of the handsome Virginians at Harvard, Adams in London exulting over the long-awaited, tragically belated, first victories of the Union armies: "Life never could know more than a single such climax. In that form, education reached its limits. As the first great blows began to fall, one curled up in bed in the silence of night, to listen with incredulous hope. As the huge masses struck, one after another, with the precision of machinery, the opposing mass, the world shivered. Such development of power was unknown. The magnificent resistance and the return shocks heightened the suspense. During the July days Londoners were stupid with unbelief. They were learning from the Yankees how to fight."

Nothing is more notorious about the *Education* than the fact that Marian Adams is never mentioned in it and that the years of her marriage to the author are eliminated. There has been much speculation concerning the reason. An obvious one is that her loss was so terrible that he could not speak or write about her. But this seems inconsistent with his continued lively interest in attractive women and his long romantic friendship with Senator Don Cameron's attractive wife Elizabeth. Perhaps he simply could not bear to contemplate the attitude toward their marriage which Marian's suicide appeared to imply. The nearest he comes to speaking of her is when he discusses the statue which Augustus Saint-Gaudens made for him in Rock Creek Cemetery. This, of course, is the famous brooding figure of indeterminate sex which was placed over the inscriptionless grave of Marian Adams and under which Adams himself now lies. Its significance has been much debated, though more in Adams's time than in ours, for enigmatic art was more of a novelty then, but "the peace of God which passeth all understanding" is probably as good an explanation as any.

Adams used to sit by the statue in springtime and listen with acid amusement to the comments of visitors. In a famous and characteristic passage he gave vent to his distaste for the world of his time: "He supposed its meaning to be the one commonplace about it — the oldest idea known to human thought. He knew that if he asked an Asiatic its meaning, not a man, woman, or child from Cairo to Kamchatka would have needed more than a glance to reply. From the Egyptian Sphinx to the Kamakura Daibuts; from Prometheus to Christ; from Michael Angelo to Shelley, art had wrought on this eternal figure almost as though it had nothing else to say. The interest of the figure was not in its meaning, but in the response of the observer. As Adams sat there, numbers of people came, for the figure seemed to have become a tourist fashion, and all wanted to know its meaning. Most took it for a portrait-statue, and the remnant were vacant-minded in the absence of a personal guide. None felt what would have been a nursery-instinct to a Hindu baby or a Japanese jinricksha-runner. The only exceptions were the clergy, who taught a lesson even deeper. One after another brought companions there, and, apparently fascinated by their own reflection, broke out passionately against the expression they felt in the figure of despair, of atheism, of denial. Like the others, the priest saw only what he brought. Like all the great artists, Saint-Gaudens held up the mirror and no more. The American layman had lost sight of ideals; the American priest had lost sight of faith. Both were more American than the old, half-witted soldiers who denounced the wasting, on a mere grave, of money which should have been given for drink."

The "education" of Henry Adams might be defined as his own belated conviction that science, for all its achievements, had not resolved the basic mystery of the one and the many, the eternal question of whether the universe is a divine unity or a composite of more than one ultimate substance, a super-sensuous chaos that no single theory can encompass. The only thing of which the author of *Mont-Saint-Michel* and the *Education* could feel absolutely sure was that in the twelfth century man had believed in such a unity and that in the twentieth his less fortunate descendant did not. All Adams could now see in the dark and dangerous era that lay ahead was the seemingly unintelligible interplay of forces.

After finishing the *Education* he devoted himself entirely to trying to make that interplay intelligible. He hoped that it might still be possible to derive some rule from these forces by which he could make a projection of the future. Defining force as anything that helps to do work, and identifying man and nature as forces, he was able to turn history, or social evolution, into a gravitational field in which man and nature constantly acted on and modified each other. The declining force of the church in the past few centuries, for example, gave place to the force of a secular society energized by gunpowder and the compass. In the twentieth century man had to reconcile himself to the loss of the concept of unity and follow the movements of the new forces of nature discovered by experiment. This following would open a new phase in history, the phase of the acceleration of mechanical forces. Adams, spending his mornings at his desk playing with magnets, became obsessed with the vision of human society approaching the ultimate forces with a dizzily accelerating speed, like a comet shooting to the sun.

His writings of this period, "The Rule of Phase Applied to History" (1908) and *A Letter to American Teachers of History* (1910), contain postulations of human life and psychical activity more or less corresponding to the physical phases of solids, liquids, and gases. He finally worked out a mathematical formula based on the law of squares by which he predicted a change of phase (following the human phases of "instinct" and "religion") in 1917 and a breakdown in human thought four years later. All of this is beyond the scope of this essay, but in the opinion of many commentators Adams went hopelessly astray in applying the laws of physics to human events so that his theorizing amounts to little more than brilliant and imaginative fantasy.

It was a waste, unhappily, of valuable energy. Adams's obsession with the mystery of the universe deflected him from the true path on which Mrs. Lodge had set him when they toured the Gothic cathedrals of northern France. Who today would give up *Mont-Saint-Michel* for "Rule of Phase"? With old age he gave in more and more to the nervous habit of questioning everything which had so irritated his friend Justice Oliver Wendell Holmes. The latter wrote this description of him to Lewis Einstein, eight years after Adams's death: "He was very keen and a thinker, but seems to me to have allowed himself to be satisfied too easily that there was no instruction for him in the branches in which he dabbed. When I would step in at his house on the way back from Court and found him playing the old Cardinal, he would spend his energy in pointing out that everything was dust and ashes. Of course one did not yield to the disenchantment, but it required so much counter energy in a man tired with his day's work that I didn't call often. And yet meet him casually on the street and often he was a delightful creation."

Mont-Saint-Michel and the *Education* were both printed privately (in 1904 and 1907 respectively) in large, handsome blue-covered folio editions, one of a hundred and fifty and the other of forty copies, and distributed to friends and a few libraries. Adams did not think the public at large would be interested; he probably thought it was not intellectually ready. He refused to allow an eager young publisher, Ferris Greenslet, from Houghton Mifflin, to tempt him with a contract for the *Education*, but he finally allowed the same firm to bring out an edition of *Mont-Saint-Michel* which appeared, with an introduction by Ralph Adams Cram, in 1913. One wonders if he would have been altogether pleased had he foreseen the enormous popularity that both books would enjoy in the next half century. Would he have been gratified to find himself a "best seller" in an age whose intellectual taste he despised?

I believe that Adams always misconceived his principal talent. He wanted the recognition of scientists for his theories in a field where he was not equipped to make any serious contribution. The picture of Adams, the descendant of presidents, a kind of early American "Everyman," a survival from the Civil War in the day of the automobile, traveling from one end of the globe to the other in quest of the absolute, pausing before Buddhas and dynamos, has so caught the imagination of the academic community that his biography, which he wrote as well as lived, has become, so to speak, one of his works, and his most fantastic speculations the subjects of serious theses. Yet to me his primary contributions to our literature were aesthetic. He is far closer to Whitman and Melville than to Bancroft or Prescott, and he is not at all close to Einstein.

In history he went as far as could be gone on the basic presumption, later repudiated by himself, that the study of trade, diplomacy, and politics can be made to reveal the sequence of human events. No historian has unraveled with more illuminating clarity the exchange of thought in chancelleries, the effects of embargoes, and the influences of electorates on legislators and administrators. If Adams's historical writing leans to the austere, it is because he was determined not to be sidetracked by the quaint, the picturesque, the sensational, or the merely entertaining. Although he denied this from time to time, as when he wrote his publishers that he had given the public a "full dose" of Andrew Jackson because of its "undue interest" in that soldier and statesman, his denial is not convincing, for nobody could think that the portrait of Jackson in the *History* is more than a minimal sketch.

Adams gave up writing American history because he did not believe, after long consideration of what he had done, that he had made any really significant contribution to the long quest for cause and effect. Yet, when he turned from the austerity of historical writing to the looser and more copious field of the novel, he discovered that he did not have the kind of imagination that operated much more easily without limitations of fact. The historian is only too evident in *Democracy* and *Esther*. Both tales are confined to the bare bones of their situations. There is almost no detail of background, and the characters are analyzed only insofar as necessary for us to understand their plotted actions. As in seventeenth-century French fiction, we are confined to essentials. Adams may have considered that in depicting his senator as a monster he was allowing himself a riot of indulgence, but Ratcliffe is given the smallest possible crime to justify his classification as villain.

It is interesting in this respect to contrast his mind with that of Henry James, a lifelong friend whose fiction Adams consistently admired. No two minds could have been more different. As Leon Edel has pointed out, Adams always sought a generalization while James sought to particularize. Adams wanted to know the law of the universe, while James was studying the effect of Paris on a single American soul. Yet each man appreciated the other. Adams loved the subtlety of James's characterizations, and James admired the sweep of Adams's reaching. James, however, would not have approved of Adams's experimentation with the novel form. To him the art of fiction was only for the totally dedicated. We know that he read *Democracy* and said of it that, despite the coarseness of its satire, it was so good that it was a pity it was not better, but he did not know that Adams had written it.

Adams did not find the medium of expression best adapted to his talents until he left the world behind and went to the Pacific with John La Farge. In Tahiti he explored the reconciliation of instinct with logic in his history of the island. There was no even seeming sequence of events to be derived from economics or diplomacy. He had to find it in legends and customs inextricably tied up with the emotions which, as a historian in the older sense, he had tried to eliminate from the field of observed phenomena. The experiment was not a success, but it was a rehearsal of what he was next to do when he came to the Gothic cathedrals of France. "Putting the feeling back" in the stones of Chartres was his goal there, and he attained it. He then proceeded to expand this goal, in the *Education*, to putting the feeling back into his own life and into the contemporary history of the United States and wrote one of the monuments of American literature.

It is not to denigrate the earlier work of Adams to say that *Mont-Saint-Michel* and the *Education* represent the finest flowering of his mind. The biographies and the *History* are not only valuable in themselves; they were indispensable preliminaries. But one may regret that Adams did not more fully recognize his own major phase. He was always determined to be valued for something other than his best.

The great bulk of his correspondence, filling three volumes, shows this. Some of the letters, particularly those from the Pacific, are as brilliant and evocative as John La Farge's water colors of the same subject. But through the ones that deal with social and political life the shrill, constantly repeated strain of dramatic and rhetorical pessimism becomes a great bore. One wonders why Adams thought that it would divert his correspondents. And then, too, he seems to take a perverse pleasure in *not* giving descriptions of people and events that one knows he could describe incomparably. Perhaps it was because all his friends knew the same people and events, but to the modern reader it is like reading Saint-Simon with the characterizations removed. If Adams had only had a correspondent on the moon to whom he had had to give an impression of our planet, a niece in space, he might have been the greatest letter writer in American literature.

His last book, *The Life of George Cabot Lodge*, was published in 1911. It was a memoir that he had written about the senator's son, "Bay," a poet who had died prematurely two years before. The memoir had been written at the request of Senator Lodge and given to him to publish or not as he pleased. It is a tactful and charming piece in which the narrative is largely used to string together quotations from the young man's letters. This is not because Adams was embarrassed by a task that he could not well refuse. He enormously liked Bay Lodge and evidently admired his poetry. But he was by nature too reticent for this kind of eulogy. Perhaps it was just as well. The letters reveal a young man whose talent must have been more in his flaming good looks and enthusiasm than in any originality of imagination or poetic aptitude. Bay Lodge's idealism and aspiration seem to have charmed the aging Adams. They went to the theater together in Paris and discussed ideas for Lodge's plays. They formed together a fanciful political party called the Conservative Christian Anarchists. Lodge was a rebel against Boston society, but he expressed his rebellion largely by appearance, in the manner of some youths today. He wore a huge black hat and gold watch around his neck and let his hair grow long. At least he was going to *look* like an artist. Perhaps he fascinated Adams because he was so exactly his opposite. Adams always dressed and acted the conservative, but his black frock coat covered the heart of a poet.

In 1912 Adams reserved passage from New York to Europe on what would have been the second voyage of the *Titanic*. This brought the disaster of her maiden trip very close to him, and he was much affected. No doubt it seemed even more a symbol to him than it did to others of the disastrous acceleration of science of our century. A week later, he was stricken with a slight stroke. Despite his conviction that he would not survive, he recovered full use of his mind and body, but it became necessary for him to have somebody to supervise the details of his housekeeping, and Aileen Tone, a beautiful young woman who was the friend of two of his nieces, undertook the job. She became his secretary, companion, and adopted niece, and remained with him until his death six years later. As a member of the Schola Cantorum she had learned piano arrangements for old French songs which she used to sing to Adams and his friends. He found in their atonalities a possibility of recapturing the music of the twelfth-century poems that he so loved. In his letters to Miss Tone, during her brief visits away to look after her mother, he made constant references to medieval France, addressing her as "Comtesse Soeur" (as Richard I had addressed his sister) and describing himself as "Robin," the shepherd in a *chante-fable*. As the end approached, he lived more and more in his chosen century.

The last year was darkened by bad war news. It seemed the long anticipated Götterdämmerung. Adams continued, however, to read, to study, to write letters and see friends. Miss Tone took him for daily drives, read to him and helped, as he put it, to keep him alive. The end came in the winter of 1918.

His family discovered the manuscript of a curious and beautiful poem in Adams's wallet. It was entitled "Prayer to the Virgin of Chartres" and was published with some of his correspondence in *Letters to a Niece* in 1920. Because of the depth of its mystical feeling, some of Adams's friends, particularly Mrs. Winthrop Chanler, to whom he had shown the poem in his lifetime, thought that he might have been turning toward Roman Catholicism. But if there is religious feeling in the "Prayer," it is heresy even by the most liberal standards of the Church today. The poem very neatly synthesizes Adams's philosophy.

He sees himself as appearing before his "Gracious Lady" to ask her aid, as simple and humble as his counterpart of seven hundred years before, in the year 1200. He identifies himself with Mary's worshipers throughout medieval history: he has prayed before her portal with Abélard and sung the "Ave Maris Stella" with Saint Bernard of Clairvaux. However, for all his devotion, he recognizes that Mary has always been helpless to help him, even back in the days of her greatness when Chartres was built:

For centuries I brought you all my cares,
And vexed you with the murmurs of a child;

> You heard the tedious burden of my prayers;
> You could not grant them, but at least you smiled.

Because Mary is impotent in the affairs of men, Adams, or Everyman, the "English scholar with a Norman name," abandons her to seek the Father, as Christ himself did, when he went about his Father's business. In this there may be a reference to Saint Thomas Aquinas restoring the Trinity to the center of creation and dethroning the Virgin. In looking for the Father Adams only loses the Mother. The Church of Saint Thomas, without the love and laughter of Mary, without the illogic of her abounding grace, is a sterile combination of cold virtue and damnation.

Adams now visualizes himself as crossing the Atlantic to the New World with a greedy band of Europeans, intent on the plunder of America. He has turned his back not only on the Virgin, the Mother, but on God the Father, too. In the secular society that man is now creating, there is no room for a deity. If man is to revere anything, it must be himself alone, even if that self is mortal without a soul to survive its body.

> And now we are the Father, with our brood,
> Ruling the Infinite, not Three but One;
> We made our world and saw that it was good;
> Ourselves we worship, and we have no Son.

But this independence is illusory. Man discovers that there is still a god to worship, not a just god, like the Father, or a loving and merciful one, like the Virgin, but one that is only force, primal force. The meter changes, and the "Prayer to the Virgin" is interrupted by the "Prayer to the Dynamo," the last of the strange orisons that humanity has "wailed."

Whether the primal force is matter or mind, the only thing man knows about it is that it is blind and cannot respond to prayer. Man and force, lords of space, may both he approaching some end or limit at a terrifying rate of acceleration. It remains only for man to wrest the secret from the atom, but here Adams, with a prescience that is more alarming in the 1970s than it may have been in 1920, sees the hollowest of victories. The victor over the atom will have little on which to congratulate himself.

Seize, then, the Atom! rack his joints!
  Tear out of him his secret spring!
Grind him to nothing! — though he points
To us, and his life-blood anoints
  Me — the dead Atom-King!

The poem now reverts to the form of the prayer to the Virgin. Adams, or Everyman, has come again to seek the help of the helpless Mary. He has no further faith in science and has fled modern man who needs the force of solar systems for his grim play. The latter, too, will find the hopelessness that Adams has found. There is nothing left but the Virgin and the barren consolation that she has to offer.

Does he mean the Virgin or his idea of the Virgin or the medieval concept of the Virgin? It seems to me that he means a fusion of the last two. Adams seems to be clinging to a faith in his own concept of a historical conception that has no current validity and that must have been only an illusion in the twelfth century. For the Virgin was helpless even then. She did not exist. She was an idea, no more, but such a magnificent idea that she could and can console men who *know* that she was and is only an idea, that, indeed, she is now only the memory of one.

In the end he prays to the Virgin to give him her sight, her knowledge, and her feeling. She must have the strength to help him, he argues, because she has had the strength to endure the failure of the very concept of God. It is on this note of ultimate pessimism that the great pessimist leaves us:

Help me to feel! not with my insect sense, —
  With yours that felt all life alive in you;
Infinite heart beating at your expense;
  Infinite passion breathing the breath you drew!

Help me to bear! Not my own baby load,
  But yours; who bore the failure of the light,
The strength, the knowledge and the thought of God,—
  The futile folly of the Infinite!

GAY WILSON ALLEN

WILLIAM JAMES

In *A Pluralistic Universe* William James declares that "a philosophy is the expression of a man's intimate character, and all definitions of the universe are but the deliberately adopted reactions of human characters upon it." Whether or not this opinion holds true for the whole history of philosophy, it was profoundly true in the life and character of William James himself and is a suggestive clue to his contributions to both psychology and philosophy. His own somatic problems led him to study psychology, and his personal concern with the relations of his mind and body underlay all his philosophical speculations.

The first and deepest influence on William James was his father, Henry James, usually called "senior" to distinguish him from his son Henry, the novelist. He was the son of William James of Albany, a self-made millionaire and pious Presbyterian. He rebelled not only against his father's theology but also against his compelling drive to acquire property and money. After he received an inheritance from his father's estate which made him independent, he devoted himself to studying and writing books on theology.

The quarrel of Henry James, Sr., with Calvinism was that it taught a natural estrangement between himself and God. But he also came to believe that all evil in the world was the result of men's overvaluation of their selfhood, and especially their pride in moral uprightness. Inverting Calvin, he declared that men are born innocent, but "fall" individually through selfish egotism, and are saved by subordinating their individual wills to the collective good of society. In early manhood Henry, Sr., had come under the influence of the French socialist Charles Fourier and later the Swedish mystic Emanuel Swedenborg. Fourier taught that man's natural instincts are of divine origin and that social ills are caused by institutions which thwart and corrupt them. If people could live in complete freedom — possible, he thought, in small communities or "phalanges" — they would follow their divine impulses and attain social harmony and personal happiness in this world. Swedenborg taught that God incarnated Himself in mankind, not one man, and that His church was not an institution but humanity. Henry, Sr., combined and adapted Fourier and Swedenborg in his theory of the origin of the world: God created the world by a prolonged and continuous exertion of His energy, first in a "formative" stage now nearing completion, and second in a "redemptive" stage ready to begin. As William James summarized his father's doctrine: "To speak very oracularly, *Nature* is for Mr. James the movement of formation, the first quickening of the void into being, and *Society* is the movement of redemption, or finished spiritual work of God."

William James (born in 1842 in New York City) received a novel but erratic education as a consequence of his father's social and religious theories, which inculcated the need for freedom, spontaneity, and innocence. The innocence of the infant should be protected as long as possible to give his innate divine creativity a chance to grow strong enough to resist the corruptions of society and institutions. In *The Nature of Evil* Henry James, Sr., declared: "I desire my child to become an upright man, in whom goodness shall be induced not by mercenary motives as brute goodness is induced, but by love for it or a sympathetic delight in it. And inasmuch as I know that this character or disposition cannot be forcibly imposed upon him, but must be freely assumed, I surround him as far as possible with an atmosphere of freedom."

However, William James's education was not as free and spontaneous as that of Rousseau's Emile. He attended private schools, had a succession of tutors, and in his father's educational experiments was shifted back and forth between Europe and America — and in America between New York City, Albany, and Newport, Rhode Island. He received a smattering of scientific training in France and Switzerland, and acquired fluency in French and German. His father did not want him to specialize or choose a profession too soon, with the result that he was late in choosing at all. He studied painting with William Hunt for a year, gave that up for chemistry in the Scientific School at Harvard, shifted to anatomy and comparative zoology, and finally entered the Harvard Medical School in 1864, only to withdraw for a year to accompany Louis Agassiz to Brazil on a zoological collecting expedition. A few months after returning from Brazil and reentering Medical School, he withdrew again for a year, ostensibly to study physiology in Germany, but partly to seek a cure for the mysterious pains in his back. Illness prevented him from doing laboratory work at Leipzig or Heidelberg, but he did attend a few lectures at the University of Berlin, acquired a command of scientific German, read the latest books in German on physiology and "psycho-physics," and became deeply interested in the possibility of a "real science of psychology." The year in Germany greatly stimulated his intellectual development.

James's poor health had begun in his nineteenth year while he was trying to decide between a career in science and one in art. Uncertainty, shame over his vacillation, and regret over his inability to understand or reconcile himself to his father's ideas, seemingly so tolerant but maintained with dogmatic vehemence, all these problems combined to undermine the young man's self-confidence and reduce him to nervous prostration, at times so strong that he contemplated suicide. In his youth and early manhood William was his father's favorite of his four sons, and Henry, Sr., wanted him to pursue science instead of art, although, paradoxically, he had a low opinion of scientists because he thought they held " a giant superstition we call Nature." In an article on "Faith and Science" he explained: "Nature, when philosophically regarded, expresses the lowest form of the human intelligence. . . . It is a mere hallucination of nascent intelligence. . . . It has no existence save to a finite intelligence, an intelligence whose knowledge is derived through the senses." To attain real knowledge, therefore, man must emancipate himself from nature and become a spiritual being, but this emancipation tempts him to assert his own individualism and self-expression, his own selfhood instead of acquiescing in the Selfhood of God. This paradox in Henry James's adaptation of Swedenborg — what might be called Henry James's substitute for the doctrine of "original sin" — was very difficult for William to understand. In *Substance and Shadow* his father wrote: "For we being absolute creatures of God are without any substance in ourselves, and hence are what we are . . . only by virtue of His infinite tenderness imparting, or, as Swedenborg phrases it, *communicating*, Himself to us; permitting us, if we please, to put His love to the basest uses, in order that at last we may through sheer disgust of our own loathsome performances, turn ourselves freely to Him and demand . . . at last the guidance of His unerring laws. . . . For the power by which all this deviltry is enacted is literally God in us."

To a friend William James wrote in 1868: "I have grown up, partly from education and the example of my Dad, partly, I think, from a natural tendency, in a very non-optimistic view of nature, going so far as to have some years ago a perfectly passionate aversion to all moral praise, etc. — an antinomian tendency, in short. I have regarded the affairs of human life to be only a phantasmagoria, which had to be *interpreted* elsewhere in the kosmos into its real significance." Fortunately, about this time William found in Goethe's "realism" a palliative for his father's unhealthy (for William) antinomianism. In his diary he wrote: "[Goethe's] endless delight in facts & details seems to be no longer the painstaking literalness of a mind which, having no inspiration or intuition of its own, and yet fearing to lose the valuable in anything, gathers the accidental & arbitrary up with the essential in one sheaf; but rather the naif delight of an incessantly active mind & healthy sense in their own operations." However, this conflict between the spiritual determinism of Henry James, Sr., and the "realism" of Goethe would continue throughout William James's life in his mind and conscience.

James finally received his M.D. degree in 1869, but had no desire to practice medicine, and saw no way opening to a scientific career. Naturally his neurotic symptoms increased, and he worried about his weak willpower, which he strongly suspected to be responsible for his physical illness. Frequent debates with a friend and neighbor, the brilliant but unknown determinist Chauncey Wright, and reading the German psycho-physicist Gustav Fechner, who claimed to have measured sensation and reduced it to a mathematical formula, aggravated James's depression. He felt "swamped in an empirical [materialistic] philosophy," his will paralyzed by forces beyond his control or comprehension. He was haunted by an image of an epileptic patient frozen in a cataleptic posture whom he had seen on a visit to a mental hospital. "*That shape am I*, I felt, potentially," he later confessed in the guise of a case history in *Varieties of Religious Experience*.

Fortunately, two experiences helped James recover hope and a measure of self-control. One was the death of an adored cousin, Minnie Temple, in the spring of 1870. Her death shocked him into a realization of "the nothingness of all our egotistic fury." He attained a kind of existential stoicism, or what Emerson called "fatal courage," and wrote in his diary: "The inevitable release is sure; wherefore take our turn kindly whatever it contain. Ascend to some sort of partnership with fate, & since tragedy is at the heart of us, go to meet it, work it in to our ends, instead of dodging it all our days, and being run down by it at last. Use your death (or your life, it's all one meaning)."

The other experience was reading a book James had brought back from Europe, *Essais* on a "théorie phénoméniste," by Charles Renouvier, an empiricist who stressed voluntarism and fideism. James recorded in his diary on April 30, 1870: "I think yesterday was a crisis in my life. I finished the first part of Renouvier's 2nd Essay and saw no reason why his definition of free will — 'the sustaining of a thought *because I choose to* when I might have other thoughts' — need be the definition of an illusion. At any rate I will assume for the present . . . that it is no illusion. My first act of free will shall be to believe in free will." He resolved also, as an experiment, to indulge less in speculation and to pay more attention to his conduct, or as he expressed it, "the *form* of my action." Very soon he observed a decrease in his morbid tendencies and a diminishing of the pains in his back. The success of this self-therapy might be called William

James's first psychological discovery, and it would influence his later philosophical thinking.

William James never found a cure for his neuroses, but he learned to live with them. He was greatly assisted by the sympathy and understanding of his former chemistry teacher, Charles W. Eliot, who became president of Harvard University in 1869. He appointed James to give undergraduate instruction in anatomy and physiology in Harvard College in 1873, and two years later James began giving a course in psychology on the physiological approach he had learned from the *Psychophysik* of the Germans. This was a new departure in America, and in 1876, James was also the first to establish a psychological laboratory, three years before Wundt opened his epochal Institute at Leipzig. James, like the Germans, worked on the Darwinian assumption that there is a continuity between animals and human beings, and though it was an accident that he began his teaching in physiology and comparative anatomy, this was a logical approach to the "new" psychology. Yet in spite of his somewhat haphazard preparation, actually no one else in his own country was as well prepared in the field. His medical courses had given him sound basic knowledge of the structure and functions of the human body, and he had extended this knowledge in preparing lectures for his courses — also for several years he was in charge of a Museum in Comparative Anatomy at Harvard. Furthermore, his command of languages enabled him to keep abreast of the latest discoveries and theories in Europe.

James's earliest writings on psychology were reviews for magazines, mainly the *Nation*, the *Atlantic Monthly*, and the *North American Review*, and consequently were written in a popular style, which he soon perfected and never lost. Almost at the start of his career he began to question the materialistic bias of the laboratory psychologists. His first contribution to a professional journal was "Remarks on Spencer's *Definition of Mind as Correspondence*," published in the *Journal of Speculative Philosophy* in 1878. Here he advanced an idea which would become the foundation of his later psychological and philosophical theories, namely, that the mind is motivated by interest and preference. Nearly twenty years later in "Reflex Action and Theism" he declared: "I am not sure that all physiologists see that it [the reflex theory of mind] commits them to regarding the mind as an essentially teleological mechanism. I mean by this that the conceiving or theorizing faculty . . . functions *exclusively for the sake of ends* that do not exist at all in the world of impressions we receive by way of our senses, but are set by our emotional and practical subjectivity altogether."

By 1878 *subjectivity* had become a term of opprobrium in physiological psychology, and in his second important contribution of that year, an essay on "Quelques considérations sur la méthode subjective," which his friend Renouvier published in *Critique philosophique*, James pointed out that "the whole theory of different local habitations in the brain for different classes of ideas with fibres connecting the localities together — so that when one locality is excited the excitement may travel along the fibres and waken up the other locality — this whole theory, I say, was originally derived from our introspective knowledge of the way in which our feelings awaken each other."

In this same important year (1878) James gave a lecture at Johns Hopkins University and at Lowell Institute in Boston on "The Brain and the Mind," in which he traced the development of scientific theories on the nature and function of the brain and the nervous system, but pointed out that no one had yet been able to explain *consciousness*. He did not question the "reflex arc," and he agreed that many of the responses in the brain to nerve-end stimuli were unconscious and seemingly automatic (as in breathing, digestion, circulation of the blood, etc.), but other conscious responses were decidedly not automatic or scientifically predictable, including the concept of "automatism": "The truth is that science and all these other functions of the human mind are alike the results of man's thinking about the phenomena life offers him. . . . I, for one, as a scientific man and a practical man alike, deny utterly that science compels me to believe that my conscience is an *ignis fatuus* or outcast, and I trust that you too . . . will go away strengthened in the natural faith that your delights and sorrows, your loves and hates, your aspirations and efforts are real combatants in life's arena, and not impotent, paralytic spectators of the game."

In "The Sentiment of Rationality" (1879) James argued strongly for the primacy of *feeling* even in the most "rational" conceptions of the philosopher. As far back as Plato (and perhaps beyond) philosophers had shown distrust of human emotions, regarding them as hindrances to the attainment of rational thought. But James asks how the philosopher knows that he has attained a rational conception, and replies that he recognizes it "as he recognizes everything else, by certain subjective marks with which it affects him. . . . A strong feeling of ease, peace, rest, is one of them. The transition from a state of puzzle and perplexity to rational comprehension is full of lively relief and pleasure." This may sound rather negative, "the absence of any feeling of irrationality," but "all feeling whatever, in the light of certain recent psychological speculations, seems to depend for its physical condition not on simple discharge of nerve-currents, but on their discharge under arrest, impediment or resistance." Just as we are unaware of breathing until there is some interference with respiration, so with cogitation: a perfectly "fluent course of thought awakens but little feeling." But "when the thought meets with difficulties, we experience a distress," which yields to a feeling of pleasure as fast as the obstacle is overcome.

Why we are so made that we are unhappy without this fluency of thought James says is an ethical question; he is concerned here with psychology, and it is "an empirical fact that we strive to formulate rationally a tangled mass of fact by a propensity as natural and invincible as that which makes us exchange a hard high stool for an arm-chair." The formulation, or *conception*, "is a *teleological instrument*" used "to satisfy the sentiment of rationality." In forming a concept, a partial aspect of a thing is seized upon to represent the entire thing, ignoring other qualities and properties which for a given purpose do not seem essential. Both in this essay and elsewhere James regards concepts as thus limited, though the conceiver tends to regard them as all-inclusive and universal. James also detects two kinds of mental dispositions, those which have a "passion for simplification," and others, probably a minority, which have a "passion for distinguishing . . . the impulse to be *acquainted* with the parts rather than to comprehend the whole." Later he calls these different responses "the two great aesthetic needs of our logical nature, the need for unity and the need for clearness." James himself prefers the clearness of "concrete reality" in all its fullness and eccentricity of detail, and this preference will lead to his philosophy of "pluralism" and "radical empiricism."

James also preferred concrete reality in its rich diversity to an abstract, simplified unity because it left more room for chance and indeterminism. In 1884 he gave an address at the Harvard Divinity School (and the audience is significant) on "The Dilemma of Determinism," in which he argued for indeterminism on psychological rather than metaphysical grounds — a foreshadowing of his later "pragmatism." At the outset he admitted that "evidence of an external kind to decide between determinism and indeterminism is . . . strictly impossible to find." In a later lecture ("Great Men and Their Environment") he amplified this impossibility: Only an infinite mind able to see all parts of the universe simultaneously could know the ultimate cause and effect of any one action or event in the universe; since it is obviously impossible for a finite mind to attain to such knowledge, the argument must be settled on other grounds than cause and effect — that is, it can never be settled.

But if we cannot *know*, we can at least see the effects of accepting one doctrine over the other. Determinism "professes that those parts of the universe already laid down absolutely appoint and decree what the other parts shall be. The future has no ambiguous possibilities hidden in its womb: the part we call the present is compatible with only one totality. Any other future complement than the one fixed from eternity is impossible." This is an "iron block" universe. "Indeterminism, on the contrary, says that the parts have a certain amount of loose play on one another. . . . It admits that possibilities may be in excess of actualities, and that things not yet revealed to our knowledge may really in themselves be ambiguous. Of two alternative futures which we conceive, both may now be really possible; and the one become impossible only at the very moment when the other excludes it by becoming real. Indeterminism thus denies the world to be one unbending unit of fact. It says there is a certain ultimate pluralism in it; and, so saying, it corroborates our ordinary unsophisticated view of things. To that view, actualities seem to float in a wider sea of possibilities from out of which they are chosen; and, *somewhere*, indeterminism says, such possibilities exist, and form a part of truth."

The real "dilemma," James told the theological students, was the inability of determinism to give a satisfactory explanation of evil in the world. "If God be good, how came he to create — or, if he did not create, how comes he to permit — the devil? The evil facts must be explained as seeming; the devil must be whitewashed, the universe be disinfected, if neither God's goodness nor his unity and power are to remain unimpugned." The determinist can make no distinctions between good and bad; things simply are, and distinctions are merely fantasies. "Calling a thing bad means, if it mean anything at all, that the thing ought not to be, that something else ought to be in its stead. Determinism, in denying that anything else can be in its stead, virtually defines the universe as a place in which what ought to be is impossible — in other words, as an organism whose constitution is afflicted with an incurable taint, an irremediable flaw." The only escape is utter indifference, or cynicism.

In an unfinished universe, bristling with chance and possibilities, both good and bad are real, and eternally at war. Not only did James see hope in such a universe, he also found it immensely stimulating. "Regarded as a stable finality, every outward good becomes a mere weariness to the flesh. It must be menaced, be occasionally lost, for its goodness to be fully felt as such. Nay, more than occasionally lost. No one knows the worth of innocence till he knows it is gone forever, and that money cannot buy it back. Not the saint, but the sinner that repenteth, is he to whom the full length and breadth, and height and depth, of life's meaning is revealed. Not the absence of vice, but vice there, and virtue holding her by the throat, seems the ideal human state. And there seems no reason to suppose it is not a permanent human state."

To the expected question from the divinity students, "Does not the admission of such an unguaranteed chance or freedom preclude utterly the notion of a Providence governing the world?" James replied by an analogy of a chess game between an expert and a novice. The expert will surely win in the end because he knows all the possible moves, but he cannot foresee every actual move the novice will make. Even this analogy may seem rather gloomy for the novice, but James replied that "it is entirely immaterial . . . whether the creator leave the absolute chance-possibilities to be decided by himself, each when its proper moment arrives, or whether, on the contrary, he alienate this power from himself, and leave the decision out and out to finite creatures such as we men are. The great point is that the possibilities are really *here*." Later, in *A Pluralistic Universe*, he would find more encouragement for human effort by speculating that God is not all-powerful, is Himself struggling against obstacles, and needs help, even from finite human beings.

During the 1880s James was trying desperately to get started on writing a textbook in psychology, for which he had signed a contract with Henry Holt in 1878. All the publisher wanted was an elementary exposition of basic principles, though of course he wished it to be as up-to-date as possible. James had thought it would be a simple matter to synthesize the recent discoveries in Germany, France, and England and write the book in a couple of years. But as he began to survey the field, he became convinced that nothing was settled, and scarcely the rudiments of a "science" had yet been formulated. Moreover, he found himself questioning the widely held theories of "associationism" which dominated British psychology and was still accepted by some of the leading German exponents of a psychology based on biological principles.

Associationism began with Locke's *Essay Concerning Human Understanding*, in which he argued that experience gives two sources for ideas (images or representations in the mind), sensation and reflection. Ideas of qualities (color, heat, sound, taste, etc.) come from sensation; thinking, willing, believing, doubting, etc., are the products of reflection. All ideas are simple or complex, the simple being a single sense impression, like the smell of a rose; the complex, a combination of two or more simple ideas, such as green (a mixture of yellow and blue). Some ideas come from two or more senses, such as sight and touch in the experience of space, figure, motion. Others, like ideas of pleasure and pain, come both from sensation and from reflection. Ideas which Locke thought to reside in the objects themselves, the basic ingredients of Newtonian physics, such as solidity, extension, motion, figure, and number, he called *primary qualities*. Qualities existing only in the senses, though produced by the effect of primary qualities in objects, he called *secondary qualities*, such as sights, sounds, tastes. Knowledge of primary qualities Locke regarded as more certain and dependable than knowledge of secondary qualities, which might vary with the state of the senses or indivdual differences. Berkeley tried to find a way out of Locke's dualism in pure idealism, and Hume ended his inquiry in complete skepticism, but British empiricists did not give up the atomic suppositions of Locke. They still tried to account for certain kinds of knowledge by combining or associating sensations by mental processes.

To William James, however, it seemed that "All our mind's contents are alike empirical," and he began conducting experiments to test this hypothesis. In "The Space Quale," published in the *Journal of Speculative Philosophy* in 1879, he summarized and evaluated the results of his laboratory investigations of sense perception of space. He agreed with the earlier theorizers that man has no special space sense, but he found that several senses give sensations of weight, intensity, interval, muscular stress, etc., which constitute primordial experience of space. In other experiments he proved that the sense of balance is controlled by the semicircular canals of the inner ear, the conclusive evidence being that deaf-mutes whose semicircular canals have been paralyzed by injury or have atrophied cannot experience dizziness or motion sickness. In this field James did important pioneer work. The perception of time he found also to be a function of various senses, including muscular tensions.

James's first publication on the will was a thirty-two-page essay in 1880 on "The Feeling of Effort," in which he argued that the incoming currents in sensory nerves are felt in consciousness (i.e., one is aware that something out there is being seen or heard or touched); but that after the brain has received the "message" and dispatched a reply, there is no feeling of the efferent discharge. If some choice needs to be made for a practical end, the mind is aware of directing the impulse to the right muscle, but "consciousness seems to desert all processes where it can no longer be of any use." Here James was close to discovering the "conditioned reflex," and perhaps missed it only because he was more interested in evidence of choice and free will in the processes. He points out that in learning to perform an unfamiliar act, conscious effort has to be exerted, but with practice the act can be performed with less and less conscious attention: "The marksman thinks only of the exact position of the goal, the singer only of the perfect sound, the balancer only of the point in space whose oscillations he must counteract by movement. The associated mechanism has become so perfect in all these persons, that each variation in the thought of the end, is functionally correlated with the one movement fitted to bring the latter about."

Because of this "principle of parsimony in consciousness," James says, "the motor discharge *ought* to be devoid of sentience. The essentials of a voluntary movement are: 1, a preliminary idea of the end we wish to attain; 2, a '*fiat*'; 3, an appropriate muscular contraction; 4, the end felt as actually accomplished. . . . The end conceived will, when these associations are formed, always awaken its own proper motor idea."

Closely akin to this view of the volition process was James's theory of emotions as "indubitably physiological," a process occurring in the motor and sensory centers. There is therefore no such thing as *an emotion*, only these combined motor processes. In an essay on "What Is an Emotion" (1884), he admits, however, that he is speaking only of "emotions . . . that have a distinct bodily expression." There are perhaps others (feelings of pleasure or displeasure, interest or boredom, etc.) which may be "mental operations," though they may be accompanied by involuntary or unconscious physical movements, as in thinking of food, one may move his tongue, moisten his lips, and involuntarily salivate.

James's thesis is "that *the bodily changes follow directly the* PERCEPTION *of the exciting fact, and that our feeling of the same changes as they occur* IS *the emotion*." We might paraphrase this by saying that perception plus bodily manifestation equals emotional feeling. When he published this essay James was not aware that a Danish psychologist named Lange had proposed the same theory, and when this fact was called to his attention he readily agreed to having it called the "James-Lange theory of apperception." In popular parlance, one does not run from a bear because he feels fear; he feels fear because he runs. This simplification sounds more paradoxical than the theory actually is: the point is that bodily activity, not an abstraction, causes the feeling of emotion. The James-Lange theory occupies a major position in James's psychology. James was not trying to reduce all psychological functions to physiological processes, but seeking to show how inseparable and interdependent the mind and body are.

These contributions to physiological psychology were first recognized and appreciated in France, where they were published in translation in *Critique philosophique*. These early essays are also important because they led James to his most important discovery, for which he became world-famous after publishing his *Principles of Psychology* in 1890. The German psychologist Franz Brentano had compared consciousness to a stream, but it was James who discovered the "fringe" of consciousness, which gave new meaning to the stream concept. He found that consciousness was not, as the epistemologists who talked of simple and complex ideas believed, awareness of separate objects in procession which the mind somehow connects by association. Instead consciousness was like a flowing river carrying all sorts of detritus, undifferentiated objects until some personal interest causes the consciousness to focus on some part of the flux. And always just beyond consciousness there is a blurry periphery of objects which contribute to the flow, the continuity, some of which never come into focus. One object leads the mind's attention to others, and we ought, James says, to speak of association of objects, not of ideas.

The mind becomes aware of many things without effort, and consciousness is never a blank, there is always a flux of something, or somethings, in it. Although this process takes place even when the will is passive, as in reverie, or in weak, halfhearted action, it is not fortuitous or haphazard. In the first place, consciousness came into existence on strictly Darwinian principles, to aid the organism to adapt itself to its environment and survive. In James's words: "Every actually existing consciousness seems to itself at any rate to be a *fighter for ends*, of which many, but for its presence, would not be ends at all. Its powers of cognition are mainly subservient to these ends, discerning which facts further them and which do not." The more attention needed, the greater the volition, but holding the object in consciousness unlocks the proper motor energy and the flow takes place. If the chosen response is no action, or delayed action, more attention is needed — more volition — and the motor energy is held in reserve, though this, too, is accomplished by switching nerve currents to appropriate circuits.

James has often been accused of inconsistencies and contradictions, and consistency was not a virtue which he cherished;

nevertheless there is such a close relationship between his theories of the will, the stream of consciousness with its "fringe," habit, the self, and the nature of reality (to name major subjects) that one theory almost implies the other.

The chapter of his *Principles* which received most popular (unprofessional) approval was "Habit." James begins with the assumption that all organic matter is plastic, nerve tissue especially. Once a particular stimulus has traveled through nerve tissue to a certain center of the brain and activated an ideo-motor response, a similar stimulus will follow the same path unless it is blocked or rerouted by conscious volition, that is, energy generated by attention with effort. Habits are, therefore, the result of "pathways through the nerve-centres," and the more often the same path is used, the deeper and more fixed it becomes.

Habits can be beneficial or harmful, James stressed, and it is very important to start and preserve the helpful habit. The practical benefit is that "habit simplifies our movements, makes them accurate, and diminishes fatigue," because each repetition demands less and less conscious effort. A great difference between man and other animals is that he "is born with a tendency to do more things than he has ready-made arrangements for in his nerve-centres. Most of the performances of other animals are automatic. But in him the number of them is so enormous, that most of them must be the fruit of painful study. If practice did not make perfect, nor habit economize the expense of nervous and muscular energy, he would therefore be in a sorry plight." This theory, like James's "stream of consciousness," emphasizes plasticity, flux, the need for choice in adjusting to new experiences, and the importance of *feeling* in the process of ideo-motor responses.

James's exposition of the "Self" makes great use of the flux of consciousness and the malleability of habits. In the first place, he finds not one self but several, all of course interrelated and interdependent. There is "the empirical self or me," and all that the "me" possesses, including not only his body and his physical possessions, but his reputation, and his social relations. Then there is the "spiritual me," the "core and nucleus" of the self, which some call the "soul." James wishes to dispense with "mind-substance" and soul, but this controlling center serves the same purpose as the older concepts of a Soul uniting mind and body. James's "self" has consciousness of a consistent personal identity, connecting states of consciousness of the past with the present state, or, as he says, "each successive mental state appropriate[s] the same past Me." Just who the *knower* is James leaves to metaphysics. He accepts the common-sense view that we have "*direct* knowledge of the existence of our 'states of consciousness' " without the hypothesis of a transcendental Soul or Mind "which thinks through us." He concludes provisionally that "the thoughts themselves are the thinkers."

James himself was far from satisfied that thoughts think themselves, but he was trying desperately to keep psychology within the realm of pure empiricism. That it was not yet a "natural science" he ruefully confessed in a Conclusion he wrote for the one-volume edition of his *Principles* which he called *Psychology, Briefer Course* (1892): "When, then, we talk of 'psychology as a natural science,' we must not assume that that means a sort of psychology that stands at last on solid ground. It means just the reverse; it means a psychology particularly fragile, and into which the waters of metaphysical criticism leak at every joint . . . a strong prejudice that we *have* states of mind, and that our brain conditions them: but not a single law in the sense in which physics shows us laws. . . . This is no science, it is only the hope of a science."

The great success of James's *Principles of Psychology* and his *Psychology, Briefer Course* made him one of the most famous men in the field of American education, and he accepted the opportunity to become a widely acclaimed popular lecturer. He had always addressed himself as much to a nonprofessional audience as to a professional one, and he now became in actual fact a popular psychologist, with a permanent effect on both his writing and thinking. Although he delivered his address on "The Will to Believe" to philosophy clubs at Yale and Brown universities in 1896, it was one of these "popular" lectures. He even called it "something like a sermon on justification by faith."

Scientists had become increasingly agnostic because part of the concept of a scientific method is suspension of belief (or conclusion) until all the evidence is in. But James had decided as early as his

"Dilemma of Determinism" that seldom, if ever, is the evidence all in, and meanwhile *some* decision often needs to be made, both for practical necessity and because prolonged indecision may be deleterious to the nervous system. His thesis in "The Will to Believe" is this: "*Our passional nature not only lawfully may, but must, decide an option between propositions, whenever it is a genuine option that cannot by its nature be decided on intellectual grounds; for to say, under such circumstances, 'Do not decide, but leave the question open,' is itself a passional decision, — just like deciding yes or no, — and is attended with the same risk of losing the truth.*" James was immediately accused of advocating "wishful thinking," but he was advocating a willful entertaining of belief only when there is a "genuine option"; further, not all optional choices need be final. All he was saying was that sometimes it is better to take a chance on a decision than wait indefinitely for elusive evidence. He also believed that at times decisive action may change the circumstances; that, to anticipate "pragmatism," *truth* can sometimes be *made*, and a man's world changed by his own efforts. If this were not so, social reform would be impossible.

The doctrine of pragmatism is almost an extension of "The Will to Believe." James first used the term in a lecture at the University of California in 1898 on "Philosophical Concepts and Practical Results." He borrowed the word from his friend Charles Peirce, who had coined it twenty years earlier in an article on "How to Make Our Ideas Clear." Peirce did not intend to present a theory of truth, only a method of using language so as to avoid ambiguity. In James's version of this method "our beliefs are really rules for action," and "to develop a thought's meaning, we need only determine what conduct it is fitted to produce; that conduct is for us its sole significance" — in *Pragmatism* he would later say its *truth*. "To attain perfect clearness in our thoughts of an object, then, we need only consider what effects of a conceivable practical kind the object may involve — what sensations we are to expect from it, and what reactions we must prepare. Our conception of these effects, then, is for us the whole of our conception of the object, so far as that conception has positive significance at all."

Peirce had strongly objected to James's "Will to Believe" because this emphasis upon conduct was too subjective for him. He was interested more in the *method* of thinking, James in *purpose* and *effect*, though he also called pragmatism a method for attaining truth (*answers* might have been less controversial), and subtitled his book *Pragmatism* "A New Name for Some Old Ways of Thinking." By "old way" James evidently meant that the dependability of an assumption can only be tested by experience. An assumption that proves reliable is a "truth," but only provisionally, for no truth is universal. This rules out "absolutes" of all kinds and makes truth relative, a concept which most philosophers of the past would have called a contradiction of terms. But James claimed that most metaphysical assumptions, such as determinism, as we have seen, can never be settled by objective proof one way or the other. Yet if a man believes he has at least some control over his destiny, he is more likely to make an effort to help out the desired result. The effort itself is good for his character and morale, and it may succeed also on the physical level of practicality. Believing in one's own strength and willpower, therefore, has pragmatic value, and the assumption is true because it works.

In *Pragmatism* James says: " 'Grant an idea or belief to be true . . . what concrete difference will its being true make in any one's actual life?' . . . The moment pragmatism asks this question, it sees the answer: *True ideas are those that we can assimilate, validate, corroborate and verify. False ideas are those that we can not*. . . . We live in a world of realities that can be infinitely useful or infinitely harmful. Ideas that tell us which of them to expect count as the true ideas in all this primary sphere of verification, and the pursuit of such ideas is a primary human duty."

Though the book entitled *Pragmatism* was not published until 1907, five years earlier James had used the pragmatic approach in his epoch-making *Varieties of Religious Experience*. In this work he is not concerned with the validity of any particular religion, only with the *life of religion*, which "consists of the belief that there is an unseen order, and that our supreme good lies in harmoniously adjusting ourselves thereto." James himself maintains a neutral position regarding these "varieties," but he does not doubt the reality of the experiences to the people who have had them and feel that they have been in a personal relation with "unseen power" of some sort. To the charge that many of the experiences he reports may have been caused by a condition of the person's nervous system, James replies that even if this is true, the experience is no less an empirical fact. He grants that religious ecstasy and insanity may be difficult, or impossible, to differentiate, but who knows what power may be working through human nerves and brains? The religious experience is phenomenally *real*.

In spite of his attempts to be scientifically objective in writing his *Principles of Psychology*, and his rejection of a Soul or transcendental world or cosmic spirit to account for the phenomenon of consciousness, James had all along harbored a suspicion — perhaps even a secret wish — that a transcendental consciousness might exist. This hypothesis colored his empiricism and made it at times almost an eccentric variety of idealism. For example, in 1898 he had given a lecture on "Human Immortality," in which he had suggested as a hypothesis, not a personal conviction, that the human brain does not *produce* thoughts, as a dynamo produces electricity, but only *transmits* thoughts, as wire conducts electric current.

Because he had never found a satisfactory or consistent theory of cognition, James now suggests that we imagine the brain to be a thin membrane separating the world of mind and matter, and that sometimes (why not always?) spiritual energy flows through it. Then, shifting his metaphor, he speaks of the human threshold of consciousness being lowered, so that a consciousness from a higher than human level flows into it. Something like this seems to take place in religious "conversion" and a "mystical experience." The physiological-psychological explanation that consciousness is in the brain had always been to James an "absolute world-enigma, — something so paradoxical and abnormal as to be a stumbling block to Nature, and almost a self-contradiction." So, as a possible way out, James suggests that "we need only suppose the continuity of our consciousness with a mother sea, to allow for exceptional waves occasionally pouring over the dam. Of course the causes of these odd lowerings of the brain's threshold still remain a mystery on any terms."

The enigma of consciousness had led James to become interested in "psychical research" while still a medical student, and he helped found the American Society for Psychical Research in 1884. Before writing his *Principles* he had attended séances, and he spent many years trying to find objective (scientific) evidence of telepathy, clairvoyance, and survival of consciousness after the death of the body. His professed motive was that claims for such phenomena should not be dismissed as fraudulent without scientific investigation, but his continued effort in the field indicated, by his own psychology, a strong passional interest. His acquaintance with hypnotism, with which he experimented, with split personality, which he observed on many field trips to insane asylums, with hallucinatory visions (both he and his very religious father had each had one almost traumatic experience of this kind) — these phenomena made him wonder whether an individual consciousness might somehow be a part of a larger consciousness (or consciousnesses) under certain conditions. He never found any scientific proof of telepathy, clairvoyance, or survival of consciousness after death; nor did he ever come to believe sufficiently in an Infinite Consciousness encompassing all finite consciousnesses to cause him to renounce pluralism for monism. He entertained this idea in various writings, but he continued to have a strong intuitive feeling that the phenomenon of consciousness was also pluralistic.

This digression is necessary for understanding the kind of book *The Varieties of Religious Experience* is. James began by collecting every record he could find of a religious nature, and it is significant that he subtitled his work "A Study in Human Nature." His procedure was as follows: first description, then comparison, classification, analysis, and finally some tentative conclusions. He wanted first of all to find out the nature of a religious experience, and whether the mass of such experiences had anything in common. His approach was, therefore, psychological, and he soon became convinced that *feeling* and not intellect or reason was the doorway to the religious life. Dogmas and systematic theologies were only the fossils of religion, sometimes surviving centuries after the life had passed out of them. If a person had to prove the existence of God by logic, that person had never had intimate knowledge of God. The only virtue James could find in theology and a church was an aesthetic one, like the symmetry of scholasticism or the beautiful architecture of a medieval church. But why had men built the cathedral, and what function did it serve in their lives? James was never more pragmatic than in his search for answers to such questions.

The one belief James found in all examples of the religious confessions was that the worshiper *felt* that he had been in communication or some sort of contact with spiritual power (singular or plural), from which he derived a charge of new energy. In all religions there seemed to be three similar techniques for tapping this psychic energy: sacrifice (of objects, self, or pleasures), confession (a "general system of purgation and cleansing"), and prayer ("every kind of inward communication or conversation with the power recognized as divine"). Of these three techniques James found prayer to be "the very soul and essence of religion." Through prayer the devotee finds purpose, guidance, and strength to endure the accidents and hardships of life, and "at all stages of the prayerful life we find the persuasion that in the process of communion energy from on high flows in to meet demand, and becomes operative within the phenomenal world. So long as this operativeness is admitted to be real, it makes no essential difference whether its immediate effects be subjective or objective. The fundamental religious point is that in prayer, spiritual energy, which otherwise would slumber, does become active, and spiritual work of some kind is effected really." And of course the "spiritual work" may also in turn stimulate the person affected to perform physical work.

The test of a religious experience, therefore, is pragmatic, and it does not matter, James says, where the energy comes from, or that science cannot account for it. "Religion, in short, is a monumental chapter in the history of human egotism. The gods believed in — whether by crude savages or by men disciplined intellectually — agree with each other in recognizing personal calls. Religious thought is carried on in terms of personality," whether by the "healthy-minded" who take their world for granted, or the "sick-minded" oppressed by a sense of guilt and inadequacy: "the religious individual tells you that the divine meets him on the basis of his personal concerns."

James himself suspected that this mysterious psychic energy might come from the person's own subconscious. But this did not, for him, rule out the possibility of contact with some sort of supernatural — or supranatural — consciousness. The subconscious might be the doorway to the supernatural — a doorway also between a science of religion and the living experience of religion, for science accepts the existence of the *subconscious*, and certain objective techniques can be used to demonstrate the flow of energy from the subconscious to the conscious mind. Of course the assumption that the subconscious is a doorway to a world of nonphysical energy is only an assumption (for James this was Fechnerian, pre-Freudian speculation), but the effects are real, and James could find no other hypothesis for their source. He admits, too, that to experience this flow of energy from the mysterious fountain in the subconscious one must have confidence in its existence, what the church calls "faith" and James an "over-belief."

Although all the transcendental metaphysicians opposed this "thoroughly 'pragmatic' view of religion," James found it to be a common view in the vast confessional literature he had collected, and he saw no reason to interpolate "divine miracles" or build an imaginary "heaven" to make religion more divine or more spiritual. "I believe," he says, "the pragmatic way of taking religion to be the deeper way. It gives it body as well as soul, it makes it claim, as everything real must claim, some characteristic realm of fact as its very own. What the more characteristically divine facts are, apart from the actual inflow of energy in the faith-state and the prayer-state, I know not."

James now held as an over-belief, perhaps influenced by his association with psychical research, the notion that "the world of our present consciousness is only one out of many worlds of consciousness that exist, and that those other worlds must contain experiences which have a meaning for our life also; and that although in the main their experiences and those of this world keep discrete, yet the two become continuous at certain points, and higher energies filter in." He was well aware of the contempt of scientists for such an over-belief, but he also now held the view of his father that "the real world is of a different temperament, — more intricately built than physical science allows. So my objective and my subjective conscience both hold me to the over-belief which I express. Who knows whether the faithfulness of individuals here below to their own poor over-beliefs may not actually help God in turn to be more effectively faithful to his own greater tasks?"

In spite of James's talk of different levels of consciousness, he never wavered in his doctrine (or "philosophical attitude," he preferred to call it) of "radical empiricism," which opposed monism, idealism, and was pluralistic. He defined the term as early as 1898 in his Preface to *The Will to Believe*: "I say 'empiricism,' because it is contented to regard its most assured conclusions concerning matters of fact as hypotheses liable to modification in the course of future experience; and I say 'radical,' because it treats the doctrine of monism itself as an hypothesis, and, unlike so much of the halfway empiricism that is current under the name of positivism or agnosticism or scientific naturalism, it does not dogmatically affirm monism as something with which all experience has got to square."

Thus by *empiricism* James means that nothing can be known except by human experience, and he postulates that "*the only things that shall be debatable among philosophers shall be things definable in terms drawn from experience*. (Things of an unexperienceable nature may exist ad libitum, but they form no part of the material for philosophic debate.)" This limitation James calls "a methodical postulate" (quoted by Ralph Barton Perry in his preface to *Essays in Radical Empiricism*). Elsewhere he says that pragmatism and radical empiricism have no necessary logical connection, but actually they use the same method for finding answers to questions, and both look for answers in particular experiences rather than general ones or in abstractions about experiences.

In 1907 James collected and placed in an envelope twelve articles, most of which he had published in philosophical journals from 1904 through 1906, which he intended to republish in a book, but *Essays in Radical Empiricism* was not published until 1912, two years after his death. Though this posthumous volume is in the nature of an anthology, it has a unifying theme in the attempt of the various essays to define the basic concepts of "radical empiricism." In the first essay ("Does 'Consciousness' Exist?") James suggests abandoning the term *consciousness*, though he means "only to deny that the word stands for an entity" and to assert "that it does stand for a function." For "consciousness" he substitutes "pure experience," which is "made of *that*, of just what appears, of space, of intensity, of flatness, brownness, heaviness, or what not." He wants to avoid the dualism of *thought* and *thing*, for "*thoughts* in the concrete are made of the same stuff as things are." This does not mean, for instance, that the thought of a chair can be measured with a tape measure, but the very thought of a chair includes all the physical qualities which make it known as a chair. James answers the old metaphysical riddle of how one object can exist in two minds at the same time by the contention that the two (or more) minds meet in the object which they experience together, just as two lines can pass through one point if they intersect at the point.

In the essay on "A World of Pure Experience" James says: "To be radical, an empiricism must neither admit into its constructions any element that is not directly experienced, nor exclude from them any element that is directly experienced. For such a philosophy, *the relations that connect experiences must themselves be experienced relations, and any kind of relation experienced must be accounted as 'real' as anything else in the system*. Elements may indeed be redistributed, the original placing of things getting corrected, but a real place must be found for every kind of thing experienced, whether term or relation, in the final philosophical arrangement." Berkeley, Hume, James Mill, and other associationists had argued that the relations or connections of things experienced are supplied by the mind.

Although at any given moment experiences may seem unrelated or chaotic, they do not come singly or detached from the stream of experience (what James had called "consciousness" and its "fringe" in his *Principles*). He calls the contents of this stream, "taken all together, a quasi-chaos." Yet, as he argues in "The Thing and Its Relations," in its immediacy, experience "seems perfectly fluent." It is only after intellectual reflection that we distinguish elements and parts, give them separate names, and discover contradictions and incomprehensibilities. " 'Pure experience' is the name which I gave to the immediate flux of life which furnishes the material to our later reflection with its conceptual categories. . . . Pure experience . . . is but another name for feeling or sensation. But the flux of it no sooner comes than it tends to fill itself with emphases, and these salient parts become identified and fixed and abstracted; so that experience now flows as if shot through with adjectives and nouns and prepositions and conjunctions. Its purity is only a relative term, meaning the proportional amount of unverbalized sensation which it still embodies."

James himself admits one difficulty in his theory of "pure experience." Experience can be "pure" only to the newborn babe or someone in a semicoma from sickness, intoxication, or injury — sensation without reflection of any kind. Normal people tend to verbalize their sensations as soon as they "think" of them. The postulation of "pure experience" is, therefore, hypothetical; we must look (or feel) quickly to get a glimpse of it before it is adulterated by thought.

In a book which he did publish himself the year before his death, *A Pluralistic Universe* (1909), James continued his quarrel with monistic idealism, a quarrel which he always admitted to be partly a conflict of temperaments, between those who want a tidy, safe universe with divine decisions already made and engraved on eternal tablets and those who prefer an unfinished, imperfect, precarious universe with the final outcome still hanging in the balance. This temperamental difference in types of thinkers was the subject of his first discourse in the Gifford Lectures at Oxford University, published as *A Pluralistic Universe* — and it is worth noting that the article "a" is more tentative and modest than "the" would have been; he does not say dogmatically that this *is* the way the universe is, but here is one man's theory of the way it is.

In his second lecture James also confesses that he prefers some variety of pantheism to a dualistic theism because it allows a greater degree of intimacy with "the creative principle": "we are substantially one with it, and . . . the divine is therefore the most intimate of all our possessions, heart of our heart, in fact," whereas dualistic theism makes man "a secondary order of substances created by God." But pantheism can be of two forms, one absolute or monistic and the other pluralistic. In the monistic form "the divine exists authentically only when the world is experienced all at once in its absolute totality, whereas radical empiricism allows that the absolute sum-total of things may never be actually experienced or realized in that shape at all, and that a disseminated, distributed, or incompletely unified appearance is the only form that reality may yet have achieved."

In Lecture III James calls Hegel an idealistic pantheist and says that "in no philosophy is the fact that a philosopher's vision and the technique he uses in proof of it are two different things more palpably evident than in Hegel. The vision in his case was that of a world in which reason holds all things in solution and accounts for all the irrationality that superficially appears by taking it up as a 'moment' into itself."

Hegel's vision was in two parts: "The first part was that reason is all-inclusive, the second was that things are 'dialectic.' " The dialectic process admits that things are in a flux, and they are often experienced as off-balance and working at cross-purposes. With this James of course agrees. But Hegel finds the equilibrium and symmetry restored in a "higher synthesis" in which opposites merge and become a perfect unity. James calls this synthesis a "treaty," and says that "Hegel's originality lay in transporting the process from the sphere of percepts to that of concepts and treating it as the universal method by which every kind of life, logical, physical, or psychological, is mediated. Not to the sensible facts as such, then, did Hegel point for the secret of what keeps existence going, but rather to the conceptual way of treating them." Even though "concepts were not in his eyes the static self-contained things that previous logicians had supposed, but were germinative, and passed beyond themselves into each other by what he called their immanent dialectic," nevertheless the "absolute" which his logic establishes transcends human experience. The arguments by which James finds Hegel's rationalism irrational are too complicated for brief summary, but regardless of the logic by which he finds Hegel illogical, his main objection is that Hegel's reasoning leads away from the "strung-along unfinished world in time" in which men actually live.

"But if we drop the absolute out of the world," James asks, "must we then conclude that the world contains nothing better in the way of consciousness than our consciousness?" His answer is that "logically it is possible to believe in superhuman beings without identifying them with the absolute at all." As an example of such a belief he turns to the panpsychism of Gustav Fechner, whose earlier

Psychophysiks had not favorably impressed him; but recently he had read Fechner's *Zend-Avesta* and *Über die Seelenfrage* and been fascinated by the German's theory of pyramiding souls, which James calls a "republic of semi-detached consciousness," presided over by a God whose limited power absolves him from responsibility for evil in the world. Fechner's philosophy can be called panpsychic because it finds a hierarchy of souls in all existing things, rising from plants and animals to human beings, planets, and still higher souls ascending to a Supreme Soul. (Query: Wouldn't this make Fechner's soul-empire a monarchy instead of a republic?) James admits that this Supreme Soul or God provides the possibility for an absolutist philosophy, but he insists that Fechner develops his details pluralistically.

James had struggled for many years to escape solipsism without postulating an absolute mind or soul in which all finite consciousnesses could exist. As he confessed in his Hibbert lecture on "Compounding of Consciousness": "Sincerely, and patiently as I could, I struggled with the problem for years, covering hundreds of sheets of paper with notes and memoranda and discussions with myself over the difficulty. How can many consciousnesses be at the same time one consciousness? How can one and the same identical fact experience itself so diversely? [He had attempted to answer this question in *Radical Empiricism* — see above page 72.] The struggle was vain; I found myself in an *impasse*. I saw that I must either forswear that 'psychology without a soul' to which my whole psychological and kantian education had committed me, — I must, in short, bring back distinct spiritual agents to know the mental states, now singly and now in combination, in a word bring back scholasticism and common sense — or else I must squarely confess the solution of the problem impossible, and then either give up my intellectualistic logic . . . or, finally, face the fact that life is logically irrational."

In Fechner (encouraged, too, by Bergson's attack on logic) James saw a possible way out, a way also suggested by the accumulated data of psychiatry regarding hypnotism, split personality or plural selves, "mystical experiences," etc., which he had studied both for his lectures in *Varieties of Religious Experience* and as an active member of the Society for Psychical Research. "For my own part," he confesses, "I find in some of these abnormal or super-normal facts the strongest suggestions in favor of a superior consciousness being possible. I doubt whether we shall ever understand some of them without using the very letter of Fechner's conception of a great reservoir in which the memories of earth's inhabitants are pooled and preserved, and from which, when the threshold lowers or the valve opens, information ordinarily shut out leaks into the mind of exceptional individuals among us. But those regions of inquiry are perhaps too spook-haunted to interest an academic audience, and the only evidence I feel it now decorous to bring to the support of Fechner is drawn from ordinary religious experience. I think it may be asserted that there *are* religious experiences of a specific nature, not deducible by analogy or psychological reasoning from our other sorts of experience. I think that they point with reasonable probability to the continuity of our consciousness with a wider spiritual environment from which the ordinary prudential man (who is the only man that scientific psychology, so called, takes cognizance of) is shut off."

James, a scientist in spite of his sympathy with mystics and mental healers, cautiously says he finds *suggestions* — not proof — "in favor of a superior consciousness." This view appeals to him because the believer in it "finds that the tenderer parts of his personal life are continuous with a *more* of the same quality which is operative in the universe outside of him and which he can keep in working touch with, and in a fashion get on board of and save himself, when all his lower being has gone to pieces in the wreck. In a word, the believer is continuous, to his own consciousness, at any rate, with a wider self from which saving experiences flow in."

Such evidence is, of course, purely subjective, but to James it has pragmatic value. And to him personally Fechner's polytheism has advantages over monotheism because it is a way of "escape from the paradoxes and perplexities that a consistently thought-out monistic universe suffers from as from a species of auto-intoxication — the mystery of the 'fall' namely, of reality lapsing into appearance, truth into error, perfection into imperfection; of evil, in short; the mystery of universal determinism, of the block-universe eternal and without a history, etc.; — the only way of escape, I say, from all this is to be frankly pluralistic and assume that the superhuman consciousness, however vast it may be, has itself an external environment, and consequently is finite." At the end of *Varieties of Religious Experience* James had used the argument for a limited God to restore man's sense of importance and give him an incentive for effort: God needs us as much as we need Him.

In his study of religious experiences James had found so much psychological and human value in them that he wanted to restore religion to intellectual respectability. So he now suggests: "Let empiricism once become associated with religion, as hitherto, through some strange misunderstanding, it has been associated with irreligion, and I believe that a new era of religion as well as of philosophy will be ready to begin. . . . I fully believe that such an empiricism is a more natural ally than dialectics ever were, or can be, of the religious life. It is true that superstitions and wild-growing over-beliefs of all sorts will undoubtedly begin to abound if the notion of higher consciousnesses enveloping ours, of fechnerian earth-souls and the like, grows orthodox and fashionable; still more will they superabound if science ever puts her approval stamp on the phenomena . . . of psychic research so-called — and I myself firmly believe that most of these phenomena are rooted in reality." This *firm belief* was an over-belief, for in his final report on psychical research (1909) James has to admit that after twenty years of reading the literature of the researchers, talking and corresponding with them, and spending many hours "in witnessing (or trying to witness)" psychic phenomena, "yet I am theoretically no 'further' than I was at the beginning; and I confess that at times I have been tempted to believe that the Creator has eternally intended this department of nature to remain *baffling*."

This candor, however, did not save James from attacks by his scientific colleagues, and his tolerance for the "wild beasts of philosophy," to use his own phrase, was responsible to a considerable extent for a decline in his reputation even before his death in 1910. He was well aware of this decline and dissatisfied with himself for never having completed an integrated philosophical system. At the time of his death James was working on an introduction to metaphysics which he had hoped would complete his "unfinished arch," but he was discouraged by this effort too and left a note with the manuscript asking his editor (his son Henry) to call it "a beginning of an introduction to philosophy." The book was published in 1911 as *Some Problems of Philosophy*. It is indeed elementary, but it is the most systematic and organized of all James's books, and in some respects makes a fitting ending for his philosophical writings.

"Philosophy in the full sense is only *man thinking*, thinking about generalities rather than about particulars," he says in his first chapter, "Philosophy and Its Critics." James very concisely and clearly defines the kinds of philosophy (mainly rational and empirical), the kinds of philosophers (for he still thinks that a man's temperament determines his philosophical preferences), and in chapter 2 neatly outlines the major problems and theories of metaphysics. In "The Problem of Being," or ontology, he says that "the orthodox opinion is that the quantity of reality must at all costs be conserved, and the waxing and waning of our phenomenal experiences must be treated as surface appearances which leave the deeps untouched." He admits, however, that "the question of being is the darkest in all philosophy."

The balance and impartiality of *Some Problems* is most evident in James's treatment of *percept* and *concept*. While arguing for his "radical empiricism" and "pluralism" he invariably showed a partiality for perception, which seemed to him nearer to "pure experience." But he now admits: "Had we no concepts we should live simply 'getting' each successive moment of experience, as the sessile sea-anemone on its rock receives whatever nourishment the wash of the waves may bring. With concepts we go in quest of the absent, meet the remote, actively turn this way or that, bend our experience, and make it tell us whither it is bound." This is essentially, again, a Darwinian theory (though James does not say so), an explanation of how human beings have adapted themselves to environment and changes. James does say, "We *harness* perceptual reality in concepts in order to drive it better to our ends."

In mathematics, the sciences, and the branches of philosophy such as aesthetics and ethics, the sense order is transformed into a symbolical rational order. "We may well call this a theoretic conquest over the order in which nature originally comes. The conceptual order into which we translate our experience seems not only a means of practical adaptation, but the revelation of a deeper level of reality in things. . . . Concepts not only guide us over the map of life, but we *revalue* life by their use." Yet if we lose ourselves in abstractions, we lose a feeling for the novelty, the variety, the excitement, and the adventure of the sensual world of experience.

In science, "The notion of eternal elements and their mixture serves us in so many ways, that we adopt unhesitatingly the theory that primordial being is inalterable in its attributes as well as in its quantity, and that the laws by which we describe its habits are uniform in the strictest mathematical sense. These are the absolute conceptual foundations, we think, spread beneath the surface of perceptual variety. It is when we come to human lives, that our point of view changes. It is hard to imagine that 'really' our own subjective experiences are only molecular arrangements, even though the molecules be conceived as beings of a psychic kind. . . . Psychologically considered, our experiences resist conceptual reduction, and our fields of consciousness, taken simply as such, remain just what they appear, even though facts of a molecular order should prove to be the signals of the appearance. Biography is the concrete form in which all that is is immediately given; the perceptual flux is the authentic stuff of each of our biographies, and yields a perfect effervescence of novelty all the time. New men and women, books, accidents, events, inventions, enterprises, burst unceasingly upon the world. It is vain to resolve these into ancient elements, or to say that they belong to ancient kinds, so long as no one of them in its full individuality ever was here before or will ever come again."

Some critics have said that William James was not a philosopher but a literary man, and it is true that in his feeling for and intuition about the infinite variety of the world he had the sensibility of a poet, and his unflagging interest in the unpredictable responses of human beings to their experiences was that of a novelist in his plots and resolutions. His deep sympathies and great imagination gave him the command of a prose style unequaled in vigor, clarity, and colloquial spontaneity by any other philosopher writing in English. His literary reputation kept his name alive long after his psychology and philosophy had faded in popularity. One of his public lectures on "The Moral Equivalent of War" was circulated in several million copies by the American Association for International Conciliation. John Dewey further popularized the term *pragmatism*, but his pragmatic philosophy was strictly functional and social — adaptation of an organism to its environment — and not directly concerned with the problems of James's pluralism. It was Dewey's, not James's, pragmatism which became a world influence in education during the first half of the twentieth century. The rise of J. B. Watson's behaviorism also further eroded James's influence, for Watson scornfully dismissed James's psychology as "introspective," which it was in part, but his theory of emotion might be regarded as the beginning of behaviorism.

James's *Varieties of Religious Experience* continued to be widely read, and both his *Letters* edited by his son Henry (1920) and the monumental *Thought and Character of William James* by Ralph Barton Perry (1935) created personal interest in the life and personality of James. But American psychologists found the *Principles* old-fashioned and moralistic, and the contradictions and lack of order in his philosophical writings were regarded by most professional philosophers as fatal defects.

It is hardly surprising that rediscovery of James had to take place in Europe, where he was first appreciated and had never been as forgotten as in his own country. It is difficult to say exactly when this rediscovery began, though the books that show it have been published only recently, the most important being Hans Linschoten's *On the Way toward a Phenomenological Psychology: The Psychology of William James*, 1968 (translated from a German version, 1961); Bruce Wilshire's *William James and Phenomenology: A Study of the "Principles of Psychology,"* 1968; and John Wild's *The Radical Empiricism of William James*, 1969.

As two of these titles indicate (and the other author would agree) what is *new* in James is the discovery that he was a forerunner of the "phenomenology" of Edmund Husserl and the existentialism of Martin Heidegger. Wilshire explains the meaning of the term: "The central thesis of phenomenology is that the world is comprehensible only in terms of its modes of appearance to mind, and that mind cannot be conceived independently of the world which appears to it. Hence, despite Edmund Husserl's aversion to the word metaphysics, the phenomenological thesis generates implications concerning the structure of reality, and must be considered an outgrowth in the broadest sense of Kant's new metaphysics of experience. It is not that the world exists only in the mind, but that the world can be specified only in terms of what it appears to be to mind. Hence, as well, the phenomenological thesis generates a philosophy of mind. Truths about the relationship are necessary and nonempirical and the discipline which discovers them is a nonempirical one. Mind cannot conceive independently of the world which appears to it. Any phenomenological psychology derives from this fundamental philosophical background."

In 1900 Husserl wrote that he had read James's *Principles of Psychology* in the 1890s: "Although I was able to read only a few things and too little of James' Psychology, it brought some lightning flashes. I saw how a courageous and original man did not let himself be shackled by any tradition but endeavored effectively to hold on to and describe what he saw. This influence was not unimportant to me." Husserl was especially grateful to James for showing him a way out of "psychologism," the view that, since thought is a psychical activity, the object of thought is subject to psychological laws. Although James started out to write his *Principles* on the commonsense, dualistic principle that he need not settle the question of the relation of the external object to a mental image of it, and could simply assume that it was *there* where it seemed to be, he soon found himself entangled in the problem of cognition.

Another definition by Wilshire will help to clarify James's predicament: "The central thesis of a phenomenological psychology is that mind and thoughts cannot be conceived independently of the world which appears to mind, and that this phenomenal world can be conceived only through a philosophical investigation of the world's own structures (in Husserl's parlance, essences) as revealed to mind. For example, material objects and formal objects like numbers fall into different regional ontologies; if thought's objects are numbers, say, then at some point in the elucidation of the *thought* a mathematician will have to be called in, not just a psychologist. Although the object belongs to thought and thought is psychical, still the object of thought cannot be given an elucidation that is exclusively psychological. Hence psychology is derivative, not ultimate."

Time and again, and especially in his later writings, James stated the impossibility of separating mind and world, and he tentatively resorted to transcendental conjectures, such as Fechner's panpsychism, but he was not able to find a way to elucidate "the world's own structures," or to see that they might have different ontologies. Thus he stopped short of a phenomenological psychology — or philosophy. As Linschoten says, "James confronts us with a doctrine of experience of the body that in many essential points was anticipation of phenomenological psychology."

Instead of regretting James's lack of a consistent system, Linschoten regards it as one of his virtues. He saw that no systematic or rational conception of the whole of reality is possible; it is too large and human experience too limited. "The real world as it is given objectively at this moment," James points out in "Reflex Action and Theism," "is the sum total of all its beings and events now. But can we think of such a sum? Can we realize for an instant what a cross-section of all existence at a definite point of time would be? While I talk and the flies buzz, a sea-gull catches a fish at the mouth of the Amazon, a tree falls in the Adirondack wilderness, a man sneezes in Germany, a horse dies in Tartary, and twins are born in France. What does that mean? Does the contemporaneity of these events with one another and with a million others as disjointed, form a rational bond between them, and unite them into anything that means for us a world?" Linschoten comments: "A system, if it wants to be a system, must be a *closed* system. And why should all those events form one system? The world is a multiversum, not a universum; a pluralistic 'whole' of infinite diversity; a kaleidoscopic stream of varieties. No system can reduce it to one single principle." In other words, "*Diverse viewpoints lead to diverse formulations.*"

James was in search of the sources of the stream of reality, which he believed to be discoverable only in perceptual experience. His "seemingly unsystematic approach," says Linschoten, "is an attempt to reach a more comprehensive system. . . . James' psychology at first shows a methodological pluralism and hence a seeming confusion of heterogeneous viewpoints and explanations. But the idea hidden behind it is the principle of complementarity." Psychology had got divided into a "mental science" and a "natural science." James desired to preserve their mutual connection. This presupposes a theory about that connection and coherence, a phenomenology of the life-world, that was at least implicitly aimed at by James. Hence his seeming lack of a systematic view. It is this which caused him to say: "It is not that we are all nature but some point which is reason, but that all is nature and all is reason too. We shall see, damn it, we shall see."

Professor Wild, a native American and a retired professor of philosophy at Yale, explains in his preface to *The Radical Empiricism of William James* that he had supposed phenomenology and existential philosophy to be exclusively European until he came to know Husserl in 1931 and studied with Heidegger at the University of Freiburg. Then he learned of Husserl's reading of James and began also to see some of the origins of existentialism in James's theories of empiricism. A friend of Wild's at Harvard, Gordon Allport, also told him that if James's *Principles of Psychology* had been fully understood, it "might have inaugurated a native phenomenological movement in the United States." Professor Wild's intention in writing his book was to "confirm a historical fact that others have suspected, namely that around the turn of the century, a native American philosopher began to think in an existential manner, and made important contributions to the phenomenological movement, in that broader sense which we are now beginning to recognize is required to understand it as a whole. But this is a relatively minor point. In my more optimistic moments I sometimes hope that by trying to see through the conventional tags and labels which have buried a great man of our past, I may have made some of his insights more accessible, and may thus indirectly help some of those who really read him not merely to think, but to think empirically in relation to our existence in the world, and thus to take philosophy seriously again."

James M. Edie, professor of philosophy at Northwestern University, declares positively in *An Invitation to Phenomenology*: "In American philosophy we are witnessing the beginnings of a radical reevaluation of the thought of William James and with it the discovery that James can be credited with more than the creation of a typically

American philosophical 'ism,' and that his thought has a more fundamental meaning for the evolution of twentieth-century philosophy than even his most partisan followers have yet claimed for it." During his lifetime William James enjoyed an international reputation as a major psychologist, but his philosophical standing — except for his popular audience — was often questioned. Today he still has his popular audience, and is steadily growing in stature among professional philosophers.

PHILIP WAGNER

H. L. MENCKEN

Henry Louis Mencken died in his sleep of a coronary occlusion on Sunday, January 29, 1956, in the row house on Hollins Street in Baltimore where he had lived most of his life. At midday on Tuesday a few people met at the neighborhood undertaker's just down the street: his brothers August and Charles and his sister Gertrude; Hamilton Owens, the chief editor of the Baltimore Sunpapers at that time; Alfred Knopf, his publisher; James Cain, the confectioner of hard-boiled fiction; the musician Louis Cheslock, most faithful of friends; and some others — fewer than a dozen in all. Hamilton Owens had been invited by August Mencken to preside. He rose, said briefly that they came together, as Henry had wanted, a few old friends to see him off, then sat down. The undertaker's men in their black suits took the body away, to the crematory, followed only by brothers August and Charlie. The company sat about uneasily for a few minutes and then scattered into the winter day.

The funeral of an unbeliever is more somber than most, since the usual remarks about a life everlasting are out of bounds. This one must have set some sort of record for bleakness, for in a way it was redundant. Mencken had been leading a ghostly life, "ready for the angels," since the day eight years before when he was knocked out by a cerebral thrombosis that affected his speech and partly paralyzed him. He recovered fully though slowly from the paralysis but was left cruelly handicapped in other ways, robbed of the ability to read and write, unable to remember the names even of his friends. Seen on one of his rare public appearances he appeared no different at first. He had been restored to what, following an earlier illness, he had called his "former loveliness": the dumpy figure that he liked to call matronly, the ruddy face, the scowl, the laugh, the popping blue eyes. But this was a deception. The croak of his voice was the same, but the words that issued were those of a stranger. The shell was intact, but the essence had been shattered; and the grim jest of it was that Mencken knew this deep inside as well as anyone else and yet was helpless to do anything about it.

But though he had to endure that long winter of wordlessness, it was surely not true that his career had been cut short. His daily newspaper work embraced better than half a century. The first and the last things he wrote for publication were printed in newspapers, and it must be remembered that Mencken thought of himself as a newspaperman before anything else. The flood of his critical writing, in the old *Smart Set* magazine mainly (the best of it republished in his *Prefaces* and *Prejudices*), swept away the deadening literary standards, and the deadly standard-bearers, of our early twentieth century and cleared the way for a tremendous flowering of new writing. As a slashing and wonderfully comic critic of American life and institutions he attained for a time a stature and influence such as no other American writer has ever known. Though he disclaimed scholarly pretensions, his *The American Language* systematically explored for the first time our native tongue as it must be distinguished from British English and provided a solid basis for American linguistics. As a political commentator he carried immense authority for a time — though this waned with the coming of that upheaval called the New Deal and was gone entirely by the time he had ceased writing. He wrote a formal treatise each on political theory, religion, and ethics. He tried his hand at verse and the drama. And the autobiographical sketches brought together in his *Days* books recreate the life of an American city, Baltimore, at the turn of the century with such gusto and uproarious humor and unabashed sentiment that their claim to immortality is secure. All this — and his letters, too. Mencken the writer was cut down cruelly, but not cut short.

Mencken was third-generation Baltimore German. Baltimore was one of the chief ports of entry for the big German immigration of the mid-nineteenth century — the Forty-Eighters. Most of them moved on to make their main impression on the land and life of the Midwest. But many found Baltimore congenial, with its already well-established German community, and went no farther. Mencken's grandfather Burkhardt was one of these. Stiff-necked, immensely proud of the Mencken family's long roll of learned men, diligent and thrifty, he prospered in the tobacco business and founded a numerous family. His eldest son August held likewise to the tobacco business, prospered, and married Anna Abhau, daughter of another German Forty-Eighter.

It was into this conventional west Baltimore German family where values were certitudes, love and discipline were dispensed with a lavish and impartial hand, and security was never in question that Henry Louis Mencken was born on September 12, 1880. Insofar as any childhood can be easy, his was. "We were lucky," he wrote many years later of this childhood, "to have been born so soon," and he looked back at his childhood and indeed at the life it had prepared the way for without any regrets at all: "If I had my life to live over again I don't think I'd change it in any particular of the slightest consequence. I'd choose the same parents, the same birthplace, the same education (with maybe a few improvements here, chiefly in the direction of foreign languages), the same trade, the same jobs, the same income, the same politics, the same metaphysic, the same wife, the same friends, and (even though it may sound like a mere effort to shock humanity), the same relatives to the last known degree of consanguinity, including those in-law." It may not be far from the truth to say that he took the lonesome integrity of his mind and spirit from tough old Burkhardt, from his father August a talent for gaiety in company, and from his mother certain qualities that rarely show in his writing, especially his unexpected gentleness, his instant sympathy for the troubled, and his devotion to family life and routine.

His education moved ahead in the Baltimore German way, which is to say with the solidest kind of family backing. At the age of six he was handed over to Professor Friedrich Knapp and his thoroughly Teutonic Institute, a no-nonsense place, and did well in most subjects. In due course he was translated to a public high school, the Polytechnic Institute, where the main emphasis was then and still is on science and technology. This change was made by his father in the mistaken belief that little Harry had an aptitude for such matters. Though in his own words little Harry "had no more mechanical skill than a cow" he was tempted for a time by the mysteries of chemistry and photography and he was graduated — he was not quite sixteen — at the head of his class, even winning the competition for a gold medal in electricity. So much for science and his formal education.

His education in letters was a parallel and separate thing. The Mencken family was not particularly bookish, but there were books around, and the magazines of the time, and his introduction to the delights of the printed word came when he was seven by way of *Chatterbox*, the hard-cover annual which started generations of young English gentlemen on their way to literacy. He absorbed it so thoroughly, Englishness and all, that in middle life he confessed to knowing "more about Henry VIII and Lincoln Cathedral than I know about Millard Fillmore or the Mormon Temple at Salt Lake City." Young Henry dutifully did all the things the boys of his neighborhood were expected to do — he was a member in good standing of the neighborhood gang, he frequented the firehouse. But such occupations had to compete with " a new realm of being and a new and powerful enchantment" and before very many years had lost the battle. The "powerful suction of beautiful letters" had caught him and he never again escaped. He tackled Grimm's fairy tales — not much to his taste. He began to explore the contents of the old glass-front secretary that stands to this day in the Hollins Street middle sitting room with most of the same books still in it, a miscellany of things pretty much beyond his ken, hence all the more intriguing. And then he came upon *Huckleberry Finn*, "probably the most stupendous event of my whole life." The story of this encounter is set down in his sketch "Larval Stage of a Bookworm." By the age of nine he had his card for the neighborhood branch library and had begun "an almost daily harrying of the virgins at the delivery desk." He was caught for fair: "I began to inhabit a world that was two-thirds letterpress and only one-third trees, fields, streets and people. I acquired round shoulders, spindly shanks, and a despondent view of humanity. I read everything that I could find in English, taking in some of it but boggling most of it. . . . to this day [at sixty] I am still what might be called a reader, and have a high regard for authors."

A second stupendous and decisive event is confessed in another of his sketches, "In the Footsteps of Gutenberg." It was the gift from his father, not long after his discovery of the magic of Mark Twain, of a toy printing press, a Dorman No. 10 Self-Inker costing $7.50 together with a font of No. 214 type costing $1.10. Mark Twain had made him a consumer of letters; this made him a producer. It put "the smell of printer's ink up my nose at the tender age of eight, and it has been swirling through my sinuses ever since." Other Christmas presents came along, to divert him momentarily — the set of water colors, the camera, the microscope, the galvanic battery, the set of carpenter's tools. But "it was the printing-press that left its marks, not only upon my hands, face and clothing, but also on my psyche. They are still there, though more than fifty years have come and gone."

His father, sensible man, saw Harry as logical heir to the tobacco business and had small patience with the notion of a career in writing or publishing. Henry was required to learn the rudiments of the business, including the way to roll a cigar. This was the cause of some friction between father and son, but there was never the slightest doubt in Henry's mind that the tobacco business was not for him, and, to cut the story short: "When, on my father's death, as I was eighteen, I was free at last to choose my trade in the world, I chose newspaper work without any hesitation whatever, and, save when the scent of a passing garbage-cart has revived my chemical libido, I have never regretted my choice. More than once I have slipped out of daily journalism to dally in its meretricious suburbs, but I have always returned repentant and relieved, like a blackamoor coming back in Autumn to a warm and sociable jail."

And so it was, four days after his father's death in 1899, that he presented himself at the office of one of Baltimore's several newspapers, the *Herald*, and was turned down. But his persistence earned him free-lance assignments, then a staff job. He soon demonstrated his ability and moved swiftly through every job in the office: police reporter, drama critic, Sunday editor, city editor, and by 1906 at the age of twenty-five actually the editor of the paper — only to see the *Herald* fail for reasons with which he had nothing to do, and to find himself out of a job.

It was then that he joined the *Sun* (locally the Sunpaper), a newspaper believed by the local gentry to be the one true source of wisdom and current intelligence, which remained his journalistic home to the end of his career. He did venture away from time to time for reasons that were various, but always returned "repentant and relieved." His connection with that paper (and its evening sister) turned into something unique in American journalism. The *Sun* provided the real launching pad for his career as a national figure and in turn gained immeasurably from the relationship.

From the beginning, however, he did not limit his writing to daily journalism, prodigious though his output for the *Herald* was. He began experimenting with verse, and selling it. He was a "stringer" providing features for out-of-town papers. He became a fabricator of short stories for most of the popular magazines of the day — formula fiction loaded with blood and thunder, done by the yard and showing small trace of the style we think of as Mencken's. He was available for hack jobs — even doing a prospectus for Loudon Park Cemetery, where, fittingly, his gravestone now stands. He didn't stop reading, either. He was sopping up the new writers who had things to say and said them well, such men as Shaw and Conrad; and always Mark Twain; and others such as Huxley and Nietzsche and Spencer and James Huneker and William Graham Sumner, the author of *Folkways*. They fixed his philosophical bearings once and for all (though these had been pretty well set already), and on them he honed his ideas and his style.

The hack period began to recede, and in 1905 he published his "first real book," as he called it, *George Bernard Shaw: His Plays* (he preferred not to count a little book of rather dreadful verse that too much fuss was later made about simply because copies were rare: the poetic muse kept clear of him always). This essay offered the first intimations of the Mencken style and his formidable critical capacity, immature though they were. It was no great success though it was well reviewed, but for him it broke the ice: he was a published critic. Mencken recalled, in his *Newspaper Days*, his enchantment on the arrival of its proofs. His editor at that time, an understanding man named Meekins, insisted that he take the day off to read them. "So I locked myself in as he commanded, and had a shining day indeed, and I can still remember its unparalleled glow after all these years."

Three years later he published his *Philosophy of Friedrich Nietzsche*, a better book and still very much worth the reading. William Manchester, in *Disturber of the Peace*, best of the several Mencken biographies and studies, says, "The subject . . . was Mencken's Nietzsche, not Nietzsche's Nietzsche. There is a difference." It is probably a better guide to Mencken than to Nietzsche, to the extraordinary toughness and stiffness of his mind beneath its lively movement at the surface. He alluded to this quality himself from time to time. In a letter to the writer Jim Tully in 1940 he said: "I never listen to debates. They are dreadful things indeed. The plain truth is that I am not a fair man, and don't want to hear both sides. On all known subjects, ranging from aviation to xylophone-playing, I have fixed and invariable ideas. They have not changed since I was four or five years." And I remember a casual remark he made to me at about the time of that letter, when his thinking was going so strongly against the national grain. Speaking of another newspaper editor he said: "John is a reasonable man. Try it on him. A good argument will always fetch him, but not me." He was not boasting. Neither was he confessing. He was stating a fact.

There was another and important branching out early in his association with the *Sun*. Mencken's duties as an editorial writer were not arduous and they used up only a portion of his energy. A chance encounter with Theodore Dreiser, then a magazine editor, led him to another chance encounter with George Jean Nathan; and out of that all-day meeting of two men as unlike as two could be, yet so surprisingly alike in their disgust with contemporary life and letters, there came a partnership that lasted better than two decades. The inspiration of the partnership was a magazine of dubious reputation, the *Smart Set*, which was about to undergo one of its rejuvenations, or reincarnations. Mencken had been invited to do a monthly full-length piece for it on books, Nathan to do dramatic criticism. The result was something like a volcanic eruption. The shallow standards and appalling inanity of most American writing and the theater of the early years of this century were the targets of both. With high spirits, total confidence in their own judgments, and a torrent of brilliant invective, they laid about them, bashing heads, pulling down idols, puncturing inflated pomposity, infuriating the sources of conventional wisdom, sweeping away the rubbish that then passed for literature and drama. Prodigious labor was required, and it was a bravura performance. Mencken's stint was a monthly article of about five thousand words, and his anthologist Huntington Cairns, adding it all up, found that from November 1908 to the end of December 1923 he performed it one hundred and eighty-two successive months for a total of better than 900,000 words. The preparatory reading involved in this may be imagined. Mencken was equal to it because he was one of those reading prodigies who can gulp down books a page at a time missing nothing of consequence.

As contributors the two dominated the magazine, which was by no means an appropriate medium for such intellectual high jinks but better than none. In due time (1914) the magazine became theirs as joint editors. As editors they wrote much of it themselves under a fragrant bouquet of pseudonyms. Betty Adler, the Mencken bibliographer, has tracked down and confirmed 23 pseudonyms and lists 13 more as probabilities; the chances are there were others, used interchangeably or jointly by the two. But they also searched out new talent, so buttressing their criticism with evidence of what they did like. Sweeping out the rubbish was not enough. They wanted non-rubbish to replace it, and this they set about discovering — a labor at which Mencken proved remarkably adept. Once he got on the scent of a promising writer he was unshakable — he cajoled, browbeat, sent gifts, fed ideas. There is a large risk of error in this hunting out of new writers, but he was equally skillful at ditching whatever failed to make the grade.

The *Smart Set* was a tour de force, a gale of fresh air across the campuses, a serial spoof, bellwether of a new generation, an object of delighted devotion.

Mencken and Nathan worked out a modus for editing which reduced red tape to zero. Nathan held down the New York office with the help of a secretary of monumental impassivity, a Miss Golde. Mencken did his reading, writing, and scouting for talent, and carried on his enormous correspondence, from his quarters on the third floor of the family home in Hollins Street, periodically taking the train to New York for a day which he and Nathan divided between merrymaking and the planning of the next issue.

But I get ahead of the story. Not long after Mencken's emergence through the *Smart Set* as a national critic of letters, things began to happen to the *Sun* in Baltimore. The *Sun* of that day was a staid institution much impressed with its rectitude and infallibility, one of the four pillars of Baltimore life, along with the Washington Monument, the Shot Tower, and Federal Hill, and just about as exciting. A victim of complacency and accumulated inhibitions, it began to go down hill even as a commercial enterprise, and it was sold to a group of wealthy Baltimore citizens headed by an aggressive publisher, formerly a competitor, who was resolved to pump some life back into it. The decision was made to spawn an evening sister, and to Mencken fell the task of providing this new *Evening Sun* with a personality and point of view, mainly by way of its editorial page. This he set about doing; and so (1911) his column, "The Free Lance," came into being. He was given a free hand, and took every advantage of this and of the title. The column swiftly became the sort of thing that no one of consequence in Baltimore dared not to read; and the subjects were whatever came into his head. Baltimore had seen nothing like it before. He was into everything: the mucky world of municipal politics, local forms of beastliness and gentility particularly when combined in the same person, new trends in writing, the deplorable condition of the sewage and water systems as reflected in the local typhoid death rate, the barbarous condition of the national culture — everything. The predominant qualities Mencken endowed the *Evening Sun* with were impertinence, riotous good humor, a high degree of literacy — with the back of the hand for every form of sham and a strenuously libertarian bias.

Mencken's output, not confined to the column by any means, was large. But thanks to the compulsive orderliness of his mind he worked with extraordinary economy. Pieces done for the *Smart Set* were reworked for the "Free Lance" column; "Free Lance" material found its way rearranged and expanded into the magazine; and much of all this eventually wound up in his books: the *Prejudices, The American Language, Notes on Democracy*, and so on. Mencken was never the man to waste a good thing on a single audience.

So things went for Mencken in the years before World War I, exuberantly, as he juggled two careers: those of a literary critic of rapidly growing stature and of a newspaper columnist knowing no bounds except those of libel and common prudence. There was no time for larger works, though these had begun to gestate in his mind; and the only thing that appeared between hard covers was his priceless little drama without words, *The Artist* (1915), which was later reprinted in his *A Book of Burlesques* (1916).

But as the war approached, he found himself under growing constraint in both careers. He was, to put the matter shortly, pro-German. As he explained his position toward the end of the war to a correspondent, the medical historian Fielding Garrison, "The fact is that my 'loyalty' to Germany, as a state or a nation, is absolutely nil. I haven't a single living relative there; I haven't even a friend there. . . . But I believe I was right when I argued that unfairness to [the Germans] was discreditable and dangerous to this country, and I am glad I did it." Other things — pride of ancestry, his bourgeois German upbringing, his philosophical underpinnings, his contempt for the quality and the personalities of American politics — contributed to his attitude. And being Mencken he said his say — loudly, bluntly, mockingly. At the *Smart Set* this was felt in the countinghouse, and as a critic he began to find himself vulnerable to *ad hominem* attacks, many of them shockingly irrelevant and abusive, from those who had smarted under his criticisms. At the Sunpapers the cleavage between his views and the ardently Wilsonian management of the papers grew so broad as to be intolerable. In 1915 his "Free Lance" column came to an end abruptly; and except for a comic opera episode as a war correspondent for the *Sun* in Germany, which ended with American entry into the war, his contributions to the paper dwindled to little and then nothing. In the literary world the counterattacks on him increased ominously with the war fever. His *A Book of Prefaces* (1917), consisting of a series of critical studies, was viciously reviewed by, among others, Stuart Sherman. Sherman was then the leading academic critic, and his far from academic attack amounted to this: the opinions of the man Mencken on prose fiction are beneath contempt because he is no patriot. Then too there was a misunderstanding with his new publisher Alfred Knopf (soon happily resolved; they were destined to have an enduring friendship). Certain other journalistic enterprises worked out unsatisfactorily, as did an interim arrangement with another publisher, his friend Philip Goodman, and the *Smart Set* found itself compelled to trim its sails.

The war years were years of misery for Mencken, carrying the brand of pro-Germanism though his loyalty as a citizen was never in real doubt. He was left with no means but his private correspondence for venting his opinions. He solved the problem — that is to say, the problem of one who must write but is constrained on all sides — by plunging into his linguistic project, *The American Language*, which had been simmering gently for a long time. The conclusion of this landmark work was being written, appropriately, as the war ended. It was a critical and popular triumph when published a year later, in 1919. The impression it made on the new college generation especially, by its syle, its humor and its lightly worn scholarship, was tremendous. That same year saw also the publication of the first volume in the series of *Prejudices*, consisting of reprints from the *Smart Set*, the *Evening Sun*, and some other sources. Each new *Prejudices* volume was awaited avidly by the new Menckenites, and the series ran to six before the curtain was rung down on it in 1927. And in 1919 too Mencken resumed his formal connection with the Sunpapers, this time as editorial adviser to the publisher and as a weekly contributor to the editorial page of the *Evening Sun*. He was also available for special assignment. (His reporting of the Scopes anti-evolutionary trial in Dayton, Tennessee, yielded some of his finest descriptive writing, including his famous account of the hysterical goings-on at a back country revival meeting; yet for some reason it was never brought together in a book.)

The *Smart Set* had somehow managed to struggle through the war years. How rough the going had been is exposed in a letter Mencken wrote to Dreiser in 1920 explaining its modest rates for contributions: "If it hadn't been for the fact that each of us has a small independent income, we'd have been down and out a dozen times. All this for your private eye. . . . I go into it simply to purge your mind of any notion that you may harbor that we are Shylocks." It now emerged basically intact, and was clearly what the new generation wanted.

In brief, the Mencken Period had begun. He offered what the times needed: a clearinghouse for the cynicism and discontents of the postwar years and a lash for their excesses wielded with alternating scorn and high good humor. The work he did in bringing out and supporting the new writers (Sinclair Lewis and Fitzgerald typically) and continuing his championing of Dreiser and Conrad and a score of others was carried on with the greatest gusto. At last he could really take literature out of the hands of the decorous and the genteel and make it something meaningful (he could not have done this had the talent not been waiting in the wings, ready for a persuasive impresario). And yet even as he reached the peak of his influence as a critic of letters he began to move out of this role and into criticism of the American mores. This was not a new role for him, of course, but it now got far more emphasis: the truth is that imaginative writing was beginning to bore him. His work for the *Evening Sun* reflected this — it ran more and more to political and social commentary. His *Prejudices* books reflected this too, the first of these being devoted almost entirely to writers and writing — what he called beautiful letters and the bozart — and the last containing hardly anything relating to current writing. The change in his interests was reflected also in the *Smart Set*, where increasingly he tacked away from literature and toward life, in spite of Nathan's persistence in the old course.

The two were in fact growing apart. In a revealing letter to literary journalist Burton Rascoe, Mencken described the bases and also hinted at the limitations of their long collaboration: "Our point of contact is our complete revulsion from American sentimentality. . . . We work together amicably because we are both lonely, and need some support. . . . we come together on several essentials, e.g. our common disinclination to know authors or to belong to literary coteries, our lack of national feeling, and (perhaps most important) our similar attitudes toward money, religion, women, etc." But Nathan the complete aesthete, absorbed as always in the theater, was cold to that "show" — the excesses and absurdities of the jazz age — which so dazzled and delighted Mencken as a theme for writing.

This is really what ended that long partnership. Though Mencken had no conscious intention of neglecting the arts he wanted the emphasis placed on American life — to him, the American comedy. In addition Nathan was fairly oblivious to the shoddy trappings of the *Smart Set*, but they had begun to bother Mencken. He hankered for a "swell" review, to be Brahmin in its typographical dress if not in its contents. Knopf stood ready to back such a review, and indeed had proposed it and offered to finance it; and so, after a sufficiency of preliminary planning and wrangling, the *American Mercury* got its name, the *Smart Set* was published for the last time in December 1923, and in January 1924 the new critical review appeared in its Garamond typeface and ultra-dignified green cover. The Mencken orbit was moving toward its apogee, and the reception of the *Mercury* far exceeded the expectations of the three principals, in circulation and in acclaim. Its first issues promptly became collectors' items. The impassive Miss Golde had somehow been mislaid and was succeeded by the efficient and self-effacing Edith Lustgarten in the New York office and the equally efficient and self-effacing Rosalind Lohrfinck (known simply as Lohrfinck though Mencken professed to be dimly aware that she had a private life and even a husband) at the Baltimore end of things. Otherwise the manner of operation was not greatly different from *Smart Set* days, though quarters were moved into the Knopf office and there was a need for more of those train trips to New York.

And yet the crack in the collaboration was widening, and becoming evident even to bystanders. In a long letter to Nathan, written before the *Mercury* was many months old, Mencken, who was uneasy about the course of things, brought the matter into the open: "Its chances are not unlike those which confronted the Atlantic in the years directly after the Civil War: it has an opportunity to seize leadership of the genuinely civilized minority of Americans. . . . Our interests are too far apart. . . ." It was a plea to thresh out their differences if that were still possible, subconsciously a bid for dominance. Nathan, seeing the course of things, accepted it with good nature. After fewer than a dozen issues he abandoned his co-editorship, though he kept on as a contributor; and before the decade was over he and Mencken had parted completely — not in anger but as intellectual and emotional strangers. Mencken carried on alone, with an assistant (Charles Angoff, who proved in the end to be no friend and whose *H. L. Mencken, a Portrait from Memory*, put out in the year of Mencken's death, was a bitter and distressing performance).

The Mencken wave swept on, with the *Mercury* riding its crest; and there was hardly a page of this but showed the hand of the editor. He was at once the most ingratiating and the most exacting of editors. Contributions were responded to with unprecedented speed, and the blow of every rejection was softened by one of Mencken's inimitable notes. Rascoe once wrote: "I have yet to meet a man under thirty-five with articulate ideas who has not a sheaf of those lively, hearty notes whereby Mencken conveys a maximum of good cheer and boisterous comment within a minimum of space." Acceptance for publication brought immediate payment, and (quite unprecedented in the experience of free-lance writers) a conveyance of copyright was forthcoming immediately after publication. This act of generosity cost nothing, yet earned enormous dividends in the good will of a whole generation of young writers struggling for recognition. He was ever attentive to the legitimate interests of his contributors, yet determined always to have his way. An article with a clumsy opening, a feeble conclusion? Out with them! In with new ones from his own typewriter, but always there was advance warning along with a plea for acquiescence when he was dealing with a style-conscious writer. He was marvelous at finding the one-article man — the jailbird or the cab driver with a story to tell. He constantly tapped the well of working newspapermen, but found it shallower than one might think; of his early newspaper colleagues he once wrote: "At least half the members of the staff had literary ambitions of some sort or another, but not one of them ever got anywhere as a writer in the years following." He ransacked the campuses and the ranks of campus journalists for youngsters of promise, and gave many of them their start.

Mencken himself did but one book from the ground up, so to speak, during this period, which was the latter half of the twenties. That was not a success: his *Notes on Democracy* (1926). Even that one was mainly a rewriting job based on previously published material. It was done in such time as he could spare from his furious magazine editing, his continuing daily journalism, and responses to the calls now being made on him increasingly in his role as a unique national figure, certainly the most hated and also perhaps the most admired American of his time. These calls were of many sorts, but mainly from academe. Here is one described in a letter to Philip Goodman: "I am lecturing at Goucher College tonight: an annual affair. The audience consists of 250 virgins. I begin on the subject of national literature, but at 8.35 modulate gracefully into the Old Subject in F sharp minor. I always advise them to marry early, as, after all, the most sanitary and economically secure way of life for a Christian girl." But of course he refused dozens for every one he accepted.

The magazine itself began to show evidence of strain, of stridency. Mencken's commentaries on books continued, and at length, but there was a forced quality in much of this now, and they tended to turn into lectures on his special brand of sociology. His waning interest in literature as literature began to show in the magazine's fiction, too: having given a whole generation of new writers the stage and the audience they needed, he had slipped out of the audience, or at least was on the way to the exit. In his preoccupation with manners and morals, he actually began to miss new writing talent, worse, to misjudge it: Hemingway, for example, and Faulkner, and Thomas Wolfe. The frantic twenties were beginning to burn themselves out, and so apparently was the chief barker of this gaudiest of side shows, though by ordinary standards the magazine continued to prosper throughout the decade.

In 1929, Mencken completed the second of his trilogy treating formally of politics, religion, and morals: his *Treatise on the Gods* (1930). As Cairns remarks, he had plowed new land when he wrote *The American Language*, which was in every sense an original work, in subject as well as treatment. Religion was another matter, a preoccupation of powerful minds since the dawn of human consciousness, the most thoroughly worked field of all: small room here for originality. What he could do, and did, was to restate the materialist-rationalist position as so thoroughly developed in the nineteenth century by Huxley and others, but in contemporary terms, bringing to bear the abundant new material of psychology and the study of human institutions. He saw the religious motive as a prudent form of hedging against the terrors of the unknown, and organized religion as an elaborate tool for bamboozling and manipulating the credulous masses, a tool of government really. There was not a trace of the mystic in him, and while acknowledging the genuineness of the mystical experience he looked upon it as one of the puzzles not yet worked out by scientific means. He came by his antireligious position quite naturally, first through his grandfather Burkhardt, then through his father, then by degrees through his reading. The constant prevalence of what he felt to be a delusion had absorbed him from adolescence on. Writing of the place of religion in his family, he commented many years later to A. G. Keller, a Yale anthropologist and disciple of William Graham Sumner, "My mother went to church now and then, but her doctrinal ideas seem to have been very vague, for I never heard her mention them. I think she went simply as a sort of social gesture. My father accompanied her no more than two or three times in my recollection, and even then he went under protest. Religion was simply not a living subject in the house." Anathema to the conventionally religious, his *Treatise on the Gods* is nevertheless a storehouse of learning and curious information; and it has ample helpings of the characteristic Mencken audacity and wit. It received a far better reception than his *Notes on Democracy*, as possibly it deserved to, and it sold well. It was his last substantial success for some time, and its appearance coincided with a sharp break in what had seemed the unbreakable pattern of his private life, the tender episode of his middle-aged courtship and marriage.

In spite of the public impression to the contrary, Mencken's personal life followed a rigorous and austere routine. At the center of it was the family house in Hollins Street presided over with quiet authority by his mother Anna. The loss of her in 1925 had affected him far more than he could have anticipated, in the small ways that so quickly add up to a big way, and his correspondence is full of references to her death. To Jim Tully he wrote, for example: "You ask if I feel lonely here. My belief is that all authors are essentially lonely men. Every one of them has to do his work in a room alone, and he inevitably gets very tired of himself. My mother's death in December, 1925, left me at a loss. My sister is keeping house but the place seems empty. It is hard to reorganize one's life after 45."

It is too pat to say that he turned to Sara Haardt on the rebound. Yet without doubt his mother's death was contributory to his growing attachment to Sara and his need for the qualities she had to give. He had met her at one of those annual lectures to the Goucher College virgins. She taught there — a young lady from the deep South, a minor but fastidious novelist and short story writer with a faint aura of the anachronistic about her, reserved and physically frail. Their marriage in 1930 took all but a few of their closest friends by surprise, and was greeted with ironic delight by editorial writers from coast to coast. That the author of *In Defense of Women* and chief railer at the institution of holy matrimony should himself succumb, and be married by a parson at that! Mencken took the public ribbing in good part, and so did Sara though somewhat nervously, as they settled down to the sedate idyll which both knew, or had reason to suspect, could not last long. It was broken frequently by her illnesses, and it ended with her death five years later — a cruel blow to Mencken however much he had anticipated and prepared for it. He told Hamilton Owens shortly after her death that the doctors had given her only three years at the time of their marriage. "Actually she lived five, so that I had two more years of happiness than I had any right to expect." It had been a precious, bittersweet thing, and life in the apartment which they had established on Baltimore's handsome Mount Vernon Place, and where Sara had indulged her bent for the Victorian style, had lost its meaning. In due course he returned "completely dashed and dismayed" to the house in Hollins Street to take up life again with his brother August, his shadow from then to the end.

In the meantime other troubles of a worldly and professional kind had been piling up on him. As the times had embraced him following World War I, so now with the crash and the onset of the Great Depression they were ready to reject him. A nation dazed and hurt by the collapse of its financial and industrial structure, by farmers dispossessed and city people caught overnight with no means of subsistence, by soup lines and apple sellers and a steady shower of overextended brokers leaping out of Wall Street windows, ceased to enjoy being described as a gaudy human comedy. That kind of talk, and writing, might be tolerable and even entertaining in a going concern. To a people on the ropes, it seemed suddenly petty and irrelevant. It was a time of shocked and bitter reaction and among the victims of this was Mencken's unchanging and unchangeable devotion to individuality, self-reliance, and limited government. To his readers he ceased abruptly to be a champion of the individual and herald of freedom and became an archreactionary — this without changing his position one iota. His newspaper polemics seemed suddenly and oddly out of date; he lost the faith and credit of the new generation of college students (that was perhaps the worst blow save Sara's death); the circulation of the *Mercury* began to slide. One does not write easily in the face of a situation like that; and Mencken's writing showed it. The familiar refrains turned stale, the variations were no longer amusing.

One blow came after another. The decision to abandon the *Mercury* was taken in 1933 and was actually welcomed by him (it lived on for a while under another editor, then passed from hand to hand, always downward). The third of his triology on politics, religion, and morals, the *Treatise on Right and Wrong* (1934), got a critical mauling and had a poor sale — a far poorer sale than the same book would have had, certainly, ten years before, for it is highly readable still.

The Depression moved into what he considered the fantastic excesses of the Roosevelt New Deal. He had voted for Roosevelt while confessing privately that he thought him "a weak sister," but quickly changed his mind. So far as he was concerned, the Rooseveltian devaluation of the dollar was on a par with the coin clipping of an earlier day, which is to say a form of refined thievery; and Roosevelt's manner of doing it, which involved pulling the rug out from under his own delegation to the London Economic Conference, the behavior of a cad. Cynical as Mencken was about the courts in general and the caliber of the men who manned them, Roosevelt's scheme for packing the Supreme Court and so ensuring the color of constitutionality for whatever he might do shocked him beyond measure. The mixture of soft-voiced paternalism and political ruthlessness so finely blended in the character of Roosevelt II (as he called him) grated on his nerves like the jangle of an out-of-tune piano. "I begin to believe seriously," he wrote to the publisher B. W. Huebsch, "that the Second Coming may be at hand. Roosevelt's parodies of the Sermon on the Mount become more and more realistic. The heavens may open at any moment. Keep your suitcase packed."

As he responded in typical vein to the course of events it became clearer day by day — and to none more clearly than Mencken himself — that he was no longer being listened to. His day as reigning critic of manners and politics was over. In journalism he continued to take special assignments for the Sunpapers but he abandoned his famous *Evening Sun* Monday articles early in 1938. War was brewing again across the Atlantic, and with his Washingtonian belief in no foreign entanglements he was bitterly against American involvement; but he saw it coming. Wishfully, he played down Hitler as a clown who could not long hold the stage. To George S. Schuyler, the Negro journalist, in 1939: "Roosevelt is hot to horn into the European mess, and his wizards believe that if he can scare the country sufficiently, it will be possible to reelect him [for a third term] next year. I am inclined to agree that this is sound political dope." He dreaded the recurrence of war fever with its intolerance, its vindictiveness, its restraints on free expression, and at the beginning of World War II he gave up writing regularly for the *Sun* though he remained as editorial adviser. Every superior journalist has feelers: Mencken's told him it was time to shut up, at least so far as public affairs were concerned.

With that durable good sense that governed him through the downs as well as the ups of his career, he had in the meantime turned to other things. One of the defenses he fell back on was the labor without end that he had made for himself in American linguistics. On returning to Hollins Street and at the bottom of his loneliness following the death of Sara, he plunged into the work of rewriting, enlarging, and in many ways reshaping *The American Language* for its fourth edition. This was published in 1936. The reception of it proved that whatever may have happened to his standing as a publicist, in this other field it was secure. Supplement I and Supplement II, massive works and complete in themselves, came along in due course (1945 and 1948).

More surprising was the way he opened an entirely new lode. Those who knew Mencken well knew how false was the impression of his personality that his no-quarter polemical writing gave. That was his battle dress. To be sure it was not exactly a mask, since he loved the give and take of public controversy. But it did conceal a much more complicated personality through which ran a broad stream of sentiment and warm humanity. His love affair and marriage with Sara had exposed this briefly to an astonished public. Now, disarmed as a controversialist, he yielded to it in his writing. He turned to the recollection of his childhood in the Baltimore of another day, that childhood for which he had no regrets, in a series of sketches written for the *New Yorker* magazine. They were by turns rollicking, mordant, warmhearted, and nostalgic; and they were greeted with surprise and delight. These were brought together in his book called *Happy Days*, published in 1940. In its preface he conceded that "the record of an event is no doubt often bedizened and adulterated by my response to it," but insisted on the essential truth of the sketches as both autobiography and social history. As props to memory he had consulted his father's old accounts, miraculously intact, and other "contemporary inscriptions."

There followed in 1941 a second volume, *Newspaper Days*. This second group of autobiographical sketches, covering his first years of newspaper life in Baltimore, he described as "mainly true, but with occasional stretchers," and he commended them to the understanding sort of reader who, in Charles Lamb's phrase, felt no call to take "everything perversely in the absolute and literal sense." Absolutely and literally true they certainly were not, as for example his deathless story of "A Girl from Red Lion, P.A." They were better than that: they caught and preserved the smells and flavor and temper of an era. The success of these two volumes inspired a project for a full autobiography to be done on a scale of one book per decade; but he thought better of it: his good sense told him that the mood could not be sustained into the years of his combative maturity. He did one more book of reminiscences, *Heathen Days* (1943), which made pleasant enough reading and did well but lacked the perfect autumnal quality of its predecessors, and called quits on this enterprise.

Mencken was coming to the end of his days as a writer. There was his book of quotations, fruit of a lifetime of clipping and marking and note-saving, and a very different thing from Bartlett's. It was published in 1940 as *A New Dictionary of Quotations.* His *Christmas Story*, a brief bit of mellow buffoonery on a sardonic theme, was published in 1946. In 1948 he returned to the Sunpapers after much urging, and reluctantly, to cover the presidential conventions of that year, including the rump convention of the Wallace Progressive party which proved to be an extravaganza made to order for his talents. The rigors of the campaign itself were no longer for him, but that fall he did contribute a few more things to the paper from home base. His last piece of newspaper writing was published on November 9 of that year, a few days after the election. It was on a subject unrelated to the election, and I will return to it a bit farther on, for it was an appropriate epitaph to a man who had spent much of his life battling for the rights of the individual.

Two weeks later he was taken by the thrombosis that ended his career with such terrible finality. One last book had occupied him toward the end of his writing years: a book of aphorisms and short statements culled from his notes. The manuscript, completed and ready for the printer, was found some years later and was published as *Minority Report: H. L. Mencken's Notebooks* following his death in 1956.

It is in character that the last four sentences of Mencken's final book (that same posthumous *Minority Report*) have to do with his style as a writer: "The imbeciles who have printed acres of comment on my books have seldom noticed the chief character of my style. It is that I write with almost scientific precision — that my meaning is never obscure. The ignorant have often complained that my vocabulary is beyond them, but that is simply because my ideas cover a wider range than theirs do. Once they have consulted the dictionary they always know exactly what I intend to say. I am as far as any writer can get from the muffled sonorities of, say, John Dewey."

It is true enough that there was never anything muffled or fuzzy (though there was plenty of sonority) about what Mencken wrote. His meaning was always transparently clear. But the passage is worth looking at closely because it illustrates how much more than that there was to the Mencken style, which is loaded with artifice. Scientific precision? On the face of it, this example is loaded with imprecisions. The word "imbeciles," for example. A great deal that had been written about Mencken's books was silly, certainly. But the men who had written about Mencken, silly though they might be, were certainly not imbeciles by any available definition of that word. Nor had they written "acres" on the subject — another flagrant inexactitude. Nor did the ignorant often complain about his vocabulary, because the ignorant did not often read him. When they did, it was not his vocabulary that bothered them. As to the elements of his vocabulary that might be complained of, resort to the dictionary was no help because they were either words of his own invention — "booboisie," "bozart" — or old words deftly provided with new meanings and bent to his special uses. His vocabulary was most definitely not beyond his readers: the complaints were from readers who understood only too well what he was saying and were responding precisely as he intended them to respond. The complaints were the flutterings of hit birds.

To write with scientific precision is to take mathematics for a model, avoiding all emotive overtones, rejecting anything that might color a plain statement of fact or interfere with the unfolding of a rational argument — to reject the art of rhetoric, in other words. But Mencken was a supreme rhetorician. Far from being scientific, his use of words was aesthetic. He used them as an artist uses color and a musician the arrangement of notes in clusters — to play upon the senses and emotions of his readers, to make them laugh, sigh, weep, go along with him, grind their teeth in fury, and to put across his point whether it was intrinsically worth making or just a piece of wayward mischief. That paragraph on style, with its deceptive bluntness, clarity, and simplicity, illustrates pretty well how much more complicated it is than he would ever admit.

For the origins of his style one can go straight back to his discovery of *Huckleberry Finn* in his ninth year, which he described as "probably the most stupendous event of my life." It was indeed. He devoured everything he could find by Mark Twain, whose manner of writing was without question the chief influence on his own. Twenty-five years later he wrote (in the *Smart Set*): "I believe that 'Huckleberry Finn' is one of the great masterpieces of the world, that it is the full equal of 'Don Quixote' and 'Robinson Crusoe.' . . . I believe that it will be read by human beings of all ages, not as a solemn duty but for the honest love of it, and over and over again. . . . I believe that Mark Twain had a clearer vision of life, that he came nearer to its elementals and was less deceived by its false appearances, than any other American who has ever presumed to manufacture generalizations. . . . I believe that, admitting all his defects, he wrote better English, in the sense of cleaner, straighter, vivider, saner English, than either Irving or Hawthorne. . . . I believe that he was the true father of our national literature, the first genuinely American artist of the blood royal. . . . He was one of the great artists of all time. He was the full equivalent of Cervantes and Molière, Swift and Defoe. He was and is the one authentic giant of our national literature."

From Mark Twain he learned many things, never to forget them, including these: that sentiment is nothing to be ashamed of though sentimentality is, that the way to meet human venality is to meet it head on, that compassion and a sense of humility need never be concealed, and that, in Mark Twain's words, "the secret source of Humor . . . is not joy but sorrow. There is no humor in heaven." From Mark Twain came the qualities that make Mencken the American humorist second only to Mark Twain himself. Alistair Cooke considers that Mencken has been overrated as a thinker and "underrated as a humorist with a deadly sensible eye on the behavior of the human animal." Mark Twain gave him that eye, or at least inspired him to use his own, and much of his apparatus as a writer.

There were other sources, all going back to his childhood and youth, for he was quick to discover that there are ways, and ways, of writing. Thomas Huxley fascinated him not only for what he had to teach but for his utter clarity, and he mentioned Huxley many years later as "the greatest of all masters of orderly exposition. He taught me the importance of giving to every argument a simple structure." In his view Huxley's prose "was the best produced by an Englishman in the Nineteenth Century."

At several places in his writing, Mencken points to the old *New York Sun*, "especially its editorial page," as an influence on his style, an influence both good and bad — "good because it taught me that good sense was at the bottom of all good writing, but bad because it . . . made me overestimate the value of smart phrases." There is a touch of irony in this, considering how Mencken lambasted editorial writers throughout his life: it turns out that his animus was against the third-raters, not against the competent ones.

He sucked up much from Nietzsche and Shaw and Macaulay, though he never failed to take a poke at Macaulay later on for his pretentiousness. Cooke summarizes their contributions almost too patly: "Nietzsche suggested the outlandish metaphors, Macaulay the feigned omniscience . . . Shaw taught him most." Both Shaw and Mencken, as he writes, "are superior popular educators who kick up a terrific dust on the intellectual middle plateau between the philistine and the first-rate scholar. What makes both of them more memorable than many of their betters is their style." But Mencken never had Shaw's malice and he wholly lacked "the shrill spinster note that in the end wearies all but the most dedicated of Shaw's disciples."

Shaw was, as we know, the subject of Mencken's first book. Mencken admitted that "there was a good deal of empty ornament" in that book, as in his early *Smart Set* work which came along shortly after, but that "afterward I began to tone down, and by the time I was thirty I had developed a style that was clear and alive. I can detect no diminution of its aliveness as I grow older." In this latter remark (from *Minority Report*) he is unduly modest. Of all his writing, the most flexible, subtle, and responsive to his demands was the autumn-blooming style of his autobiographical sketches.

Of stylistic characteristics peculiar to him, there were many. I mention four.

One of these was his belief that the function of criticism — coming ahead even of the discovery of the true and the beautiful — was to be interesting. He never forgot the man on the receiving end: the reader. Always before him as he wrote was the vision of a reader who might fall into a doze with a book, one of his, in his lap; or of the newspaper reader who might pause for a moment over what he had written, yawn, and move on to the next column.

Corollary to this was the care he took to be always on the offensive. He had discovered early that what the public likes is a fight. His first purpose being to catch and hold the interest of the reader, he always charged. This made for difficulties if in all honesty he was compelled to bestow praise. But he had a way around that, too. "When I have to praise a writer, I always do it by attacking his enemies."

Another was his constant resort to the *reductio ad absurdum*, which as James Farrell says he often handled not only cleverly but even brilliantly. The object was to make his victim a butt of ridicule. Here he was most plainly Mark Twain's disciple, who saw laughter as the one really effective weapon of an honest man in an imperfect and on the whole inattentive world. Other weapons might, with time and diligence, make some impression on humbug, but as Mark Twain said, "only laughter can blow it to rags and atoms at a blast."

The fourth was the care with which he placed his readers, those he wanted to persuade, on his side in any argument. He wrote, as he never tired of assuring his readers, for "the nobility and gentry," for "the truly civilized minority." Anyone taking the trouble to read him could therefore consider himself complimented. By inference his readers could never possibly be identified with the bores, shams, and neanderthals whom he delighted to take apart, or share in the slightest their meanness of spirit, their stupidity, their ignorance, and their wrongheadedness. Before going into battle, Mencken always saw to it that the cheering section — his reader — was in good heart and ready to back him. He was a master at this sort of rhetorical sleight of hand.

In discussing "the Mencken philosophy," let us begin by acknowledging that Mencken was not a philosopher. Cairns calls him a positivist, and though the word is probably the right one if Mencken must be given a philosophical label, it seems curiously formal and inappropriate for one of such commonsensical cast of mind. And the tag "skeptic" used in its philosophical sense is even less appropriate. The philosophical skeptic has an open mind, he is a doubter, but he stands ready to be convinced by rational argument — if he can't break down the argument. Philosophical skepticism is apt to be the refuge of timorous but clever men since philosophical arguments can be quite easily destroyed, by the cheap and easy device of questioning the major premise if by no other, and the skeptic is thus spared on high philosophical grounds the inconvenience and vulnerability involved in taking a position on anything. Mencken was abundantly skeptical of the motives of men, especially when they purported to be lofty, and of the postures assumed by public figures. But he was no skeptic: he had a set of convictions as unshakable as Gibraltar. He knew his own mind, and as I have suggested he was not prepared to allow anyone to change it.

The point is that he was simply not interested in first causes or fine-spun theories of knowledge: metaphysics bored him; more, it enraged him, since efforts to prove the unprovable by word-defining and logic-chopping (which is the self-assigned task of metaphysicians) struck him as being the vainest of all parlor games. His view is put with utmost starkness in a famous letter to Burton Rascoe: "My notion is that all the larger human problems are insoluble, and that life is quite meaningless — a spectacle without purpose or moral. I detest all efforts to read a moral into it." But his disgust with philosophy's efforts to account for the universe and its contents, including man, did not, as I say, leave him a skeptic. He believed (and this is where the word "positivism" comes in) in the tangible, the measurable, the verifiable. He described himself once as "a materialist of the materialists," and put it another way in a letter in which he wrote of his "congenital dislike of Plato" and his preference for feet-on-the-ground Aristotle. What science could discover and verify, that he believed; and it must be admitted that during the past several hundred years science has taken a lot of territory away from philosophy.

This gave him all the base he needed for his work as what he called a "critic of ideas." It was the shooting box from which he blasted away at organized religion. It provided him with his political position, which was at once antidemocratic and passionately libertarian.

It was from this point of view that he saw human beings and the whole rickety structure of human institutions.

Pushing aside formal philosophy, then, Mencken started with the proposition (certainly verifiable) that the human organism despite its manifold wonders is a badly botched job. ("God nodded," he once exploded in the midst of the hay fever season, "when he designed my nose.") From that he moved on to the proposition (also verifiable) that all men are not created equal. Equal they may be, or should be, before the law, and equally entitled to opportunity; but demonstrably they are not equal in their native physical and intellectual endowment. The natural incompetence and gullibility of the masses he held to be a matter of simple fact, confirmed every day and everywhere, and the existence in much smaller numbers of superior men a matter equally beyond dispute.

And from this, though he had nothing better to offer ("I am interested in pathology, not therapeutics"), came his criticism of democratic theory and practice. The mass of men, buffeted by forces beyond their strength and understanding, do not yearn for freedom but for security. They turn automatically to the man who promises this. They are the natural prey of demagogues always ready to exploit them for their own purposes, and no system is better adapted to demagoguery than popular democracy. Democracy always and inevitably tends toward mobocracy.

But nothing could be more mistaken than to assume from this that Mencken would have preferred any totalitarian form. He detested Hitler and Mussolini and every other kind of demagogue either hard or soft. His concern was simply that under popular democracy, in which decisions are so often motivated by appeals to envy and promises of something for nothing, the victims are the superior man, the creative man, the self-respecting man — "the only sort of man who is really worth hell room, to wit, the man who practises some useful trade in a competent manner, makes a decent living at it, pays his own way, and asks only to be let alone. He is now a pariah in all so-called civilized countries." Mencken's bill of particulars against democracy boiled down to his simple belief that democracy, given its head, dislikes and hamstrings the producer and the creator.

Though he never put it that way, Mencken was in fact a strict constitutionalist. Given a constitution beyond the reach of easy amendment, that is to say a set of rules that did really restrain the mob and its masters, that put limitations on government and made them stick, kept speech free, and provided equal justice, the superior man probably had as good a chance as under any other conceivable system. But where is the constitution that is invulnerable to the mob when it has really been inflamed? His own experience as a critic of national policy in two world wars left him with small faith in the protections of the United States Constitution or any other. It is interesting that Mencken's political ideas are taken far more seriously in Europe today, among those familiar with them, than they are in his native land. Europeans have more, and more bitter, memories of curdled democracy than Americans do.

A study of Mencken's political ideas necessarily begins with his *Notes on Democracy*. But this is marred by a certain stridency and an overindulgence in bathos and paradox. His ideas somehow come out better in his topical writings on political issues and personalities. Most of the best of these things are brought together in *On Politics: A Carnival of Buncombe*, edited by Malcolm Moos, and in *Prejudices: A Selection*, edited by James T. Farrell. They amplify the comments on his philosophy which are offered above.

Mencken's ingrained habit of calling things and people by their right names, and his clear-eyed refusal to confuse what is what with what ought or ought not to be, led people into false inferences about his likes and prejudices. What he disliked above all was pretense. "As I say, all my work hangs together. Whether it appears to be burlesque, or serious criticism, or mere casual controversy, it is always directed against one thing: unwarranted pretension." Thus he referred to Jews as matter-of-factly as he referred to Methodists, jested about Jewish traits that to him seemed comic, criticized specifically Jewish activities that he thought harmful. This to L. M. Birkhead, a Unitarian pastor, is illustrative: "I believe there is another difficulty in the anti-Semitic question. After all, a man who believes sincerely that the Jews are a menace to the United States ought to be allowed to say so. The fact that he is wrong has got nothing whatsoever to do with it. The right to free speech involves inevitably the right to talk nonsense. I am much disturbed by the effort of the New York Jews to put down criticism. It seems to me that they are only driving it underground, and so making it more violent." This was Mencken talking free speech, not anti-Semitism. He cared nothing for racial or social stigmata and looked past them to the man. A small expression of this is that one of the two well-known paintings of him was done by a Jew, the other by a Negro.

And so it was with his jocosities about "the colored brethren" which reflected the mores of his time and the culture of the Negro community in Baltimore then and throughout the country generally. He didn't pretend not to notice differences. And yet the very last thing he wrote, the article in the *Evening Sun* of November 9, 1948, which I have already mentioned, was an angry protest against the conviction of a mixed group of seven who had challenged Baltimore's segregation ordinances by staging what he called "an interracial tennis combat" on the courts of a public park. "Is such a prohibition . . ." he asked, "supported by anything to be found in common sense and common decency? . . . My answer . . . is a loud and unequivocal No. A free citizen in a free state, it seems to me, has an inalienable right to play with whomsoever he will, so long as he does not disturb the general peace. If any other citizen, offended by the spectacle, makes a pother, then that other citizen, and not the man exercising his inalienable right, should be put down by the police."

No sturdier defender of civil liberties has ever lived, and it was in character that he should have ended his writing, as a newspaperman grinding the grist of the news, with a simple statement supporting them.

The public Mencken, as I hope I have made clear, was different in many ways from the private Mencken. To the public generally, and especially after the press took to quoting him on anything and everything in the late twenties and early thirties, he was a roistering fellow who had an acid tongue and a club in his hand and was given to every sort of excess. He went along with this cheerfully, and even encouraged it. Why not? It gave him an instant audience, one running into the millions, for anything he might want to say. Others might coat their pills with sugar: he used a tart and astringent coating and found the public equally ready to swallow it. His role as the archenemy of Prohibition gave him a supplementary reputation as a fearful boozer.

His manner in company somewhat fortified that larger, vaguer reputation. In a gathering that was large and mixed he could be subdued and even ill at ease, but among men whom he found congenial he was a marvelous companion — exuberant, boisterous, often ribald. I recall his daily visits to the Sunpapers back in the days when I was a green young editorial writer. His loud greeting was at once gay and gruff. He would disappear into one sanctum or another, that of the editor or the publisher, and from behind the door would issue muffled roars of laughter. It wasn't the response to a monologue, quite. He dominated, but he knew the difference between conversation and a one-man show. He enjoyed practical jokes, and often gave them a sharp edge — as for instance that fake institution known as "The Loyal Legion of American Mothers," which was "dedicated to avoiding foreign entanglements and keeping American womanhood pure." Much mischief was done under that and other equally grotesque letterheads.

But all this exuberance, and much of his enormous correspondence, were the compensations of a lonely man, a loneliness implicit in his work. In his *Minority Report* there is this: "I know a great many more people than most men, and in wider and more diverse circles, yet my life is essentially one of isolation, and so is that of every other man. We not only have to die alone; we also, save for a few close associates, have to live alone." And the bleakness of his view of the nature of things only fortified the loneliness and pessimism. "The natural state of a reflective man," he wrote in another context, "is one of pessimism."

His private life, save for some exceptions to be noted, was orderly and austere. After breakfast his day began with an hour or two of dictation to Lohrfinck, his secretary. When she had gone, he worked until noon on his notes and files and some writing; following luncheon he put on his public manner for his daily visit to the Sunpapers, with arrival punctually at two o'clock. By mid-afternoon he was in Hollins Street again to work on his papers until about five. Then a book, or the better part of one, perhaps a brief nap, the return of

Lohrfinck with a load of letters to sign and seal, and a short walk to the mailbox before his supper (his concession to exercise); after supper, which was finished before eight, came his main bout of writing for the day in his third-floor quarters, which normally stretched on to about ten o'clock; then downstairs to unwind, usually with his brother August, or out to Schellhase's, a *gemütlich* little restaurant, for a couple of glasses of beer with an old friend or two; and then home to bed not long after eleven o'clock, to read until he fell asleep.

There was not much room in such a routine for roistering. His weekly letdown came on Saturday nights with an odd assortment of cronies who made up the Saturday Night Club. They met in the early days above Al Hildebrand's fiddle shop, to grind out music together, Mencken at the piano with a heavy hand. Later they had a second-floor room at Schellhase's; and after the music there was beer and merriment. Music was Mencken's avocation, his companion and pleasure throughout his life: "I'd rather have written any symphony of Brahms' than any play of Ibsen's. I'd rather have written the first movement of Beethoven's Eroica than the Song of Solomon. . . . In music a man can let himself go. In words he always remains a bit stiff and unconvincing." His musician friend Louis Cheslock, possibly a prejudiced witness, always insisted that "in the same sense that Beethoven was aware of the language of sound, Mencken was aware of the sound of language."

His other recreation, growing out of his hypochondriacal temperament, was hospital visiting. Ill health, to him, was the great human curse and calamity; and that sympathy for human suffering, that compassion for the lot of man in general which he kept so well concealed from his larger public, got its release out of visits to the sick. He was a familiar figure in the halls of Johns Hopkins Hospital and of all the other local pesthouses, as he liked to call them.

He traveled occasionally, but the preparations had a way of turning into crises, and the chief effect of such holidays was to make him long for the familiar ambiance of Baltimore and the routine of home.

As for his reputation as a formidable boozer, it was without basis. As a youngster on the police beat (he tells in one of his sketches) he learned the lesson from a tough old fire department surgeon whom he came to know and admire that alcohol is not a stimulant but a depressant: "His words . . . continue to lurk in my mind, to this day. In consequence . . . I employ it of an evening, not to hooch up my faculties but to let them down after work. Not in years have I ever written anything with so much as a glass of beer in my system. My compositions, I gather, sometimes seem boozy to the nobility and gentry, but they are actually done as soberly as those of William Dean Howells." He was always from adolescence onward a "cagey" drinker — the first to raise his glass, but the last to empty it. He had no real taste for spirits and was forever finding excuses to avoid them.

A man always strict with himself, a disciplined man who severely rationed his pleasures, this was Mencken. To James Farrell he once said this: "Farrell, if you want to develop further as a writer, there are three things to stay away from. Booze . . . women . . . and politics." If he said that to one young writer, he said it to a hundred; and he followed his own prescription.

Mencken's output was prodigious. The Adler bibliography runs to 349 pages, and even this formidable listing excludes his letters. Guy Forgue, in the preface to his admirably edited selection of these letters, estimates that those deposited in public libraries and private collections must run to around 15,000. It is an estimate very much on the low side. Some years ago I discussed the output of Mencken letters with his brother August and mentioned 50,000 as a not unlikely number. August had lately made an estimate — not by trying to count, but by weight — of the number of letters addressed to Mencken in connection with a single work, *The American Language*, and came up with the figure of 65,000. Although this was an estimate of letters received, it also meant 65,000 replies, because Mencken's red-letter rule was to answer all letters and on the day of their receipt. What the total output of all kinds must have been, long ones and short ones, others amounting to essays, is anyone's guess. And the odd thing is that every one of these, no matter how perfunctory, was relieved by a phrase, a suggestion, a sharp comment, a touch of grotesquerie that made it hard to throw away. As for his longer letters, when he rolled up his sleeves and really went to work, some are Mencken at his best, as critic of life and letters and as self-revelation. Forgue's collection, of letters to writers mostly, is in fact one of Mencken's most absorbing books.

Mencken has been spared, fortunately, the deadly Collected Edition which abandons discrimination for comprehensiveness and which serves as a tombstone for so many writers whose work, in part, might otherwise live. As a newspaperman he wrote most of the time for the moment; but as Alistair Cooke quite properly insists there is a great deal of life, maybe immortality, in a fair bit of that stuff. The thing to do is to let time winnow it. The process is well begun in the several selections of his *Prejudices* and newspaper political pieces by Cooke, Farrell, and Moos and in Cheslock's gathering of his pieces on music. A much fuller anthology by Huntington Cairns, called *H. L. Mencken: The American Scene*, ranges all across his work and with sound judgment. Certain storehouses of Mencken material, notably the Mencken room in the Enoch Pratt Free Library of Baltimore and the New York Public Library collection, offer ripe pickings for the future.

Of his formal treatises — his *Notes on Democracy*, *A Treatise on the Gods*, and *A Treatise on Right and Wrong* — what is likely to be the verdict? He obviously put great store by them as a distillation of his views on the three abiding human preoccupations, with politics (or the art of living together without too much trouble) and with religion and morals (together, the art of living with oneself). But neither as a corpus nor individually can they really be called successful. The first, as suggested already, is badly organized, undisciplined, and shrill despite many a penetrating and cathartic paragraph. It overstates. It leaves the reader, shall we say, not quite persuaded. Its leading ideas are set forth better anyway in his posthumous *Minority Report*, a book which will continue to appeal to readers with a taste for the aphoristic form, and in his journalism, where they are illuminated by concrete issues and people. As for *A Treatise on the Gods* and *A Treatise on Right and Wrong*, both smell too strongly of the lamp, which is to say that they seem somehow concocted. The reading that went into them was extraordinarily wide. They contain much curious information. But Mencken's concern to make them *interesting*, to "fetch" the reader, seems inappropriate to what at bottom were intended as sober and deadly serious treatises. One is left with the conviction, again, that his leading ideas were better put by the thinkers from whom he absorbed them, that he added relatively little of his own beyond the form of the statement, that in any case they are far better stated in his topical writing and that he is not at his best in the sustained development of ideas. Mencken was simply not a systematist.

The one exception to that generalization is his great *The American Language*. And it is not hard to see why. Here Mencken the stylist, Mencken the word-juggler, is at work investigating the raw materials of his own great talent and constant preoccupation. He is studying his native tongue, his own means of communication — its origin, its evolution, the springs that feed it, its marvelous suppleness and fluidity. The theme needed systematic exploration, for it had never been given this before; and it took a man sensitive to every nuance of speech and writing to do it. Mencken was that man; and his fascination as well as his supreme capacity for the task shows through as it does nowhere in the three efforts at systematization mentioned above.

Yet *The American Language* comes up against another fate. It deals with a living and changing thing. Even in the course of its four editions (the first in 1919 and the fourth in 1936) the growth and change of the language required many modifications, including modifications of the central thesis. The American language having grown away from British English, the two had begun to coalesce again through a reverse process: the modification of British English along American lines by extensive borrowings. McDavid's one-volume abridgment (1963) required much more than abridgment: it required extensive updating. The original *American Language* will live as a period piece, a monumental work of scholarship fixing the language as of its time, like a still shot from a film, and full of wit and wisdom. But the title shows signs of developing a life of its own, like Bartlett, Webster, Roget, and even Fanny Farmer.

If we leave out this singular case, the surest candidates for immortality seem to be his *Happy Days* and *Newspaper Days*, redolent of a life that is gone yet no more to be forgotten than the Wild West, and done in a style ripened and purged of excess, a style that as Cooke says is "flexible, fancy-free, ribald, and always beautifully lucid; a native product unlike any other style in the language." Those books and the best of his "transient" work: they are the essential Mencken. They are what he gave to our literature which time is least likely to tarnish or erode.

SHERMAN PAUL

RANDOLPH BOURNE

THE BRIEF career of Randolph Bourne began in 1911 when he published in the *Atlantic Monthly* a rejoinder to one of those perennial animadversions on the younger generation. In its February issue the magazine had featured "A Letter to the Rising Generation" by Cornelia Comer, a frequent contributor. Adopting a Roman sternness and a sarcastic religious voice, she censured the young men of good families for abandoning the ways of their fathers. She knew that new conditions would not produce the sort of men the old conditions had, that the rising generation had been "conceived in uncertainty [and] brought forth in misgiving"; to be "nobly militant" would be difficult for a generation victimized by educational experiments and the eroding belief and authority of the elders. Yet everything about these young men annoyed her: their "agnostic-and-water" religious viewpoint, their Whitmanian notion of Personality and Shavian delight in the liberation of the natural will, and especially their experimental approach to ethics and advocacy of socialism, which she indicted as justifications of irresponsibility. The younger generation, she believed, lacked force and fortitude, was "soft," was deformed by "mental rickets and curvature of the soul."

Mrs. Comer's annoyance indicates the extent to which communication between fathers and sons had broken down. She accurately observes the postures of these "Whitmanshaws" but considers them "cheap"; she will not have them enjoy without a large outlay of pain. She says that "the final right of each generation to its own code [of manners] depends upon the inner significance of those manners," but she does not search — to the limit of an elder's sympathy and power — for that significance. This, to be sure, only the new generation itself can fully express, thereby declaring itself and adding its increment to human history. Meanwhile, failing to understand that she is disturbed by the role of youth — by the fact that change, as Erik Erikson says, is "the business of youth and . . . challenge the essence of its business" — she prophesies: "It may easily happen that the next twenty years will prove the most interesting in the history of civilization. Armageddon is always at hand in some fashion. Nice lads with the blood of the founders of our nation in your veins, pecking away at the current literature of socialism, taking out of it imperfectly understood apologies for your temperaments and calling it philosophy — where will you be if a Great Day should really dawn?"

In replying to Mrs. Comer, Randolph Bourne had one of the few advantages in the confrontation of generations: he understood her generation more fully than she understood his. Her viewpoint and tone were as familiar to him as Bloomfield, New Jersey, the old respectable middle-class town in which he was born (in 1886) and raised and which, all his life, bitterly attracted him. He confessed to a correspondent, whose small-town plight was similar to his, that he owed most of his political, social, and psychological education to Bloomfield, that "its Church, its social classes, prejudices, conservatism, moral codes, personalities — all furnish the background against which I throw all my experience, and in terms of which I still see life and suppose always shall." In his master's thesis he studied the effects of suburbanization on the social life of the town, explaining that the process was slower there than in nearby Glen Ridge and Montclair because the "Calvinistic religion was bred in the bone of the town, and it [would] take much urban sophistication to get rid of it." And, perhaps to find a purchase for himself and others after the war, he began an autobiographical novel of which only the chapter on his sixth year in Bloomfield was published — a chapter with which the monthly *Dial* was launched.

In everything except money, Randolph Silliman Bourne belonged to the "comfortable classes" for whom and to whom Mrs. Comer spoke. The quarrel between them was a family matter, an affair almost entirely of the middle class. He was, in fact, one of the "nice lads" of worthy native ancestry and good family whom she threatened with class-displacement and the rough discipline of "life." He, however, was already intimate with both. His birth, as he said, had been "terribly messy"; inept forceps-delivery had left his face scarred and misshapen. Then, in his fourth year, he had been ill with spinal tuberculosis, had been stunted and bent, "cruelly blasted," he once complained, "by the powers that brought him into the world." (According to his passport, he was five feet tall, had brown hair and a medium complexioned long face with blue eyes, a large nose, straight mouth, and receding chin. A close college friend reported that it was not his deformed back, which he learned to hide with a black cape and by carefully seating himself, but his malformed ear — "a rudimentary appendage" — that repelled people, and that Bourne himself disliked his "sloping chin.") He also knew a disability more common in his generation of writers: the failure of the father, itself a sign of the crumbling edifice of Victorian middle-class values. His father, Charles Rogers Bourne, had failed in business and had consented to leave home when his brother-in-law made this the condition of his support of Sarah Barrett Bourne and her four children. A cruel banishment! A martyrdom, Van Wyck Brooks might have said, to the "acquisitive life," and one that would have impressed the boy with the inexorable Calvinism of the household and with the belief, for which he said he "suffered tortures," that failure was always the result of moral weakness. Genteel impoverishment and dependence is perhaps the worst affliction of the respectable — to have to live constantly, as Bourne remembered, under the "awful glowering family eye of rich guarding relatives," who also, as far as he was concerned, remained "dumb and uninterested." An aunt and grandmother were warm sustaining presences, but his mother's unhappiness, a proper disposition in such circumstances, established the ground tone of what he called his "doleful home."

Perhaps the absence of his father confirmed the gentility of his upbringing. Like Miro, the fictive hero of "The History of a Literary

Radical," he found in his environment little genuine cultural nourishment but much cultural devoutness. In his home, as in many more, the classics, in Eliot's exact description, "Upon the glazen shelves kept watch"; only the metropolitan newspaper opened to him a portal to the world, and to it he attributed his real education. He was a well-behaved boy whose success as a student had been due, he admitted, to "my moral rather than my intellectual sense." Indeed, in the few pages of the diary he began in his fourteenth year, he reveals himself to be the phenomenon he later thought appalling, the "good" child. Here he records the eager steps of a culture-famished, priggish youth intent on success and social acceptance: he and his sister have joined the church ("Mamma wants us to very much"); he has begun to excel in school ("Wonder of wonders! I got 100 in a Greek exercise that I did tother day. I have never gotten it before"); he has been elected class president, though "not very popular in the school and very little known"; he has begun to collect stamps and well-printed and -bound books — Lowell's and Whittier's poems, *Ivanhoe* and *The Vicar of Wakefield* — and to record his literary opinions ("I have just finished reading 'Eben Holden.' It beats 'David Harum' by a good deal. . . . The love story is about the prettiest and sweetest I have ever read"); and he has discovered that babies are "cute," has sent his finest valentine to a girl named Grace Wade, has gone to a "very dainty and lovely" luncheon, and has been taken by his Aunt Fan to *Lohengrin*.

The career of respectability begun here might have continued had Bourne been able to enter college on graduating from high school in 1903. But his uncle was unwilling to provide this privilege, and he was turned out to work, learning, as he said in "A Philosophy of Handicap," that "the bitterest struggles of the handicapped man come when he tackles the business world." He worked for six years: in an office, as an accompanyist and music teacher (he was a competent pianist), and as a "factory hand" perforating music rolls for player pianos, an indelible experience of the piecework system that he described in "What Is Exploitation?" Desperate to escape such lower depths, he finally practiced the "dodging of pressures" he preached to those similarly trapped: "I solved my difficulties only by evading them, by throwing overboard some of my responsibility [he was the eldest child]." At the age of twenty-three, he entered Columbia University on a scholarship, to discover, gratefully, that "college furnishes an ideal environment where the things at which a handicapped man . . . can succeed really count."

In 1909, Columbia was already a great metropolitan university and headquarters of modern thought. In many departments, its professors belonged to the vanguard: Franz Boas, in anthropology; John Dewey, in philosophy, psychology, and education; Charles Beard, in political science; James Harvey Robinson, in history — to mention only those most frequently considered in the history of American revolt against formalism. There, Bourne was befriended by his teachers, especially by his "great hero-teacher" Frederick P. Keppel, who helped him financially, and was surrounded by bright, sympathetic young men many of whom shared with him the editing of the *Columbia Monthly*. There, he declared, he found a spiritual home. The congenial intellectual world and the fresh atmosphere of ideas represented for him the valuable "college education" that then, as now, was overwhelmed by "college life." "What we all want the college to be" — he later wrote in "What Is College For?" — "is a life where for youth of all social classes the expressions of genius, the modern interpretations of society, and the scientific spirit, may become imaginatively real." Having quickly abandoned fusty literary studies for the "intellectual arena" of the social sciences, he got what he said a student should: "a fused and assimilated sense of the world he lives in, in its length and breadth, its historical perspective and social setting." Columbia, he told a prospective student, had revolutionized his life.

When he wrote this to Prudence Winterrowd of Shelbyville, Indiana, he was thinking mostly of the thwartings he had known in Bloomfield and the heady release Columbia had provided him. But it had revolutionized his thought and, in a more modest way, his action. He had a certain notoriety because he protested such things as the exploitation by the university of its scrub women and page boys. If not a big man on campus, he was an older, notable one: a socialist, an editor of the highbrow literary magazine that in his time had repudiated *fin de siècle* symbolism for critical realism. On the magazine he had served a valuable apprenticeship, had found his vocation; and after his appearance in the *Atlantic Monthly*, he had the glamour that invests the undergraduate who arrives in the real world ahead of the rest.

Bourne's praise of Columbia was not extravagant because, with his inability to set himself in motion, he owed much of his achievement to its stimulus. In the struggle to get a foothold, he explained in "The Experimental Life," "the difference is in the fortune of the foothold, and not in our private creation of any mystical force of will." Columbia was a fortunate foothold, which he did not readily give up; it had awakened his capacity, produced activity and success. Dean Frederick Woodbridge, for example, had suggested that he reply to Mrs. Comer and had forwarded his essay to Ellery Sedgwick, the editor of the *Atlantic Monthly*, who served Bourne, for as long as he permitted, as literary counselor. Bourne acknowledged that the magazine was his "good angel" and "coddled" him. Sedgwick prompted several essays — some of Bourne's most significant essays and a large proportion of his best work were printed by him — and Sedgwick made the magazine another foothold. With his help, Houghton Mifflin Company published Bourne's first book, *Youth and Life* (1913), a collection of *Atlantic* and *Columbia Monthly* essays, and so he established himself. Columbia postponed the crisis of vocation and prepared him for it by enabling him to spend a year in Europe; and when this crisis was again at hand, Sedgwick and Charles Beard secured a place for him on Herbert Croly's new liberal weekly, the *New Republic*.

To the psychological and intellectual weather of these exciting turbulent years, *Youth and Life* is excellent testimony — "thoroughly and almost uncannily autobiographical," Bourne ruefully admitted. Walter F. Greenman, a Unitarian minister in Milwaukee, one of the many educated people (social workers, ministers, teachers, and idealistic housewives) the book inspired, believed it to be "the truest interpretation of Youth to itself" that he knew. It made him feel "as if my beloved Emerson had had a reincarnation in the 20th Century," and he told Bourne that it was "the most innocent looking sweetest stick of dynamite anybody ever chewed." In these essays, which include the reply to Mrs. Comer, is the full statement of the case for the younger against the older generation. The reviewer in the *Columbia Monthly* praised them highly as a declaration but complained that the essay form had eliminated the poetry of youth. Yet no other book of this time expresses so well, even while making youth an ideology to which to be loyal, the precarious condition and the virtues of this season of life. For all of its faults, deriving mainly from reliance on the rhetoric of uplift — a rhetoric, however, that in conjunction with candor and fresh ideas effectively expresses the new idealism — it is an irreplaceable book of this generation, like the war essays of Bourne's *Untimely Papers*, and belongs with his best work.

The title itself brilliantly states the issues, which, because of Bourne's fidelity to experience, address every younger generation as well as his own: the confrontation of youth, a new generation, with "life"; the resources of life, which youth bears; and the responsibilities it has for its replenishment. At the very moment in Western history when Ortega announced that the theme of our time was the restoration of life to its proper relation with culture, Bourne called the young men and women of his generation to life and showed them an open and daring stance toward the world, one flexible yet resilient, that would enable them to master and enjoy the "experimental life." Using these essays as a form of self-therapy — they are continuous with his remarkable correspondence — he investigated his identity crisis, one of more than usual significance because profound historical changes contributed to it. In doing this, he either anticipated or confirmed the advanced thought of men like Ortega, Erikson, and Paul Goodman, for he recognized the concept of the generation and its historical, social, and psychological components. He knew what it meant to grow up absurd and how much absurdity was due to an older generation; he knew that life had stages, each with its necessary virtue, and that in the cycle of generations youth, having the regenerative function, was especially important; and he knew that for psychological and social reasons the conflict of generations was as inevitable as it was necessary, yet sometimes irreconcilable, because beneath the rebellion over child rearing and education, philosophies and values, was the stark fact of power — that the older generation, as he said, wished "to rule not only their own but all the generations."

The first three essays specifically treat these themes, although the remaining essays, by way of exploring the thoughts and solutions of youth, consider them too. The general case gives way to particular applications, and the book concludes with the most intimately personal essay, "A Philosophy of Handicap," which had stirred the readers of the *Atlantic* and Sedgwick had insisted Bourne reprint — an essay that now certified the book by giving it a signature and fastened to the younger generation the virtue of unassuming courage.

As Bourne describes it, youth is a condition, the result of a profound psychological crisis and coming-of-age when one is "suddenly born into a confusion of ideas and appeals and traditions" and enters a "new spiritual world." Whether or not this crisis is fruitful depends on awareness and spiritual force, on finding release for oneself not in "passion" but in "enthusiasm." For the way of passion is not "adventurous"; it is the way of "traditional" youth, who, like most of those friends of Bourne's youth in Bloomfield whose social life excluded him, pass easily through the crisis by avoiding it, by following pleasure and settling for as well as into established routines. To seek security at the expense of consciousness is to forfeit youth, and Bourne does not speak for these young people but for those radical ones, like his Columbia friends, who have not been cautious and have exposed themselves "to the full fury of the spiritual elements." These adventurous youth discover the precious gift of life and become the responsive ones who, if they continue to seek and search, alter the sensibility of the age. Only the young, Bourne says, "are actually contemporaneous; they interpret what they see freshly and without prejudice; their vision is always the truest, and their interpretation always the justest." Not burdened with stock moralities, they follow the open road of experience, always susceptible to the new, eager for experiment, ready to let ideas get them. Their enthusiasm is for fresh ideals to which to give their loyalty, and nothing angers them more than the spiritual torpor and "damaged ideals" that, in this account, define old age.

The attack on the elders is directed to this condition. As in *Walden*, so here: "Age is no better, hardly so well, qualified for an instructor as youth," Thoreau says, "for it has not profited so much as it has lost." What it has lost, essentially, is the spontaneity of being — "the soul's emphasis," in Emerson's wonderful phrase — that sustains the virtue of each season of life and impels one's moral growth. Age has lost the very condition of youth, which Bourne believes to be the epitome of life. It has forsaken the "battle-ground of the moral life" to which childhood familiarization with the world opens and all subsequent stages of life, to be worthy, must contribute support. Just as toward children the duty of elders is to refrain from imposing moralities and, by permitting natural growth into the world, to prepare them for the vital morality of self-mastery, so toward youth the duties of middle and old age, respectively, are to "conserve the values of youth" by living up to them and then, in relinquishing power, wisely to understand "the truth and efficacy of youth's ideal vision."

The aim of this gospel of youth is "to reinstate ideals and personality at the heart of the world." Tested by this gospel, the older generation has failed. The older accuses the younger generation of being soft when, in fact, it is palpitant, for the virtue of all its virtues, the passion for justice, has been kindled by the kind of world the elders have given it. To them Bourne attributes the cardinal fact about the younger generation: that it has had to bring itself up and, accordingly, has learned to judge by its own standards. The education provided it has not fitted the needs of its freer social life and wider awareness of the world. The formulas of the elders have not been helpful, and their models of success have not been attractive. It finds distasteful the routine, chicanery, and predation of the business world to which they would guide it, regrets the lack of individual social responsibility in the increasingly corporate economy, and is hampered by the high cost of professional education. In every way the elders refuse it confirmation, deny it by evading with "nerveless negations" the issues raised by its "positive faith" in social reform. And so, at the pitch of his indictment, Bourne says, "the stupidities and cruelties of their management of the world fill youth with an intolerant rage."

What is hardest to understand about another generation is the very thing Bourne tried to explain in the body of his book: its way of being in the world. He begins, in "The Life of Irony," by defining its point of view, the "comic juxtaposition" it has adopted in order to revivify the world. Irony, to be sure, is deadly accurate and reveals the absurdity of many things; it has a negative power and, as Bourne's friends complained of his use of it, is often accompanied by "malicious delight." Yet for Bourne it was much more than a hostile critical weapon: it was a social mode of being, his way of embracing the world and finding in it a field for vital intelligence. He speaks of irony as the "science of comparative experience," as "a sweeter, more flexible and human principle of life, adequate, without the buttress of supernatural belief, to nourish and fortify the spirit." It is the foe of both "predestined formulas" and spiritual apathy, unfixing things, restoring fluidity, and, at the same time, bringing "a vivid and intense feeling of aliveness." It admits to experience the "noisier and vivider elements" that the New Humanists wished to exclude, and is therefore "rich" and "democratic." Like Whitman's mode of acceptance, irony requires that one take another's position and contact the world. It is an "active way of doing and being" that confronts one with his own firsthand experience, occasions "surprise," and brings with it (in one of Bourne's favorite words) the "glow" of life.

Of greatest significance in this redefinition of irony is the fact that it weaves itself "out of the flux of experience rather than out of eternal values." But of greatest moment to Bourne is the fact that the experience he has in mind is social and that what he needs most to nourish it are friends. This relish for friendship is not merely the reflection of the life he was living at Columbia; it is also an affirmation of temperamental need. To the deprivation of everything else, he says, he is invulnerable; and Clara Barrus, a friend of John Burroughs and student of Whitman, when she read the essay on friendship was moved to send him Whitman's poem "I Saw in Louisiana a Live-Oak Growing." Bourne used his friends, as Emerson did, to discover aspects of himself, but he did not demand of them, as the transcendentalists did, a running together of souls. He asked much, but on a lower plane: the excitement that generates thought; not binding spiritual relations so much as lively intellectual occasions. His conception of friendship was social where their conception was personal; he was the least of solitaries, a thoroughly social being, and the sociality he required of friendship he required also of the great community. His personal need for friendship inspired his correspondence and, after the camaraderie of Columbia, his search for another rewarding form of social life. But it also inspired, as a similar need had in Whitman, the vision of a pluralistic fraternal society that fired his generation.

Bourne's feeling for the possibilities of an intensely individual yet socialized life generated the gaiety of spirit that, in spite of his awareness of the world of fright, characterizes his book. He is familiar with the despair of naturalism, but he knows that the adventure as well as the precariousness and peril of life is grounded in this condition. To alleviate the sickness of scientific materialism, he proposes a new idealism, scientific in method but mystical in scope, such as he had found in Whitman, Maeterlinck, and William James — an idealism whose newness he suggests when he writes that youth "must think of everything in terms of life; yes, even death in terms of life." In addition, he limits responsibility to social rather than metaphysical evil, to those evils that human "interests" and "ideals" can remedy, and, by explaining the appeal of the "social movement," defends the radicalism of the younger generation while rousing in it his own desire to "ride fast and shout for joy."

In behalf of his generation, Bourne presents an objective that enlists loyalty, that satisfies the claims of both social action and religious sentiment; and, implementing it, he offers a new conception of success and strategy for achieving it. He treats success in "The Experimental Life" and finds its touchstone in the readiness of spirit that contributes also to the adventurous life of irony. "I love people of quick, roving intelligence, who carry their learning lightly, and use it as weapons to fight with, as handles to grasp new ideas with, and as fuel to warm them into a sympathy with all sorts and conditions of men" — this remark (and self-portrayal) in a letter describes the achievement of a way of being, the transformation of personality that for Bourne constitutes success. He detests the doggedness and prudence of planning one's life, for life is not plan and cannot be taken frontally. One must go roundabout, must consult his "interests" (the solicitations of the world) and stand "poised for opportunity." Life is not a battle, as the elders believe, but an experiment. "Life is not a rich province to conquer by our will, or to wring enjoyment out of with our appetites, nor is it a market where we pay our money . . . and receive the goods we desire," Bourne says, repudiating the notions of the older generation as well as those of the still younger generation of Fitzgerald and Hemingway. "It is rather [as Thoreau demonstrated] a great tract of spiritual soil, which we can cultivate or misuse."

Bourne upholds the intrinsic success of self-culture. He believes as firmly as any transcendentalist in the primary duty of living one's own life — like Thoreau, he hugs himself. The unpardonable sin is "treason to one's self," the easy self-betrayal of letting outer forces arrest the development of one's inner nature. He says that "convention is the real enemy of youth" and advises them to dodge the pressures that "warp and . . . harden the personality and its own free choices and bents." Of these pressures, the most formidable and intolerable is the family, for intimacy compounds its force. In a letter to Prudence Winterrowd encouraging her to leave home, Bourne writes bitterly of the spiritual cannibalism of parents who demand that their children sacrifice their lives for them. He tells her that he wants "independent, self-reliant, progressive generations, not eating each other's hearts out, but complementing each other and assuming a spiritual division of labor."

Now Bourne does not incite youth to rebellion for light and transient reasons. He is aware of their obsession with sex, but mentions it only to set them the task of taming it; his advice is to neglect rather than repress this desire. (He himself was disturbed by desire because he felt debarred from its fulfillment and was still Puritan enough, as "The Major Chord" indicates, to divide the claims of soul and body and imagine them in the conventional terms of light and dark lady. In this unpublished dialogue, the cool, luminous light lady stands for the pleasures of mind and spirit — for the kind of intellectual relations Bourne actually has with women. The dark lady, warm and naked, represents the body, "the surge and passion of life," and the imperious injunction to live in the body: "You must live, my poet, / And the body only lives." The poet admits his sexual hunger, but does not take the dark lady. Instead he confronts the light lady, whom he notes resembles the dark lady, with his desire and compels her to be both body and soul and to yield a safer passion: "Not the smoky fires of passion," "Not the voluptuous fumes . . ." Certainly what Bourne told a confidante, Alyse Gregory, was true: that the struggle with unrealized desire hampered him, yet colored "all his appreciations," motivated "his love of personality," and filled his life "with a sort of smouldering beauty." And considered along with all Bourne said in support of desires of other kinds, his solution to the problem of sexual desire confirms Dorothy Teall's statement that the sexual revolution of their generation was more a matter of "refreshment of emotion . . . than a revolution in morals.") Bourne does not treat this problem, except by sympathetic indirection in sketches like "Sophronsiba." The liberation he preaches is neither sexual nor an end in itself but a means to a new "spiritual livelihood." Youth, he says, "must see their freedom as simply the setting free of forces within themselves for a cleaner, sincerer life, and for radical work in society." He asks youth to find socially productive vocations, to contribute to reform *in their vocations* — by following journalism or art, medicine or engineering, not the law, ministry, or business. They must pursue their self-culture in society and stake the fulfillments of self on social reconstruction. He announces these ends in "For Radicals," his directive to the American Scholar, and calls the "idealistic youth of today" to the work of reform that Emerson had spoken of as "the conversion of the world."

The Reverend Walter Greenman wondered how long Bourne would go on using the antithesis of youth and age, and told him to guard against the assault of age and the drying-up of literary material by finding a "new cleavage." The advice was needless. *Youth and Life* was not quite the "charmingly immature book" Norman Foerster, a New Humanist professor, thought it, for youth and age, as Bourne used them, were exactly what Van Wyck Brooks meant by opposed catchwords that correspond to genuine convictions and real issues. Bourne may have approached these issues youthfully, but they were issues of profundity and scope and, followed out, disclosed an abyss in American culture.

Two years before the publication of *Youth and Life*, Santayana had spoken of America, in "The Genteel Tradition in American Philosophy," as "a country with two mentalities, one a survival of the beliefs and standards of the fathers, the other an expression of the instincts, practice, and discoveries of the younger generations." These mentalities were represented, in Stuart Sherman's adaptation of Emerson's phrases, by the Party of Culture and the Party of Nature; and the battle between them, long in preparation, was the bitterest in our cultural history because the insurgent modernists were at last strong enough to attack the entire nineteenth-century orthodox inheritance. Since Emerson's time, the Party of Nature had returned to society; the "nature" in its title was merely a New Humanist slur-word designating its archfoe, naturalism. This party was in fact Emerson's Party of Hope, inspired anew by the possibilities of social reform. Radical in its theories of education, socialistic in politics, cosmopolitan and urban, this party exuberantly embraced contemporary America. The Party of Culture, on the other hand, was what Emerson had called the Party of the Past, renamed in tribute to Matthew Arnold, and rightly, because it looked to "culture" to maintain its traditional social and religious values. It was predominantly eastern, Anglo-Saxon, professorial; it spoke for the good families of native stock, for the established and wealthy. To these parties Bourne fixed the distinctions of youth and age, for in the battle between them he saw "the struggle of the old to conserve, of the new to adapt" — that "overlapping of the generations, with their stains and traces of the past" that, instead of evolution, accounted for social change.

Ortega has said that a generation is not a succession but an argument. The truth of this observation is especially evident at those times when assumptions are exposed by loss of conviction and points of view alter radically. The transcendentalists had engaged in such an argument about the nature of human experience and creativity and the ends of American life — an unfinished argument resumed in Bourne's time. He put the issue when he said that his generation wanted "a new orientation of the spirit that shall be modern." And Walter Lippmann, another spokesman for this generation, put it in another way when he wrote in *Drift and Mastery* (1914), a book Bourne greatly admired: "The sanctity of property, the patriarchal family, hereditary caste, the dogma of sin, obedience to authority, — the rock of ages, in brief, has been blasted for us. Those who are young today are born into a world in which the foundations of the older order survive only as habits or by default." Industrialization had changed precipitately the ways of economic and social life, and since the 1880s thinkers — a whole literature — had been assailing the modes of thought supporting the old order. Its guardians, however, seemed neither prepared nor willing to meet the challenge of "experience" — to fulfill new needs and, in Lippmann's phrase, restore the "moral texture of democracy."

The enemies of those who at every stage of our history have responded to the moral imperatives of democracy have been cowardice and complacency, the moral deficiencies Bourne attributed to the older generation. Here, it was most vulnerable because of its assumption of virtue, and Bourne, often with devastating lightness, continued to attack it. He drew its several portraits — caricatures, perhaps, when compared with his tender sketches of the young — in "One of Our Conquerors," "The Professor," and "The Architect."

The conqueror, barely disguised, was Columbia's president, Nicholas Murray Butler, one of the "sleek and successful elders" who was "against everything new, everything untried, everything untested." With his ideal of service and gospel of success, his Anglo-Saxon prejudices, absolute idealism in philosophy, and Republican political rectitude, he was the representative public man of the older generation, an intellectual Horatio Alger, the Captain of Learning who, in the *Columbia Monthly*, had told the undergraduates, "Don't Knock! Boost!"

The professor, drawn appropriately with delicate irony, was John Erskine, also of Columbia. This professor of English had acquired from Henry Van Dyke and Charles Eliot Norton the "ideals of the scholar and gentleman" and protected the "chalice of the past." Himself free from "philosophic or sociologic taint," he deprecated (as Bourne personally knew) "the fanaticism of college men who lose their sense of proportion on social questions."

The architect, an American whom Bourne had met in Italy, shared the professor's gentility and cultural colonialism, for he was an exponent of the Gothic style and a devotee of art for art's sake. Both belonged with the Arnoldians treated in "The Cult of the Best" and "Our Cultural Humility" — those, Bourne said, who believed that "to be cultured . . . mean[s] to like masterpieces" and whose reverential, moralistic attitude toward art closed their eyes to the "vital." Of their company — indeed, with Irving Babbitt, one of their spokesmen — was Paul Elmer More, whose *Aristocracy and Justice* prompted one of Bourne's sharpest replies to the older generation. More, he claimed, not only completely misunderstood modernism and was out of touch with "the driving and creative thought of the day" — was derelict as an intellectual — but was an intellectual partisan of plutocracy, a defender of class exploitation, a judgment More never lived down.

The common want in all of these members of the older generation was the social conscience, which, Bourne said, was "the most characteristic spiritual sign of our age." His generation, he believed, had shifted its spiritual center from the personal to the social. It sought social rather than individual salvation — did not, as he trenchantly explained the religious motives of the older generation, accumulate personal virtue by morally exploiting others and condone social evil as a foil for individual goodness. The older generation believed "in getting all the luxury of the virtue of goodness, while conserving all the advantages of being in a vicious society." Its ideals were selfish and did not appeal to the young who, Bourne said, had begun to "feel social injustice as [their] fathers felt personal sin" and had been converted to a belief in "the possibilities of a regenerated social order."

Youth could no longer be contained in a world "all hardened and definite," by "tight little categories," as he said of More. For More's ethics of repression was the ethics of a "parsimonious" world and had no place in a new world of "surplus value, economic and spiritual." The young had responded to the appeal of a more abundant life, and their response was complete — economic, spiritual, aesthetic. Like More, however, the elders were as insensitive to aesthetic as to moral experience. They did not see that the vision of the social movement was very much an aesthetic one, and their deficiency of social conscience was compounded by "genuine anesthesia," an inability to respond to the petitionings of life and deliver themselves, as Bourne claimed he had, "over to the present."

Bourne's generation had been able to do this because it had acquired from the pragmatists a "new philosophical vista," as Santayana said of the thought of William James, one "radically empirical and radically romantic." Ralph Barton Perry, in *Present Philosophical Tendencies*, an excellent review of contemporary systems that the bright young men of the *Columbia Monthly* considered elementary, treated pragmatism as an especially significant sign of the spirit of the age. Negatively, he wrote, pragmatism represented a "reaction against absolutism, long enthroned in academic and other orthodox circles"; positively, it represented the "'biological' imagination," the conception of an exigent naturalistic environment from which, in the need for adaptation, knowledge and religion themselves arise as "modes of life." Pragmatism, however, was not a philosophy of renunciation or despair, but an enabling melioristic philosophy of collective human effort: "It teaches that the spiritual life is in the making at the point of contact between man and . . . nature" and that knowledge is instrumental, a power that, guided by desire and hope, may "conquer nature and subdue the insurrection of evil." Santayana said that this philosophy was "a thousand times more idealistic than academic idealism" and observed that it was the "philosophy of those who as yet had had little experience"; Perry concluded that it was the philosophy of "impetuous youth, of protestantism, of democracy, of secular progress — that blend of naïveté, vigor, and adventurous courage which proposes to possess the future, despite the present and the past." Such, in any case, was the philosophy which, Santayana announced, had "broken the spell of the genteel tradition, and enticed faith in a new direction."

Bourne had discovered pragmatism at Columbia, where, he told Prudence Winterrowd, "we are all instrumentalists." To her, in fervent letters explaining this "most inspiring modern outlook on life and reality," he also related the story of his conversion. He had moved from Calvinism ("I began in the same way as you") to Unitarianism ("mild and healing") to rank materialism ("I . . . took great delight in lacerating a rather tender and green young man whose delight was in Emerson and Plato, whom I despised"). Then, in 1911, in a course with Professor Woodbridge, the "virus of the Bergson-James-Schiller-instrumental-pragmatism" got into his blood; and now, two years later, he preached James as a prophet. In view of his later relationship with Dewey — his discipleship and apostasy — it is interesting to note in these letters Bourne's failure to mention Dewey and, in other letters, his low opinion of Dewey's courses. He was not fired by Dewey; James was his man because he had what Bourne missed in positivism — "the verve, the color, the music of life." He told Miss Winterrowd that James kept alive for him "a world where amazing regenerations of the vital and spiritual forces of man take place . . . [a world at once] so incorrigibly alive and so incorrigibly mystical." James's world was one of "fluid, interpenetrating, creative things," and Bourne described its appeal when, in a letter to Brooks, he distinguished between mere intellectualism and the "warm area of pragmatic life."

Pragmatism satisfied both the old, now bereft, religious sentiment and the new clamorous scientific spirit. It mediated the extremes of idealism and naturalism. It provided scope for faith and action — and for faith in action. Grounding everything in experience and toward everything proposing an experimental attitude, it upheld the prerogatives of personality at the same time as it encouraged social reform. Itself a product of the biological imagination — a life philosophy — it stimulated the sociological imagination and the faith in salvation by intelligence that were then characteristic of liberal thought. It inspired men to master social drift in the way that the votary Lippmann suggested, by substituting "purpose for tradition," by deliberately devising means for achieving chosen social ends. And to those who adopted its method, it also imparted a democratic vision — it laid, as Bourne said of the new social sciences, "an inexpugnable basis for the highest and noblest aspirations of the time."

How fortunate for Bourne that, finding at home no work for himself equal to these aspirations, he was able to nourish his social imagination elsewhere. Having been awarded a Gilder Fellowship, a handsome patent for sociological investigation, he embarked on July 5, 1913, on the *Rochambeau* for a year's stay in Europe. There he did not follow a course of intensive study so much as a course of extensive travel; he allowed himself a true *Wanderjahr*, rushing over the Continent during the first summer, settling in England and France for most of the autumn and winter, and resuming in the late spring the travels that ended, on the eve of war, with a midnight escape from Berlin to Sweden.

"Impressions of Europe, 1913–1914," the report he reluctantly wrote to satisfy the terms of his grant, is the summary account of this year, the year in Bourne's life, however, for which his correspondence, diary, and articles provide the fullest record. In contrast with the amplitude and immediacy of these materials, the "Impressions" seem thin and belated. Bourne had by this time told his story too often, and he now chose to tell it differently (for which it is valuable), from the perspective of war and in the light of "the toddlings of an innocent child about the edge of a volcano's crater." "Impressions," in any case, was the right word because he was honest enough to claim no more for his researches and, in a genuine sense, had been another Irvingesque saunterer. He called his travel articles to the *Bloomfield Citizen* "Impressions of a European Tour" and told a friend that he liked "to go sauntering about the streets, looking at all sorts of charming and obscure scenes." He enjoyed the picturesque, as on his journey from Paris to Italy, appreciated the formal achievements of European culture, and knew how to extract the flavors of experience. But he also knew how to grasp a city as a living form by searching out the close textures of its actual social life. He knew that culture was not only the artifacts to which Baedekers were guides, but a process, a present way of life, with which he must make contact. His vision was seldom indolent and, whether sauntering or rushing about, he saw sharply with the eye of a social psychologist.

For Bourne this year abroad was especially formative. He considered it a good test of the experimental life and admitted that at times he was not up to its demands. He missed most his close little world of friends, and to some extent the degree of his success in finding similar groups colored his judgments of England and France. His need and tenacity — and his range of response — are evident in his voluminous correspondence. To Arthur Macmahon and Carl Zigrosser, former roommates at Columbia, he wrote, respectively, of political events and art; to Henry Elsasser, reputedly the most brilliant of his Columbia friends, he sent his profounder speculations; and to Alyse Gregory, whom he had met shortly before his departure, he wrote about socialism and suffragettism — and about himself, for during this period of his life, she was the woman in whom he had chosen to confide.

One of the books that he read with appreciation at the beginning of his travels and soon felt confirmed his European experience was Henry James's *The American*. For Europe immediately forced him to measure his personal resources and those of America, and offered the occasion of a slight, which, one suspects, was more damaging to Bourne than he let on because he never "literized" it as he usually did his experiences. He had been rudely turned out of the country house of S. M. Bligh, a Welsh psychologist to whom he particularly looked for sponsorship in intellectual circles. The smart set he met there did not, it seems, delight in his kind of irony. "My prophetic strain would come out," Bourne wrote Elsasser, "and my Socialism appeared as wild and hair-raising, if not actually mad, in that society of tough British and class-prejudice." His values were turned upside down: "Ideals of militarism, imperialism, moneymaking, conservation of old English snobberies and prejudices, all swept before me in an indescribably voluble and brilliant flood, and I was left, as you may surmise, stranded like a very young Hosea or Amos at the court of some wicked worldly king." To another correspondent he confessed that he had had "a hell of a time emotionally" — he had indeed been shocked and wounded, and nothing he later experienced in England mollified him. He made his way eventually, meeting the Webbs and Wells, listening to Shaw and Chesterton, studying garden cities, visiting at Oxford, attending the meetings of suffragettes at Knightsbridge. But England made him feel "just about ready to renounce the whole of Anglo-Saxon civilization." The only live thing, he told Carl Zigrosser, had been the suffrage movement. Otherwise, he found "the whole country . . . old and weary, as if the demands of the twentieth century were proving entirely too much for its powers, and it was waiting half-cynically and apathetically for some great cataclysm." By contrast, he exclaimed in a letter to Alyse Gregory, "How my crude, naive, genial America glows!"

Although Bourne had reason to feed his grudge on England, his attitude was characteristic of the younger generation, which discovered in England and France the cultural representatives of the battle it was waging at home. What better example of the Victorianism it had rejected in the Genteel Tradition than old Anglo-Saxondom itself, with its "fatuous cheerfulness" and "incorrigible intellectual frivolity" and "permanent derangement of intellect from emotion"? What better example than France of its youthful modernism — of its delight in quick intelligence, its ardent fraternal sentiment, its responsiveness to social issues and capacity for social change, its pleasure in the taste and color and movement of life? When Bourne turned from London to Paris in December, he entered, he said, "a new world, where the values and issues of life got reinstated for me into something of their proper relative emphasis." To this world the reading of Rousseau's *Confessions* had been his introduction, for it had, he wrote Alyse Gregory, "cleared up for me a whole new democratic morality, and put the last touch upon the old English way of looking at the world, in which I was brought up." It had opened to him the culture of France, which, within less than a month, he felt had completed the "transvaluation of values begun ten years ago when my Calvinism began to crack."

Kept from much about him by his poor command of French, Bourne, nevertheless, established a more satisfactory life in Paris than he had in London. He settled near the Sorbonne, whose greatness he contrasted to "poor little Oxford." The intellectual orientation was agreeably sociological and psychological, and he read sociology in the Bibliothèque Ste. Geneviève and attended the lectures of Bouglé, Delacroix, and Durkheim. He associated with students who were as representative of Young France as he was of Young America (at this time, Youth was an international movement) and he was invited to speak to them about their ideals, the philosophy of William James, and the poetry of Whitman, who had influenced Jules Romains, the author of *La vie unanime*. Although he had complained at first of the lack of feminine society and in desperation took tea with a silly married American woman — his description of her in a letter to Alyse Gregory is choice — he eventually found a French girl with whom he enjoyed an "intellectual flirtation," the girl of "Mon Ami," his most radiant portrait of youth. The campaign for parliamentary election aroused his political sympathies where the weary Liberal politics of London had not, and, if what and how much he wrote is any measure, the culture of France stimulated him more profoundly than that of any other country.

After France, he did not settle long anywhere because the pace of his travels increased and European life itself was unsettled. In Italy the political activity was as coruscating as the light, as clamorous as the marketplace. Bourne attended most to the mind of Young Italy through which, it seemed to him, "Nietzsche was raging": to the students demonstrating for Italia Irredenta, to the futurists in art, to the signs of modernism that, he believed, promised for Italy a "new renaissance of the twentieth century." He witnessed in Rome the violent three-day general strike of June — his taste of revolution — and was pleased with the solidarity of the radical classes; and he observed election night in Venice, which, he noted in his report, perhaps with mischievous intent, confirmed "the economic interpretation of politics." Working northward, he returned for the Bern Exposition to Switzerland, his land of delight, "a country . . . that knew how to use its resources for large social ends!" And then he went to Germany, where he studied enthusiastically its planned towns and housing schemes, its new architecture and decorative arts — the evidence of an efficient municipal science that was curiously "undemocratic in political form, yet ultrademocratic in policy and spirit" — but was troubled by the people, by their "thickness and sentimentality and . . . lack of critical sense." There his travel plans were altered and much that he hoped for came to an end. On July 31, he arrived in Berlin, where he experienced the hysteria and outbreak of the war under whose shadow he was to live for the remainder of his life.

The most important result of Bourne's travels was a clearer awareness of the nature and diversity of culture. This was the very thing he emphasized in his report as a corrective to the American tendency (especially dangerous in time of war) to consider the picturesque aspects rather than the fundamental emotional and intellectual differences of foreign countries. "My most striking impression," he said, "was [of] the extraordinary toughness and homogeneity of the cultural fabric in the different countries. . . . Each country was a distinct unit, the parts of which . . . interpreted each other, styles and attitudes, literature, architecture, and social organization."

The three essays that he published in the *Atlantic Monthly* during the summer and fall of his homecoming probe this theme. "An Hour in Chartres" is an essay on cultural style — on "the way things hang together, so that they seem the very emanation of a sort of vast over-spreading communal taste." "Maurice Barrès and the Youth of France" considers the cultural foundations of nationalism and the role of youth in its preservation and advancement. In this essay, Bourne expresses admiration for what Brooks, in *Letters and Leadership*, would call "the collective spiritual life." He knows the evils of nationalism, yet seeks the "intimate cultural fabric" so lacking in America; and he offers a conception of nationalism, emotionally powerful but still somewhat vague, that enhances the quality of life by satisfying social and mystical needs. Although he understands the origins in French military defeat of Barrès's idea and recognizes its essential traditionalism, he finds it overwhelmingly attractive: ". . . the nourishing influences of a rich common culture in which our individualities are steeped, and which each generation carries on freely, consciously, gladly the traits of the race's genius, — this is a gospel to which one could give one's self with wistfulness and love!" Here, for Bourne — and youth — national culture has become an object of loyalty.

Finally, in "Our Cultural Humility," he applies the idea to America, where the very appreciation of European culture (Arnold's "the best") keeps us from engaging in the vital process of our own culture and from producing indigenous art. He asks us, therefore, to foster a national culture of our own: "This cultural chauvinism is the most harmless of patriotisms; indeed it is absolutely necessary for a true life of civilization." We have already, as he himself had been learning, an indigenous tradition of great artists; he mentions here and in letters Emerson, Thoreau, Whitman, William James, Henry James, Edward MacDowell, and Augustus Saint-Gaudens. (Brooks, whose *America's Coming-of-Age* would be more influential in forming this generation's sense of the past, mentions favorably only Whitman.) Now all we need do, he advises, is "turn our eyes upon our own art for a time, shut ourselves in with our own genius, and cultivate with an intense and partial pride what we have already achieved."

The substance of this culture is conveyed best in another essay of this time, "A Sociological Poet," where Bourne speaks of Unanimism as Whitman "industrialized" and "sociologized." He advocates the larger collective life of "democratic camaraderie," the replacement of the old individualistic life by a new "mass-life" to be lived in the city; and he carefully distinguishes the emergent group feeling he desires from the herd instinct, which fear rather than the warm social conscience feeds. Bourne considers the metropolis to be the "human" milieu and maintains that "the highest reality of the world is not Nature or the Ego, but the Beloved Community"; and he believes, as he wrote later in "American Use for German Ideals," that the pragmatism of James and Dewey and the social philosophy of Josiah Royce strengthen the possibility of such a democratic socialized life.

Bourne derived the functions of this culture from his experience in France and its form from his study of the civic art of Germany. Whenever he defends German ideals or culture, as in the essay cited above and in "A Glance at German 'Kultur,'" he has in mind the civic art that he once told Carl Zigrosser was "the king of the arts, because of its completely social nature." He placed Hampstead Garden Suburb above any planned town in Germany, but he placed Germany above all other nations, "in the very vanguard of socialized civilization." In this respect, Germany epitomized the twentieth century, which explained, Bourne thought, American hostility toward her: she challenged our attitudes and social habits, and, in repudiating her organization and collectivism, we were repudiating the "modest collectivism" of our own progressive movement. Wherever he went in America — to the Midwest, for example, whose urban chaos he described in "Our Unplanned Cities" — he appreciated anew the achievement of Germany: "I love with a passionate love the ideals of social welfare, community sense, civic art, and applied science upon which it is founding itself. . . . I detest . . . the shabby and sordid aspect of American civilization — its frowsy towns, its unkempt countryside, its waste of life and resources. . . ."

Fed by subsequent experience and urged by the intense pressures of wartime, the lessons of the European year took form in Bourne's most important essay on American culture. "Trans-National America" (1916), which the admirably tolerant Sedgwick accepted for the *Atlantic*, was at once Bourne's most incisive analysis of the failure of the older generation and his clearest, most challenging directive to the younger generation. It presents his vision of the kind of culture to which America should aspire and the redeeming role such a culture would enable America to play in the debacle of European nationalisms; and when set up as an alternative to participation in the war ("the war — or American promise" of Bourne's "A War Diary"), this vision of culture provided the test of pragmatic sociology. Bourne's vision anticipated the program of *The Seven Arts*, the magazine that Robert Frost said died "a-Bourning," and first disclosed the landscape described in books such as Waldo Frank's *Our America*.

This deeply personal vision has collective sources. In *The Promise of American Life*, Herbert Croly had spoken of "an over-national idea" and had cited Crèvecoeur's account of the melting process that made the American a new man. To this notion of Americanization, Israel Zangwill's play *The Melting-Pot* had given currency and approval; but Horace Kallen, whom Bourne knew, had repudiated it and proposed instead a "federation of nationalities," or "cultural pluralism," as he subsequently called it. During these years, cosmopolitanism, associated with the city and its immigrant populations, was a cultural stance toward America as well as Europe. H. W. L. Dana, a teacher at Columbia whose dismissal during the war Bourne protested, wrote him, in 1914, that Columbia was "more than national," more than "Anglo-Saxon"; and writing from Europe to Edward Murray (a friend described in "Fergus") Bourne had observed that "the good things in the American temperament and institutions are not English . . . but are the fruit of our far superior cosmopolitanism." As a child, he had been offended by the unattractive Polish girls who worked in the kitchens of Bloomfield; but now he appreciated immigrant life, the Italian settlement, for example, at Emerald Lake (similar to the Guinea Hill district of William Carlos Williams's nearby city) which, he said, injected "sudden vitality into our Puritan town."

"Trans-National America" faced directly the problem of immigration and the making of Americans that had become a conspicuously serious issue of our culture when the show of loyalties provoked by the war revealed our cultural diversity. Sedgwick disapproved of the essay — he called it "radical and unpatriotic" when informing Bourne of the many commendations it received — and insisted that America was "a country created by English instinct and dedicated to the Anglo-Saxon ideal." One recalls another editor of the *Atlantic*, another "hereditary American" (the phrase is Van Wyck Brooks's) who warned us to guard the gates; and Brooks put their fears very well when, in *America's Coming-of-Age*, he retold the story of Rip Van Winkle, the story of an innocent old America that hears in its sleep, not Henry Hudson's men, but "the movement of peoples ["Jews, Lithuanians, Magyars and German socialists"], the thunder of alien wants." Bourne, speaking, he said, as an Anglo-Saxon, threatened the Anglo-Saxon hegemony by announcing that "America shall be what the immigrant will have a hand in making it, and not what a ruling class . . . decides that America shall be made," by questioning the efficacy of Americanization and redefining the meaning of Americanism.

Bourne's most damaging charge is twofold: that the Anglo-Saxon has not transformed the "colony into a real nation, with a tenacious, richly woven fabric of native culture" and that its theory of Americanization is destructive of this very possibility. For Americanization has not produced socialized men but insipid mass-men, "half-breeds," he says, who have been deprived of their native cultures and given instead "the American culture of the cheap newspaper, the 'movies,' the popular song, the ubiquitous automobile." In this way, Americanization contributes to the wreckage rather than creation of culture:

"Just so surely as we tend to disintegrate these nuclei [various immigrant cultures] of nationalistic culture do we tend to create hordes of men and women without a spiritual country, cultural outlaws, without taste, without standards but those of the mob. We sentence them to live on the most rudimentary planes of American life. The influences at the center of the nuclei are centripetal. They make for the intelligence and the social values which mean an enhancement of life. And just because the foreign-born retains this expressiveness is he likely to be a better citizen of the American community. The influences at the fringe, however, are centrifugal, anarchical. They make for detached fragments of peoples. Those who came to find liberty achieve only license. They become the flotsam and jetsam of American life, the downward undertow of our civilization with its leering cheapness and falseness of taste and spiritual outlook, the absence of mind and sincere feeling which we see in our slovenly towns . . . and in the vacuous faces of the crowds on the city street. This is the cultural wreckage of our time. . . . America has as yet no impelling integrating force. It makes too easily for this detritus of cultures."

This eloquent passage arises from the deepest tensions of Bourne's social imagination: "I must be interpreting everything," he once said, "in relation to some Utopian ideal, or some vision of perfection." It suggests some of the values he hoped to restore by means of "an enterprise of integration." The new peoples were "threads of living and potent cultures, blindly striving to weave themselves into a novel international nation." Having at their disposal the very agencies that had transformed Bourne and enabled his vision, they might, with its help and practical civic measures of the kind he outlined in "A Moral Equivalent for Military Service," someday achieve it.

"Trans-National America" was not published in the *New Republic* because its editors, as Sedgwick recognized, never gave Bourne space enough to work out his ideas and because, from the start, as Bourne complained, they never gave him any say in policy. When he returned from Europe, the *New Republic* was being organized and staffed; it was the forum he had been seeking, and it gave him a place at $1000 a year. These wages, he felt, were minimal; he was, so he told Alyse Gregory, "a very insignificant retainer." Though he attended the weekly luncheons of the editors, he found his relations with them uncomfortable and remained outside their circle. Sedgwick had warned him of the dangers of magazines — that most are not "loyal to ideas" and are "treacherous to taste" and that radical ones often "set their sails to other breezes." Of Croly and crew, he said: ". . . they are the solemnest procession that ever marched. . . . They can celebrate a Puritan Thanksgiving, but whether they will make the Fourth of July hum, remains to be seen." When Bourne expressed disappointment at Croly's reluctance to "go in instanter for smashing and quarreling," Sedgwick counseled him to give the magazine time to develop a soul. He did, maintaining a connection with the *New Republic* until his death, but he was dismayed.

On coming home, he had tried to reestablish his Columbia life. For a time he lived with Carl Zigrosser at the Phipps model tenements on East 31st Street and socialized — and fell in love — with Barnard girls. But eventually his center shifted. The *New Republic* set the boundaries of his intellectual world: the Public Library, the Russell Sage Foundation, and Greenwich Village. And there he began to meet other people, Elizabeth Shepley Sergeant, for example, who introduced him, in the summer of 1915, to the elite New England summer colony at Dublin, New Hampshire. ("Housekeeping for Men," a light essay, describes the cabin life that was sustained by dinners and evenings with worthies like Amy Lowell and the Abbott Thayers, the latter of special importance to Bourne because through them he met Scofield Thayer who tried to promote his interests on the *Dial*.) He also met Elsie Clews Parsons, a vigorous, intelligent anthropologist and sociologist, who offered him a haven at Lenox, Massachusetts. His typically full social life is recorded in a datebook for 1916, where one now finds the names of Agnes de Lima, a social worker, and Esther Cornell, an actress, the one the guardian spirit of his life and legacy, the other, her friend, the beautiful girl who would have married him and with whom, at last, he entered a mature emotional life. With them, and Frances Anderson, he shared a house at Caldwell, New Jersey, the summer of 1916. Agnes de Lima recalls that "it was a delicious setting for R., the center of attention with three devoted and high spirited girl companions paying him obeisance"; and she conveys the quality of devotion that still enshrines Bourne's reputation when she writes that "we all adored him of course, fascinated, stimulated, enormously fired by his brilliant intellect, his thrilling range of interests, his unique flair for personal relationships." (One is grateful for Edward Dahlberg's not so foolish surmise that Bourne was "a sensual gypsy Leporello with [to?] women." All remember his piano-playing — music, he once approvingly noted in a book review, was an emotional equivalent for otherwise unexperienced raptures.) Of male friendships he said very little, but one sees, in his relationships with Paul Rosenfeld and Van Wyck Brooks, that they were strong and good, founded on the conviction of a common intellectual enterprise.

For the *New Republic* Bourne wrote almost one hundred pieces, nearly half of them reviews, the remainder articles, portraits, and editorials. Occasionally he was permitted to write about war issues, but he had been recruited to write about other matters, and most of his work was confined to education and a small but significant amount to city planning. Many of his essays on education were reprinted in *The Gary Schools* (1916), a study of the work-study-and-play schools that William Wirt, a disciple of Dewey, had organized in the new steel town and was proposing for New York City, and in *Education and Living* (1917), a general collection held together by Bourne's insistence that the long process of education be a living now, not a postponement of life. These books contributed to Bourne's reputation as (to cite one reviewer) "the most brilliant educational critic of the younger generation," but neither has the solidity of achievement that makes reputations permanent. In the first, he was encumbered by the publisher's demands that he write for teachers and superintendents and subdue his enthusiasm for Wirt; in the second, repetition drains away the force some of the essays have singly. These books, however, represent the mastery of a field. They develop the primary themes of *Youth and Life* and bridge Bourne's personal and social concern for human fulfillment. And in them one begins to appreciate the extent to which Bourne has become a publicist of the kind he admired in J. A. Hobson — a man with "immense stores of knowledge, poise of mind, and yet radical philosophy and gifts of journalistic expression."

In retrospect, Agnes de Lima depreciated these books, remarking, however, that Bourne was finely perceptive about the needs of children, a truth confirmed by "Ernest: or Parent for a Day," a charming *Atlantic* essay that readers may find sufficiently representative of this strand of his thought. Yet there is value (and pleasure) in reading more: the realization of the alliance of educational with modern thought, of the place of education in democratic society as an essential and democratic process, as a revivifier of its faith and instrument of its reform. *Democracy and Education* — such was the title of Dewey's challenging book of 1916, when education had become an urgent domestic issue and no other social enterprise seemed to partisans like Bourne so hopeful, rational, and democratic. "To decide what kind of a school we want," he said, "is almost to decide what kind of society we want" — a disclosure of faith that may explain the presence among his unpublished papers of an essay (of 1918) extolling the efforts of the British to prepare for social reconstruction by initiating educational reforms during the war.

Much of Bourne's work before and after America entered the war was educational, either about education or in the interest of overcoming what, in 1915, he called our "mental unpreparedness." War had been the means, he explained, of shocking even his up-to-date generation into an awareness of a world where war happens, and it had given the intellectuals the task of replacing the "old immutable idealism," no longer credible, with a "new experimental idealism." "We should make the time," he told them, "one of education." Instead of military preparedness, our need, he said, was "to learn how to live rather than die; to be teachers and creators, not engines of destruction." Before war was declared, he had worked for peace, the essential condition of democratic reform; for the American Association of International Conciliation he edited a symposium of peace proposals and programs, *Towards an Enduring Peace* (1916). And he had been a leader of the Committee for Democratic Control, which tried to halt the descent to war by publishing in the newspapers (and the *New Republic*!) antiwar advertisements and appeals for popular referendums. With war declared — "the effective and decisive work" that the editors of the *New Republic* claimed had been accomplished "by a class which must be . . . described as the 'intellectuals' " — Bourne took on the role for which he is most often remembered: he became the critic of the war strategy and, especially, of the intellectuals who had broken faith with pragmatism and had closed out the promise of American life by eagerly joining "the greased slide toward war."

It is fashionable now to admire Bourne's unyielding spirit and intellectual rectitude but to pity him for assuming that the drift of things is susceptible to human mastery. When depressed by the penalties of lonely opposition, he also indulged himself in deterministic views (see "Old Tyrannies"). Yet however much in a metaphysical sense drift may be a true account of things, it is not a true account of the diplomacy that led to war. Here events seemed to have their own way but were actually chosen and, as Bourne maintained (see especially his comments on the presidency in "The State"), other choices might have prevailed. The question seldom raised by those who, curiously, speak up for intellectuals but impugn their force is the one with which Bourne in effect challenged the boastful intellectuals of the *New Republic*: had the intellectuals taken Bourne's position, would the outcome have been otherwise? By assuming that it would, one grants Bourne the condition of justly understanding him.

The wayward course of the war strategy and the policy of the *New Republic*, which Bourne cogently analyzed in five essays published in 1917 in *The Seven Arts* (collected in *Untimely Papers*, 1919), is now of less interest than his assessment of pragmatism and inquiry into the motives and roles of intellectuals. War taught Bourne that pragmatism was not so much a philosophy for fair weather as one requiring for its survival an open world of alternatives. Where choice is impossible, pragmatism ceases to exist, for intelligence ceases to have a function; in "total" or "absolute" situations like war, it is without leverage. This was the point Bourne directed specifically to John Dewey, whom he had once petitioned in an essay of praise to become an intellectual leader in "the arena of the concrete," and who, since 1916, had done so by becoming the philosopher-statesman of the *New Republic* and *The Seven Arts* (until July 1917, when Bourne and Brooks replaced him) and of the *Dial*.

To read Dewey's essays is an uncomfortable experience, wholly justifying Bourne's judgment that the philosophy of Dewey "breaks down . . . when it is used to grind out interpretation for the present crisis." Dewey speciously justified the use of force and was concerned more with winning intellectual assent to participation than clarifying the values for American national life that he claimed would come of it. Once committed to war, he wished only to get the job done in a "business like way." He insisted that "an end is something which concerns results rather than aspirations," and considered pacifists, including Bourne, "passivists," victims of "moral innocency" and "futility." Yet aspirations were the issue. For Dewey, father of a noble conception of America and leader of the educational work to be done, had himself chosen war, had turned from his own best vision and had become, as Bourne, feeling betrayed, said, a fatuous instrumentalist who believed naively that he was controlling the "line of inevitables" war brings. "It may be pragmatism to be satisfied with things that work," Bourne wrote in an unpublished essay, "but it is a very shallow one." Pragmatism was always for him a philosophy in which ends count, and he remained true to it by demanding alternative courses of action and by keeping in view the "American promise" — and nowhere so demonstrably as in these *timely* papers, where, in the exercise of intellectual responsibility, he mastered his materials, argument, and tone in writing of unusual incandescence.

As Dwight Macdonald recognized (in *Politics*, his personal attempt to propose courses during another war), Bourne had "continued along the way [the pragmatists] had all been following until the war began." They, however, took the path Bourne describes in "The War and the Intellectuals." Feeling that to be out of the war was "at first to be disreputable and finally almost obscene," they assumed "the leadership for war of those very classes whom the American democracy has been immemorially fighting." Joyfully they accepted this leadership and willingly abandoned criticism for propaganda, "the sewage of the war spirit." Neutrality had put the intellectuals under the strain of thinking; it was easier to act; and action brought relief from indecision. So the thinkers, with their "colonial" (Anglo-Saxon) sympathies and their eagerness to be responsible for the world, with their "emotional capital" idle for want of domestic spending but ready for investment in Europe, "dance[d] with reality." And this reversion to "primitive" ways, though understandable, was not only costly beyond measure ("the whole era has been spiritually wasted") and supremely ironic (for how can war and democracy be coupled?) but especially shameful because it led the intellectuals to repudiate everything that becomes the intellectual and to impugn the work of the few who were peace-minded. Included in their company, moreover, were those younger intellectuals of a different kind whom the elder pragmatists had trained: those "experts in the new science of administration" hailed by Lippmann in *Drift and Mastery*, whom Bourne now found "vague as to what kind of society they want, or what kind of society America needs, but . . . equipped with all the administrative attitudes and talents necessary to attain it."

Bourne himself accepted the role of the "excommunicated," of an "irreconcilable." He tried to make his apathy toward the war "take the form of a heightened energy and enthusiasm for the education, the art, the interpretation that make for life in the midst of the world of death." But the role, which he defined in such therapeutic essays as "Below the Battle" and "The Artist in Wartime" (unpublished), was a very hard one, requiring, as Croly long before had warned the intellectuals, "sharp weapons, intense personal devotion, and a positive indifference to consequences." In a sense, Bourne was a war casualty, unwounded, he bravely said, by "all the shafts of panic, patriotism, and national honor," yet deeply dispirited. He suffered — more, according to Elsie Clews Parsons, from the renegation of the intellectuals than from personal exclusion — and he was hurt by the bitterness that he predicted would grow and "spread out like a stain over the younger American generation." He frequently expressed the wish to escape to the "great good place" and, as if desperately fighting to attain it, struck out, in the book reviews to which he was limited in his last year, at those who seemed to stand in his way: he quarreled with Dewey over a disciple's book; discredited Sedgwick's judgment by slashing at Paul Shorey's strident defense of the New Humanism; turned on Dean Keppel, who was currently working for the War Department, by gratuitously pointing out that "his mind is liberal and yet it serves reaction"; and needlessly punished Brander Matthews in order to express his misgivings over wartime Columbia.

Yet what is impressive in Bourne's career, finally, is the attempt to master disillusionment and despair by recovering the very history of his generation, by learning the lessons it had to teach and plotting the course it might take. Bourne never shirked the responsibility of thought and began the "anxious speculation" that he told Brooks "should normally follow the destruction of so many hopes." The most ambitious project of this kind was the long unfinished essay, "The State," in which he vented the "scorn for institutions" that had once combined "with a belief in their reform." This essay, overrated by those who consider it an especially prescient political treatise, has the frantic quality of one whom events have forced back on himself — its companion work was the unfinished autobiographical novel. Bourne did not write it because the state, as legend claims, coerced him, but because he needed to understand the social behavior of the time: why, for example, an apathetic nation goes to war and centralization of power contributes not to the creation of social wealth (as Croly had once said it would) but to its spoliation in war. The essay exhibits a sharp analytical power but also a conspiratorial mentality: Bourne makes the Anglo-Saxons the betrayers of democracy throughout American history and explains the failure of reform in his "ephemeral" time by ascribing it to an evil power which he thinks simply awaited the war to make itself known. The cynicism of the essay is protective and, like its bitterness, was accepted too uncritically by the next generation. Bourne appeared to put too high the odds against idealism, ruling out the very agency that he still believed to be necessary and efficacious.

"Bourne was keenly conscious of lost values," Elsie Clews Parsons wrote, "but he was resourceful in compensations." And by way of exemplification, she noted the suspect but important strategy of his essay: "In his essay on the State he had begun to battle for distinctions between State, Nation, and Country, in which the State became the conceptual scapegoat for the sins of patriotism, leaving Nation and Country immaculate and worthy of devotion."

Bourne's goal had not altered, only the way. War taught him what any crisis may teach a reformer: that society is not as plastic as the ideas in our minds, that freedom runs into limitation, that wholesale social reconstruction must submit to the slower processes of education. It did not destroy his faith in political action, although it made him distrustful of the "cult of politics" and increased his appreciation of the social uses of personal expression — of the resources "malcontents" might find in art and criticism. His own essays in criticism such as "The Art of Theodore Dreiser" and "The Immanence of Dostoevsky" reveal a maturing critical sense and represent the kind of criticism he defined in "Traps for the Unwary" and in the closing pages of "The History of a Literary Radical." As he had pointed out earlier in a review of H. L. Mencken, Puritanism was no longer a significant cultural issue; criticism had work to do more important than moralizing. For the real enemy of art was the widening, responsive, but still genteel public that wanted "the new without the unsettling."

A "new criticism," accordingly, was needed to rectify "the uncritical hospitality of current taste" and to give the artists, who promised, he believed, "a rich and vibrant literary era," an "intelligent, pertinent, absolutely contemporaneous criticism, which shall be both severe and encouraging" — the latter to be obtained only when "the artist himself has turned critic and set to work to discover and interpret in others the motives and values and efforts he feels in himself." This criticism, Bourne explained to Harriet Monroe, editor of *Poetry*, was not aesthetic in the sense of being merely appreciative or of providing "esoteric enjoyment" (what she called "pink-tea adulation"), nor did it treat art wholly in terms of itself or move "hazily in a mist of values and interpretations." He insisted that it also be social criticism — that it take into account "ideas and social movements and the peculiar intellectual and spiritual color of the time." To have conceived of these requisites of criticism and of a "new classicism" demanding "power with restraint, vitality with harmony, a fusion of intellect and feeling, and a keen sense of the artistic conscience" is evidence of Bourne's unfailing sensitivity to the direction of his culture and, although the critic he seeks had need of the strengths of an Eliot, Pound, and Edmund Wilson, evidence of his awareness that the work he set himself should be less prophetic (not like that undertaken by Brooks and Waldo Frank) and nearer to his developing capacities.

In an autobiographical essay, "The History of a Literary Radical," he called himself a literary radical chiefly to distinguish the intellectual type of his generation from that of the older generation. The literary radical possesses an imagination at once aesthetic and sociological. He wishes to nurture his art in society and to use it to reform and enhance social life. His most common difficulty is the adjustment of aesthetic and social allegiances. In his own case, Bourne told Elizabeth Shepley Sergeant, "the reformer got such a terrific start in my youth over the artist that I'm afraid the latter is handicapped for life." But he knew, as he said with respect to his friend John Burroughs, that the "eternally right way and attitude of the intellectual life" is to look at the world with "the eye of the artist" and to employ one's science to "illumine . . . artistic insight"; and this he always tried to do by being radical in another sense: by going back to the root of perception. For all of his science, Bourne remained an essayist who addressed the world in the first person and in his writing attempted to reproduce the atmosphere of discussion that he valued so much, and whose style, as Alvin Johnson noted, possessed "warmth with light [and] logical straightforwardness combined with charm and sympathy." He had, to borrow a phrase from Santayana's applicable discussion of romantics and transcendentalists, "a first-hand mind." Autobiography was the mode he cherished, the staple thread of all his work, his way of being true to himself and his circumstances and of bearing witness, which makes his true inheritors not so much those who took over his topics as those who discovered for themselves the necessity and resources of an autobiographical method. The autobiographical novel upon which Bourne was working at the time of his death is not of interest as a novel but as an example of what, at the beginning of his career, he said was needed: "true autobiographies, told in terms of the adventure that life is."

Bourne began "An Autobiographic Chapter" by telling how, when he was six, his family had moved from a house on a back street to another house offering a life more spacious: "And his expanding life leaped to meet the wide world." This characteristic fronting of the world with "its new excitements and pleasures" was, he wrote, "like a rescue, like getting air when one is smothering." This image was perhaps more premonitory than he knew when, in the last dismal months of his life, he used it to describe the sense of relief he had felt on the occasion of his first rescue; for on December 22, 1918, in his thirty-second year, with the war over and new prospects before him, he succumbed to influenza.

The legends about Bourne that almost immediately arose created the impression of martyrdom that his example of intellectual courage neither sustains nor needs, and hindered a just appreciation of his work. He deserves the prominent place he has acquired in the history of his generation and, because his actual literary achievement was small, a modest place in the literary tradition that in his time he was one of the few to value. At the end of "The History of a Literary Radical," he speaks of "a certain eternal human tradition of abounding vitality and moral freedom" that may be found in such American writers as Thoreau, Whitman, and Mark Twain. This is the tradition he served.

WILLIAM WASSERSTROM

VAN WYCK BROOKS

THE displacement of Van Wyck Brooks from the center to the farthest margins of literary influence today is surely a stunning shift of taste. In 1920 Brooks was regarded as the undisputed heir of the great tradition in American thought — the radical, reformist, prophetic, "organic" tradition which adopted Emerson as its source of inspiration, took "The American Scholar" as its point of departure, and envisioned as its point of terminus a civilization in which the creative spirit, in all its social and imaginative forms, might flourish. To this old enterprise Brooks had brought intransigent zeal and incomparable flair — a genius for clarifying thought, said his comrade-at-arms on *The Seven Arts*, James Oppenheim. Today, Brooks's sovereign role in the transmission of this classic American tradition, his *oeuvre* of inquiry into its bearing on modern letters in America, is either ignored or disdained.

"The most interesting American books," Richard Poirier observes in his presumably definitive study of this tradition, *A World Elsewhere* (1966), "are an image of the creation of America itself, of the effort, in the words of Emerson's Orphic poet, to 'Build therefore your own world.' " For reasons of ignorance or disdain, I guess, Poirier excludes Brooks from his study — even though Brooks had acquired, a half-century ago, an international fame and following as the leading spokesman for Emerson's idea, as a most compelling opponent of those younger writers who decided that American genius could flourish only outside the United States. At first he shared their view. But eventually he came to think that America, by virtue of its history and ideology, not only was itself the very emblem of the creative life but was, too, the best place on earth to locate the republic of letters. And he composed a series of books which monumentalized Emerson's Orphic vision. Suddenly, when his art had achieved certain marvels of transformation, he lost voice, heart, taste, courage for the task. Somehow he lost the thread of his own passion and found himself in an abyss of his own devising. A really major figure in the seedtime of modern thought, he became a minor figure in the time of efflorescence — victim of the very forces he had discerned, named, and condemned. Although he turned out to be a critic of divided mind, a man whose life was broken in half, in one respect his career was all of a piece: from first to last he sought to transform America from an industrial jungle into a place fit for the realization of Emerson's romantic dream.

There was no sign of faltering will in those early books, published between 1908 and 1925, which introduced a prodigy endowed with audacity of learning, fluency of speech, an apparent assurance of mind, and a cosmopolitan experience unmatched in American criticism of that day. Born in Plainfield, New Jersey, in 1886, educated there and in Europe where his family had spent a year in 1898, Brooks had entered Harvard in 1904. Completing work for his degree a year early, in 1907, he had gone on a second European journey, to England, where for eighteen months he had lived as a free-lance journalist and where he had written and published *The Wine of the Puritans* in 1908. He came back to New York that year and remained until 1911 when he went to California. There he married Eleanor Kenyon Stimson, whom he had known as a friend of childhood and youth and whose own life, both before and after Wellesley, had been spent going back and forth from Europe: "we were both in love with Europe and always had been."

Returning to England in 1913 with his new family — a son had been born in 1912 — Brooks published the work written during his California years, *The Malady of the Ideal.* This and *The Wine of the Puritans* make a pair quite as the next pair, *John Addington Symonds: A Biographical Study* (1914) and *The World of H. G. Wells* (1914), were conceived and composed in concert. The four, taken together, provide initial statements of those ideas, passionately held, which were to shape Brooks's critique of and program for America in the celebrated essays, *America's Coming-of-Age* (1915) and *Letters and Leadership* (1918), and the psychological studies, *The Ordeal of Mark Twain* (1920) and *The Pilgrimage of Henry James* (1925). In these eight interconnected pieces of work, representing nearly two decades of resolute and concentrated labor, Brooks focused his whole energy on a single theme. He sought to penetrate the conditions which devastate and to disclose the environments which nurture the springs of art in Europe and the United States.

I speak of these intricate things as if there is no problem in reducing a thousand pages of intense prose — and hundreds of pages of criticism of Brooks's prose — to a simple formula. But the very resourcefulness of Brooks's mind and the opulence of comment on Brooks's books have obscured certain obvious matters about which it is, at this late stage of judgment, no great task to be forthright. Indeed, a certain likeness from book to book has always been fairly plain. Stanley Edgar Hyman, for example, describing Brooks's distinction between the actual "wine" of the Puritans and the "aroma" of wine, recognized in this play of metaphor an embryonic version of those distinctions between highbrow and lowbrow on which Brooks was to build the myth of America's coming of age. If you read backwards from lowbrow you discover Brooks maintaining that it was the Puritans' taste for the material life of the New World which led in later centuries to a sheer and bald commercialism: "wine." Read backwards from highbrow and you find Brooks arguing that it was the Puritans' simultaneous joy in the "aroma of the wine, the emphasis on the ideal, which became transcendentalism." The essential questions raised in *The Wine of the Puritans*, then, introduced a perplexity which was ever to vex Brooks, a man who retained all his life the habit of formulating modern questions in an archaic language. If art is defined as the Soul's perception of the Ideal, how can art enrich a society which was itself created out of a breach between Soul and Body, between Ideal and Real? Could America be made into a place where the life of thought and the life of action might be reconciled?

These were the lofty problems, invariably cast into pairs of metaphor, which led Brooks in *The Malady of the Ideal* to contrast the temper of German thought with the French. The French temperament, fixed firmly in the real world and engaged by the problems of social order, he called *rhetorical.* In contrast, the German mind, concerned with "truth, good, and beauty," the realm of the Ideal, was *poetical* in its drift. The true poet, rooted in the Real, fixed his attention unwaveringly on the Ideal and became therefore a great source of reconciliation, a visionary of order on earth. A rhetorician, however, was committed to the study of exterior consistency alone. "He takes his point of departure from an idea which in its primitive form is a sincere expression of himself. The next day looking deeper he perhaps discovers a new idea that cuts away the ground from under his former idea. But he is a practical man — he . . . therefore forces a consistency between the two ideas." As the circle of his thought arcs farther and farther away from that first, genuine perception, finally "he achieves a logical consistency; his work has a compact, finished quality. But where is truth?" Illustrating the practical effects of his theory, Brooks referred to Senancour and Maurice de Guérin, and arrived at last at Amiel, "true child of Geneva," in whom French and German influence came to a standoff, a sterile, immobilizing "fatal mixture of the blood." Neither German enough, "foolhardy" enough, to trust in intuition, nor French enough, rhetorical enough, to rely on disciplined rationalism, Amiel sat "like a spider in a kind of cosmic web spun from his own body, unable to find himself because he could not lose himself."

Before long, as we shall see, Brooks himself was to arrive at the condition in which *The Malady of the Ideal* leaves Amiel. Ironically, too, his next books, on Symonds and Wells, mark the emergence of Brooks the rhetorician, the practical critic whose work was compact and self-contained and consistent but — said his critics — Where was truth?

A disappointing book to read in 1914, the study of Symonds is an especially rewarding book to read now. For Brooks was only superficially preoccupied with his ostensible subject and was deeply engaged inquiring into his essential subject — himself. In its tiniest detail and in the sweep of its theme, the biography of Symonds is a clairvoyant essay in self-appraisal and self-revelation. Taking up the subject of his *Malady*, applying its theoretical system to English letters, Brooks presents Symonds as a victim of neuroticism so acute as to render him blind to the distinctions between "mundane and visionary values," between Real and Ideal. Symonds to his credit possessed a visionary mind; to his discredit, so Brooks believed, he was incapable of bearing the cost of vision and he turned instead to rhetoric, to the study of the humdrum. In order to support this reading, Brooks adopted a strategy which led him away from the ordinary pursuits of literary criticism and plunged him into the first of his exercises in the psychology of failure, the sociology of despair. Whatever else must be said, it cannot be gainsaid that this was pioneer work of a most taxing kind. And what has hitherto been left unsaid about Brooks is that his pioneering studies in literary psychology were informed by his reading in a single source, Bernard Hart's *The Psychology of Insanity*. This famous handbook was first published in England in 1912, shortly before Brooks's third European and second English sojourn in 1913. As he later told Robert Spiller — who repeated the anecdote to me — Hart's little book represented all that he knew of psychoanalysis. Whether or not he read Freud or Jung too, whom he mentions in print now and then, is uncertain. But there is no mention of Hart's work in Brooks's writing — a strange omission in the light of his remark to Spiller.

The Psychology of Insanity is a historic work. It is the first essay, both technical and lucid, which incorporates Freud's views on the general subject. This book, Hart wrote, "does not really occupy any definite place in the direct line of Freudian history, but is at once narrower and wider in its aim." It is narrower in that it deals with certain selected aspects of Freud's thought (Hart adopted the unconscious and the concept of repression but rejected Freud's views on sex) and it is wider "in that it attempts to bring those aspects into relation with lines of advance followed by other investigators." In its own right a remarkably sage and balanced essay, it is typical of its period, too, in its tone of wonder and certainty — wonder that some classic riddles of the psyche had been solved at last, certainty that some tentative propositions would turn out dogmatic truth.

In Hart's habit of discovering simple trauma behind complicated events, Brooks found sanction to support his own custom of searching out a "causal complex" which would simply explain everything. As applied to Symonds, this habit led Brooks to ascribe neurotic failure to a state of war between reason and action, passion and thought. Symonds's thought could not satisfy appetites generated by Symonds's passions; nor could Symonds, for reasons of health and "conscience," translate thought into action: "it was this complex [which] remained with him to the last" and ended ultimately in breakdown. Upon recovery, he discovered Whitman and through Whitman acquired "a lusty contempt for purely intellectual processes." Symonds struck a bad bargain with his instincts, Brooks said, and in consequence was transformed into a "congested poet" and *vulgariseur*, a maker of scholarly books which struggled to do what "only poetry can do" and are therefore best described as "high fantasy" not high accomplishment in humane letters.

Reading this comment on Symonds, anyone with even the skimpiest knowledge of Brooks's career must recognize in the pattern Brooks ascribes to Symonds's life the very pattern which best describes Brooks's life — including the rediscovery of Whitman. If I seem to be forcing a consistency where there is resemblance alone, Brooks's peroration dispels all doubt. The portrait of Symonds, chronology altered but otherwise changed only to include metaphoric rather than literal detail, could stand as a self-portrait: "Neurotic from birth, suppressed and misdirected in education, turned by early environment and by natural affinity into certain intellectual and spiritual channels, pressed into speculation by dogmatic surroundings and aesthetic study, his naturally febrile constitution shattered by over-stimulation, by wanting vitality denied robust creation, by disease made a wanderer, by disease and wandering together aroused to an unending, fretful activity — the inner history of Symonds could be detailed and charted scientifically."

After completing this book and publishing it in 1913–14, along with *The Malady of the Ideal* and *The World of H. G. Wells*, Brooks left England once again for New York. This time, however, the decision to return signified at last an end to wandering, an end to the disease of indecision which had plagued him since his departure from Harvard. Brooks's wanderings during this period of his life are not just of documentary interest. Nor do these represent mere sprightliness of curiosity on the part of a provincial bright young man. It is a rather more radical thing. For it was during these half-dozen years of inquiry into and contrast of certain American and European styles of life that Brooks cast about for reasons why he should remain at home or return abroad to live in determined rather than tentative exile. In these early works he sought to resolve a disquietude more pressing than troubled Amiel or Symonds. It is useful, therefore, to present a detailed chart of the inner history of Brooks's mind at the moment when he achieved his greatest fame and widest influence.

A "wanderer, the child of some nation yet unborn, smitten with an inappeasable nostalgia for the Beloved Community on the far side of socialism, he carried with him the intoxicating air of that community, the mysterious aroma of its works and ways." These are Brooks's words, written in eulogy to his beloved friend Randolph Bourne. But again biography and autobiography fuse: the sketch of Bourne is also a work of self-portraiture which intimates the state of Brooks's mind in the period beginning in 1914. Completing the book on Wells, whom he called a man of "planetary imagination," an "artist of society," Brooks convinced himself that America was ripe for rebirth on the far side of socialism. Smitten with an inappeasable nostalgia for utopia, he convinced himself, too, that a socialist America would be the place in which the life of the mind (the realm of the Ideal) and the life of action (the Real) might be brought to equilibrium. America, he said, was H. G. Wells "writ large."

Brooks at mid-decade was by no means a man of composed mind but was instead a man of divided will: the chief obsession of his divided mind was Europe. This obsession he shared, strangely, with the man he most despised, T. S. Eliot. To say that Brooks despised Eliot is no exaggeration. Although his published comment is restrained, his private comment, particularly in the later days of fascism, exhibits a barely controlled revulsion. The "Elioteers" are almost as bad as the Germans, he blurted in a letter (November 1941) to Bliss Perry. Brooks was peculiarly fierce not just because he despised Eliot's ideas but because, deep down, he shared Eliot's taste for the well-upholstered life of a European man of letters.

In Brooks's instance and Eliot's, in Pound's and Conrad Aiken's, John Gould Fletcher's and H. D.'s — that first wave of expatriate

American writers — the dream of literature was inextricable from the dream of Europe. In the world Brooks knew as a child, that well-heeled and well-placed society of the eastern seaboard, Henry Adams's world, "a voyage to Europe was the panacea for every known illness and discontent." Unlike his compatriots who had few second thoughts about cloaking themselves in the "iridescent fabric" of Europe, Brooks was deeply torn. The causes of conflict lay in the special circumstances of his early life, that family life which was at once in harmony and in conflict with the Harvard cult of Europe, incarnate in Santayana. Why am I abroad, he had forced himself to think in 1908, when I believe in living at home? Part of the answer was by no means complicated — though it did involve some complications within his family. He was determined to escape Plainfield, New Jersey, and to avoid the "sadness and wreckage" which diminished the lives of his father and brother. In that town where Brooks's neighbors were the "quiet solid men of money," he had never been at home. Nor had his brother, Ames, who had solved the problem of displacement by placing himself as far as possible from Plainfield. "He walked in front of the early commuters' train one morning at the Plainfield station." Nor indeed had Brooks's father — a man of business, doomed to invalidism, yearning for Europe — ever been at home in that suburb of Wall Street. "Had my father's practical failure in life over-affected my own mind, as his European associations had affected it also, so that perhaps his inability to adjust himself to existence at home had started my own European-American conflict?"

Although Brooks's thought tends often to lunge toward the pat answer, he did come to adulthood within a family in which Europe was represented as the solution for everything. But if his family proved anything it proved that Europe solved nothing. Eventually, believing that "deracination meant ruin," Brooks found himself impaled: "the American writer could neither stay *nor* go, — he had only two alternatives, the frying-pan and the fire." And Brooks made a self-conscious and brave choice: "the question was therefore how to change the whole texture of life at home so that writers and artists might develop there." All tremulous with misgiving he took on the truly formidable task, as Sherman Paul has observed, of making America Europe. Or, said in the terminology Brooks had devised, he would bring Ideal and Real, visionary imagination of the Germanic kind and cogency of systematic thought of the rationalist French sort, into a new and radically American balance. Returning to this country at a time of "Arctic loneliness for American writers," perhaps he would escape the wreckage his own family suffered.

This decision, a thing of high drama, was less momentous for American literature than the acolyte of art could have imagined and far more portentous for his inner life than he could have foreseen. Embracing a flimsy but plausible notion — deracination meant ruin — he returned to America almost in Puritanic renunciation of his deepest want. As is well known but ill understood, the scheme worked from 1914 when it was completed until 1925 when it and Brooks himself collapsed. In virtual casebook display of what Freud called the return of the repressed, Brooks in breakdown was haunted by the apparition of Henry James, by nightmares in which James "turned great luminous menacing eyes upon me." It was the figure of James that turned the screw of nightmare in the late twenties. But many years earlier, in childhood, it had been not James but a Hindu who appeared in the "earliest dream I remember," a "dream of flight." On the lawn a Hindu suddenly appeared, dressed in a suit of many colors, and chased the child Van Wyck with a knife. Just as he approached, running, "I soared into the air and floated away, free, aloft and safe. On other occasions, the fiend was not an Oriental, he was merely a nondescript minatory figure that pursued me, and I was not even anxious when I saw him approaching, for I knew I possessed the power to float away." That power — flight — deserted Brooks during the years of crisis when his intricately conceived scheme to evade wreckage was itself wrecked. And that figure, neither Oriental nor nondescript but now a most elegant avatar of deracination, of ruin, terrified Brooks with the minatory lesson: he who would evade himself is lost.

If this seems too fanciful a proposition, consider the trope to which Brooks resorted in all moments of crisis throughout his life, the image of seafaring, of journeying through troubled waters. It appears first in a pamphlet, *The Soul* (1910). "An Essay toward a Point of View," it is composed of some forty gnomic, Emersonian paragraphs on the transcendent subject, Art. The genius of poetry, that "ancient companion of the human soul," is its capacity to console: "in literature, I seemed to see a refuge." Safe harbor too, literature, for a man to whom in fantasy human existence appeared as a "vast ocean which contained all things known and unknown . . . without a bottom." The lives of men, "like so many ships," were "sailing, tacking, drifting across the ocean. Some sailed swiftly . . . as if they steered for a distant shore: but this ocean had no shore." Now and then a pilot would drop a line into that bottomless sea and as it struck he "would take his bearings from this depth, supposing it to be the bottom. But this bottom was in reality, though he did not know it, only the wreckage of other ships floating near the surface." Then with a startling reversal of intent in what was conceived as a fantasy of consolation, Brooks says, "I will be this ocean: and if I have to be a ship I will be only a raft for the first wave to capsize and sink." That is to say, he would settle for nothing less than absolute literary triumph but he feared cataclysmic defeat.

Given this expectation of disaster, it is understandable that similar thoughts and images should have tortured him during that "time in the middle twenties when my own bubble burst. . . .. What had I been doing? I had only ploughed the sea." The wretchedness of those years is understated in Brooks's published reminiscence but the letters, especially certain exchanges between Mrs. Brooks and Lewis Mumford, record a state of sheerest horror all round. I must refer again to this unhappy matter, for it is a storehouse of images which connect Brooks's writings with the lower depths of Brooks's mind. Thoroughly "bedevilled," Brooks in print was later to say, he had seen himself as a "capsized ship with the passengers drowned underneath and the keel in the air. I could no longer sleep."

For five years he was unable to rest or work. Before then, from 1915 to 1925, he had achieved renown as the most metaphysical mind, the most urbane and eloquent voice, the most poised and coherent theorist of diverse movements in literary nationalism which flourished in the day of Resurgence. First with a group of pacifist, Wilsonian radicals on *The Seven Arts* — Bourne, Waldo Frank, Oppenheim, Paul Rosenfeld — and later as literary editor of Albert Jay Nock's paper, *The Freeman*, he acquired unparalleled authority among American intellectuals committed to one or another program of literary reform. Beginning in 1915 with *America's Coming-of-Age*, he contrived to sail a brave course across the "Sargasso Sea" of American literary and social history, that "prodigious welter of unconscious life, swept by ground-swells of half-conscious emotion . . . an unchecked, uncharted, unorganized vitality like that of the first chaos." Then came *Letters and Leadership* in 1918, the noted essay introducing Bourne's posthumous *History of a Literary Radical* in 1920, and the last of these studies, "The Literary Life of America," which was published in Harold Stearns's symposium *Civilization in the United States* in 1921 and which prepared the way for the appearance of his climactic work, the book on Mark Twain. At mid-decade, barely forty, he had acquired national eminence as the leading spokesman for the Beloved Community, remorseless in his attack on a society which subverted the creative life in favor of the acquisitive life. Unlike H. L. Mencken, who chose the easy target of official Philistine culture, Brooks assailed his colleagues for having assisted at their own sacrifice. Jolted by and thankful for this shock of recognition, they had presented him with the *Dial* Award (for service to American letters) and offered him the editorship of that distinguished magazine. In print his many admirers expressed their gratitude for his labors in their behalf.

Brooks's fame represented a matchless moment of coalescence between the man and the epoch. His enterprise coincided with a general attack on the outrages of capitalism, with a rising labor movement, with an emerging Socialist party. Brooks, a socialist-pacifist who shared Woodrow Wilson's sense of mission, hoped to inspire, to exhort the American people to fulfill its destiny by presenting to the international community of nations a model of disinterested service to mankind. Simultaneously, he himself presented to the nation at large and to a special circle of rebel-intellectuals in small, a bill of particulars listing the reasons why Americans would be hard-pressed to realize Wilson's program. Conflict within the national consciousness thus ran parallel to a polarity of will within Brooks's own consciousness.

As he wrote those works which, as Mary Colum said, helped to create "the conditions in which the artist can work and flourish as a free spirit," he discovered in classic American letters "two main currents running side by side but rarely mingling." In America "human nature itself exists on two irreconcilable planes"; its poetry, deprived of organic life, is therefore denied the right to fulfill its true office. In contrast to Europe, where art is the source of rapture and where artists mediate between the material and the spiritual life of man, Americans prefer the state of rupture. Two kinds of public, "the cultivated public and the business public," pursue divergent tastes which perpetually widen the gulf that separates them. The highbrow public exists on the plane of "stark intellectuality" and the lowbrow public exists on the plane of "stark business," of flag-waving and money-grabbing. Under these conditions poetry cannot harness thought and action, cannot transform the great American experiment "into a disinterested adventure." Brooks, having come this distance by way of his customary route — the language of dualism — ended his essay *Letters and Leadership* with his characteristic imagery. "So becalmed as we are on a rolling sea, flapping and fluttering, hesitating and veering about, oppressed with a faint nausea, is it strange that we have turned mutinous?"

In *Three Essays on America* (1934), he would seek to prepare the way for a guild of artists, men of "exalted soul" who would fuse the life of poetry with the life of action so that America, unified at last, would realize its old dream of utopia. But before this program of salvation could be properly carried forward, its theory wanted testing. And Brooks conceived a trilogy of books on classic American writers, Mark Twain and Henry James and Whitman, which would exhibit the full effects of all those patterns of disjunction — of wine and the aroma of wine, of French temper and German, of rhetoric and poetry, of Real and Ideal, of lowbrow and highbrow — he had traced during more than a decade's study. The books on Mark Twain and James would exhibit the consequences of lowbrow debasement and highbrow attenuation of spirit in American literature. And a final book would present Whitman as the very model of a perfect poet, a very Antaeus of a man who, "for the first time, gave us the sense of something organic in American life." Brooks substituted Emerson for Whitman, so the story goes, when he learned of Whitman's homosexuality. On hearing this at lunch with Malcolm Cowley in the Harvard Club he left the table immediately.

However that may be, the revised project was greeted by members of his circle as the proper work of a man whose learning and eloquence were more than equal to the labor of representing what was then called the Young Generation in its debate with received opinion. And indeed by 1925 Brooks had discredited a whole tribe of university scholars who conducted literary affairs according to laws of taste which excluded the new criticism, the new poetry, the new painting — the new age. Reading Stuart Pratt Sherman on Mark Twain, Bourne told Brooks in a letter (March 1917), "made me chortle with joy at the thought of how much you are going to show him when you get started. You simply have no competition." Sherman "hasn't an idea in the world that Mark Twain was anything more than a hearty, healthy vulgarian. . . . But you will change all that when you get started." Stuart Sherman, Irving Babbitt, Paul Elmer More — these were the men whom Edmund Wilson listed high among those Brooks cast out of authority.

The book with which he most outraged that older generation was *The Ordeal of Mark Twain*. Despite the fury this work roused among ritual cultists of Clemens, the *Ordeal* remains a compelling book. Securely placed among specialist studies of Mark Twain, it has an even more imposing place among benchmark books in another kind of literature. For all its humorlessness, its ax-grinding and thesis-mongering, the *Ordeal* bore some marvelous first fruits of inquiry into the connections between neurosis and art, unconscious motive and literary act. And particularly as it raised some radical questions about the discontents of civilization in the United States, questions which its chief critic Bernard De Voto failed to discredit, has it earned its fame and proved its worth.

Mark Twain was no frontiersman of American jollity, Brooks argued, but was deep down afflicted by a "malady of the soul, a malady common to many Americans." His "unconscious desire was to be an artist; but this implied an assertion of individuality that was a sin in the eyes of his mother and a shame in the eyes of society." In fact the "mere assertion of individuality" was a menace to the integrity of "the herd," incarnate in that mother who "wanted him to be a businessman." This "eternal dilemma of every American writer" Mark Twain solved by choosing the mode of comedy even though he felt that as a humorist he was "selling rather than fulfilling his soul."

His "original unconscious motive" for surrendering his creative life had been an oath, taken at his father's deathbed, to succeed in business in order to please his mother, Jane Clemens. This first surrender had been followed by another, to his wife Olivia, who imposed on her "shorn Samson" the prissy rules, sterile tastes, and vacant intelligence of the genteel tradition. Until then surrender had been half- not whole-hearted. But when he married Olivia his life took permanent shape. Mark Twain, as his somnambulism indicates, became a "dual personality."

Somnambulism, gloom, obsession with double identity — these represent the effects of a "repressed creative instinct" which it is "death to hide." Repressed, Mark Twain's "wish to be an artist" was supplanted by another less agreeable but inexpungible want: to win public approval and acquire great wealth by conforming to public opinion. The impulse to conform clashed with the impulse to resist. This struggle, which implicated two competing wishes or "groups of wishes," undermined the genius of a man in whom "the poet, the artist, the individual" barely managed to survive. Because the poet lived on in cap and bells, the man managed to maintain a small measure of self-respect, to acquire high accolade and vast fortune, and preserve balance enough to outlast the despair which almost overcame him in the end. "I disseminate my true views," Mark Twain said in 1900, "by means of a series of apparently humorous and mendacious stories." The remark is given in Justin Kaplan's biography, *Mr. Clemens and Mark Twain* (1966), and Mr. Kaplan adds that at this time in Mark Twain's life "fiction, dreams, and lies had become confused, and he could not tell them apart. They were all 'frankly and hysterically insane.' " Mr. Kaplan's is a fine book, incidentally, which dispenses both with Freud and, unnecessarily, with Brooks — even as it takes up, amplifies, modifies the thread of Brooks's thought. What was hastily argued in 1920 is pursued at leisurely pace in 1966: *Mr. Clemens and Mark Twain* ends with the old man at the instant before his final coma talking about "Jekyll and Hyde and dual personality."

On publication, *The Ordeal of Mark Twain* split its readers into two camps which engaged in guerrilla warfare until Bernard De Voto in 1932, the year Brooks published a revised edition, offered in rebuttal

Mark Twain's America. Accusing Brooks of having initiated a "fatally easy method of interpreting history," De Voto condemned him for incompetence in psychoanalysis, for "shifting offhand from Freud to Adler to Jung as each of them served his purpose," and (I refer to Stanley Edgar Hyman's view of the affair) for "contradictions, distortions, misrepresentations, and unwarranted assumptions on page after page." Following De Voto nearly two generations of critics have taken up the debate. And in consequence today neither Brooks's wholesale derogation of Mark Twain's genius nor De Voto's wholesale condemnation of Brooks's thesis is quite acceptable.

Brooks's 1932 revision of the *Ordeal*, itself a product of his own years of desperation, represents a retreat from some hard-won positions. Far more ground was given up than is accounted for in a simple arithmetic of words changed or phrases dropped. This particular matter, comparison of texts, has been amply studied and I shall not reproduce details. It is true, however, that the ground he conceded was easily surrendered, and its loss did not appease those of his critics who admired the shape of his thought, as Gamaliel Bradford said in a letter (June 1923), but were distressed by the way he had used Mark Twain as a mannequin to hang a garment on. Brooks's tendency was to falsify — just a trifle maybe, Bradford agreed, but a trifle all the same. Brooks responded with an apology and a promise: he was very keenly aware of his evil tendency to impose a thesis on an individual. He agreed that the *Mark Twain* suffered from this, but promised that the *Henry James* would not, even if he had to spend two more years on the book.

The Pilgrimage of Henry James was to be an exercise in many kinds of self-discipline but it would confirm not correct iniquity. Brooks wrote both books in barely muted stridency of distaste for America, in an unrecognized and unwelcome ecstasy of longing for Europe. But the *Ordeal* was irretrievable for another, plainer reason: Brooks had lifted its skeleton from Hart's book on insanity. He was therefore flatly unable to accomplish the sort of radical revision which friendly critics would have admired. And since he chose not to identify Hart as his source of psychological learning, he left his critics to make out, with good guess and bad, the origins and ends of his thought. "Like the Freudians," Alfred Kazin remarked, "Brooks was writing to a thesis; but it was not a Freudian thesis." Nor was it an idiosyncratic pastiche, as other critics complained. It was Hart's composite portrait of the life of the psyche, Hart's synthesis of four schools of psychological thought — Freud's, Janet's, Adler's, Jung's — which Brooks adapted to his study of Mark Twain's psychic life. And it could not be jettisoned.

I have already remarked on Hart's contribution to Brooks's understanding of psychology. But this does inadequate justice to the tightness of connection which binds *The Ordeal of Mark Twain* to *The Psychology of Insanity*. Here is one of those rare and fortuitous instances in the history of ideas when direct and presiding influence, one work on another, is incontrovertible. Reading Hart today, you can recapture a measure of the excitement Brooks must have felt as he found in this handbook the key which unlocked the riddle of Mark Twain's life, of the creative life in America. In Hart's two chapters on "Repression" and "Manifestations of Repressed Complexes," he learned all the Freudian theory he needed in order to understand the principle of unconscious conflict. And in Hart's chapter on Janet, on "Dissociation," Brooks was given a ready-made system and language which accounted for some hitherto unaccountable traits of Mark Twain's character. The conception of dissociation enables us to represent the mental state of those patients, Hart said, whose delusions are impervious to facts. "They pursue their courses in logic-tight compartments, as it were, separated by barriers through which no connecting thought or reasoning is permitted to pass." One main form of dissociation was somnambulism; another was the commonly known one of "double personality." Illustrating the origins of somnambulism, Hart used an example offered by Janet: Irène, a young woman whose mother's death had been peculiarly painful, developed "an abnormal mental condition" whose symptoms resembled "those exhibited by the ordinary sleepwalker." Irène "would live through the deathbed scene again and again, her whole mind absorbed in the phantasy . . . oblivious of what was actually taking place around her."

What a thrill of recognition Brooks must have felt as he sorted out Hart's ideas, then reshaped Hart's pattern to match the design of

Mark Twain's life and art. Retelling Albert Bigelow Paine's version of the deathbed oath — to which Brooks clung even though Paine's account, relying as it did solely on Mark Twain's recollections, was an undependable report of what Mark Twain chose to remember or misremember — Brooks let out the stops. "That night — it was after the funeral — his tendency to somnambulism manifested itself." It is "perfectly evident what happened to Mark Twain at this moment: he became, and his immediate manifestation of somnambulism is the proof of it, a dual personality." Now that psychology has made us "familiar with the principle of the 'water-tight compartment,' " we realize that Mark Twain was the "chronic victim of a mode of life that placed him bodily and morally in one situation after another where, in order to survive he had to violate the law of his own spirit." Having submitted to his mother's will, he assumed the character and attitudes of a "money-making, wire-pulling Philistine," a "dissociated self" which was permanently at odds with his "true individuality."

In explanation of the reasons for Mark Twain's submission, Brooks relied on Hart's paraphrase of ideas drawn from another prestigious work of the time, W. Trotter's *The Instincts of the Herd in Peace and War*. Trotter demonstrates the existence of a fourth instinct, Hart said, "of fundamental importance in the psychology of gregarious animals," a herd instinct which "ensures that the behaviour of the individual shall be in harmony with that of the community as a whole. Owing to its action each individual tends to accept without question the beliefs which are current in his class, and to carry out with unthinking obedience the rules of conduct upon which the herd has set its sanction." In "these struggles between the primary instincts and the beliefs and codes enforced by the operation of the herd instinct, we have a fertile field for mental conflict." What Trotter called herd Freud called superego. But Hart preferred Trotter to Freud on this subject, and Brooks followed Hart. Repression of Mark Twain's creative instinct was accompanied by the rise "to the highest degree" of his "acquisitive instinct, the race instinct." His individuality sacrifices itself, "loses itself in the herd," and in the end becomes the supreme victim of that epoch in American history, the pioneer, when "one was required not merely to forgo one's individual tastes and beliefs and ideas but positively cry up the beliefs and tastes of the herd."

Obviously Brooks's thesis was neither Freudian nor a pastiche of Freud and anyone else. *The Psychology of Insanity* provided a system of ideas on individual and social behavior which Brooks absorbed, paraphrased, and exploited in his programmatic study of both Mark Twain and Henry James. It was a matter of lock, stock, and barrel. To have tampered with this system would have been to dismember Hart's thought. Revising the *Ordeal*, Brooks could correct a howler or two, tone down or play up: pure cosmetics.

Revision of that book was his last sustained essay in the psychology of literature. A few years earlier, attempting to carry on with his projected three-book series of standard American authors, he had applied the techniques of psychology to the biography of Henry James — a work which he looked upon as a Purgatorio, following the Inferno of Mark Twain and preceding the Paradiso of Whitman: strange fruit of the Harvard cult of Dante. In *The Pilgrimage of Henry James*, he had incorporated other aims as well. He had intended to examine the validity of James's view that the artist cannot thrive in the American air — an intention which he took very seriously indeed. For in this way, as he described the project to Bradford, he would rescue James from the Jacobites and show that James spoke the sober truth about the "immense fascination of England (applied to himself, that is, and in consequence of certain weaknesses in his own nature)."

In order to rescue James, Brooks was compelled to show that the great man, confronting frying pan and fire, had deliberately chosen the frying pan, Europe. The choice had been a bad one but James's judgment of the fire's heat had been accurate indeed. For James was "the first novelist in the distinctively American line of our day: the first to challenge the herd-instinct." Unlike Brooks, who immersed himself in the primitive American community, who fought it out with the "herd" — James fled. Flying, he "lost the basis of a novelist's life." He laid down a siege of London, won the war, lost himself. English society cut him "in two" and the public Henry James emerged, a "vast arachnid of art, pouncing upon the tiny air-blown particle and wrapping it round and round." Like Amiel, James spun large circles around the tiniest molecules of nuance. This was the James adored by the Jacobites, the Old Pretender whose play of style, a "mind working in the void," represented the ruin of art. Tracing ruin to James's deracination, Brooks concluded that a writer without a country of his own must sink in "the dividing sea."

Mark Twain the infernal lowbrow and James the expurgated highbrow were victims of a civilization which it was Brooks's holy mission to reform. This was all the truth he cared about, his Dantesque vision of America. Perhaps, too, the study of James was intended to serve as a lesson in self-admoniton at the very moment in the twenties when the fascination of Europe was irresistible to nearly all Americans. Having denied himself that refuge, Brooks had chosen literature as his safe harbor. But suddenly, shortly after he published this book, his ship capsized. And during the next five years as Eleanor Brooks and Lewis Mumford consulted physicians, enlisted friends, desperate for an effective way to restore Brooks to himself, he went from asylum to asylum in search of extinction, haunted by Henry James.

Until this time of crisis he had said marvelous things about the nature of conflict within the social and literary imagination. Out of his divided mind had come a new and stirring — though hyperbolic — account of polarity in the national experience. He had invented an ingenious vocabulary of antithesis, had analyzed diverse forms of dualism in England, on the Continent, and in America where, at last, he addressed to the Young Generation a full-fledged psychology, sociology, and philosophy of literary reform. A guild of evangels, these men and women would create a poetics of the body politic which would harness art and action.

Out of duality, singleness; out of diversity, unity; out of unity, wholeness; out of organic wholeness, order; out of order, utopia — this sequence of ideas served as the theme of Brooks's rhetoric until 1925. One fixed idea suffused the lot. Drawn from German and English Romanticism, it proclaimed that the creative life, the life of art, the artist's stubborn instinct for self-realization — "self-effectuation," Brooks said — must inspire individual beings to resist the herd. In this way the artist in America, Emerson's Orphic poet incarnate, would furnish all mankind with an exemplary figure of obstinate honor and untrammeled will.

Brooks's timing could not have been worse. He arrived at this stage of thought at the moment least auspicious for its exaltation. War had killed *The Seven Arts*; strain of will and gloom of spirit along with influenza had killed Randolph Bourne. And it was at this grim time of general disillusion that Brooks, completing his allegory, found himself at a loss. Unable to visualize that heaven which his prophecy had forecast, he was left with rhetoric alone. In 1925, when anybody in his right mind could see that an artist could really thrive virtually anywhere outside the United States, Brooks found himself utterly unable to contend that Emerson had prospered in an American atmosphere. Having proved that an artist is doomed if he stays here and damned if he leaves, having arbitrarily decided, for consistency's sake, that Emerson not Whitman would embody the triumph of American genius — having shifted from Whitman whom he adored to Emerson whom he had earlier half-reviled as dried manna of Concord — Brooks reached exactly that state of impasse he had observed in Symonds's life. First cul-de-sac, then breakdown. Having negotiated the Inferno and scaled Purgatorio, he found himself stalled at the gates of Paradise.

In the state of emotional collapse which followed we can discern some strange but telling conjunctions between Brooks's Dantesque allegory of the American soul, its progress from damnation to salvation, and Brooks's despair. In breakdown, his whole terror was fixed on the certainty of reprobation. Speaking with one of his closest friends, the scientist-adventurer-writer Hans Zinsser, whom Lewis Mumford brought East from California to consult and advise, Brooks tried to convince Zinsser that he, Brooks, was doomed to die of starvation in jail. In that panic time of guilt and self-accusation, he foresaw one sure end: punishment in hell. Much later, in autobiography, he was able to turn terror into a figure of speech, "Season in Hell," but in the late twenties he had no taste for conceit. What had begun as a term of rhetoric had become infernally real.

A man who accuses himself of crimes he does not commit must surely be convinced he is condemned for some reason. When we remember that Brooks, a man of Puritanic conscience — "a conscience that was like a cancer," as he said in another connection — was terrorized by the apparition of Henry James, we cannot be far wrong if we guess that Brooks feared retribution induced by his "evil tendency" to falsify, to impose a thesis. And no advice could redeem regret or could assuage guilt or diminish the sense of evil. Mary Colum, for example, later told Brooks that in 1927 in Paris she had spoken with Janet — the theorist of dissociation — and Janet had said that Brooks's cure hinged on an end of meditation, of inquiry into the laws of his own inner being and into the inner nature of all other general laws of whatever kind. But he could scarcely disown overnight two decades of forensic, of meditation on the laws governing the creative life in Europe and America. Then too William A. White, another distinguished psychiatrist, gave contradictory advice. He told Mrs. Brooks that her husband should be encouraged to round out his work, should be urged to complete the book on Emerson. Indeed, apart from Janet, everyone was convinced that Brooks would be miraculously restored to health if only he could finish that third volume. If the Emerson succeeds, Mrs. Brooks wrote to Mumford, he will be cured. Only Brooks himself was unconvinced.

The problem he alone understood and could not resolve — whatever his physicians, wife, friends said — was not simply how to get on with Emerson but how in heaven's name could he speak of salvation when he felt himself cast out, condemned, disgraced. That this feeling was unreasonable is hardly worth saying: the strongest complaint that anyone could register against his work was that it was tendentious or, as Gorham Munson in 1925 maintained, that his kind of social and "genetic" criticism too often substituted moral fervor for formal analysis. But what drove him to distraction was loss of faith in his power of vision. The condition of life in America, he decided, was sheer hell from which there was no escape — neither in the classic American and paternal solution, flight to Europe, nor in immersion in private fancy. The only thing he could do was wait for the descent of that Hindu's knife, fit punishment for a faithless man.

External evidence in support of these speculations is scanty, but internal evidence is plentiful. For when *The Life of Emerson* (1932) did finally appear, it expressed no reassertion of faith, but rather displayed Mrs. Brooks's, Mumford's, and the publisher's, Dutton's, faith in the healing power of love. This triumverate sought to do for Brooks what he was incapable of doing for himself, raise him from the slough of despond. Mumford's role is especially notable in that he performed a variety of literary tasks with exactly the kind of fidelity he brought to bear on multitudinous works of friendship during these hard years. For it was he who undertook to arrange for treatment by Jung, who assured Mrs. Brooks that money would not be permitted to interfere with therapy. Advising her that, contrary to Brooks's belief, the book was finished — that the final chapter summarizing Emerson's philosophy could not be tacked on because it was incompatible with Brooks's intention to re-create the quality of Emerson's life by relying on Emerson's own words — Mumford worked to persuade everyone concerned with Brooks's affairs to go ahead with the book. "Believing that a financial lift would help Brooks's condition, and might make him willing to publish the work," Mumford says in a letter (September 6, 1968) intended to set right some statements I had made in print, "Maxwell Perkins and I approached Carl Van Doren and got him to accept it for the Literary Guild, without its having been offered to them by Dutton. (John Macrae, up to then, had been so irritated by having his offerings turned down by the two book clubs that he had vowed never to submit another manuscript to them: so we had, somehow, to break down both Brooks's resistance and Macrae's.) Van Doren, on his own responsibility, gallantly accepted the book; and after that, Brooks's acquiescence — and Macrae's too — was easy to achieve."

It is this book, momentous for its value in helping to restore Brooks's health, his first to have a wide popular sale, which both pleased and disconcerted its admirers. "Your pictures of Emerson are perfect in the way of expressions," Santayana wrote Brooks; "but just how much is quoted, and how much is your own?" *The Life of Emerson*, Stanley Hyman said, flatly, harshly, "marked the end of his serious work." Whether or not this book marked the end of Brooks's important work, it was the first of many books which exploited a style of work that marks the breach in Brooks's career. "Instead of thundering like a prophet," Cowley said in 1961 — in an essay which Mumford says that Brooks especially liked — "he became a scholar quoting unobtrusively from Emerson's writings and weaving together the quotations into an idyllic tapestry." Cowley is accurate indeed, and generous. But I suspect that Brooks adopted this method of composition in order to vanish from his book quite as, upon recovering from malaise, he banished from his mind any notion of completing his allegory.

"May I say one further word about the method I have pursued," he was to comment in *The Writer in America* (1953). Answering Santayana's question, responding to those critics who treated the five volumes of literary history as "a sort of irresponsible frolic or brainless joyride," Brooks described his method as that of a novelist whose every character, scene, and phrase were "founded on fact." But a more important word on method he left unsaid, its attribution to H. G. Wells whose habit of composition in 1914 he had cited and approved. "I make my beliefs as I want them," Wells wrote. "I make them thus and not thus exactly as an artist makes a picture. . . . That does not mean I make them wantonly and regardless of fact." From Wells, Brooks learned to make brushstrokes of the intuitive imagination which, he hoped, would lift the writing of history to the loftiest conceivable realm, the realm of visionary art.

The season in hell ended shortly before *The Life of Emerson* appeared. Why it came to an end, what discoveries or disclosures eased his spirit, Brooks's autobiography does not reveal. Brooks's family and friends agree that private financial crisis had triggered his despair. And it is clear from Brooks's correspondence that the matter of money, all during those painful, passionate, and occasionally distraught years preceding his marriage, had plagued him beyond reason. Even after he had returned to the world, in 1940, as Eleanor Brooks told Mumford, the sight of a bill always destroyed, temporarily, his ability to write. By then, however, the external problems had been pretty well resolved, as we learn from Charles Van Wyck Brooks, whose letter (October 22, 1968) describes the special arrangements which finally, in the early thirties, released his father from external causes of despair. "The fact is that my mother's rich relatives raised a sum of almost $100,000 as a trust fund for the two of them, and I do not doubt that this was the proximate cause of his recovery. His feelings must have remained very ambivalent about it. He could never bear to speak of money, and I never knew at any time at all what his finances were." Not really concerned to pry further — to go deeper is impossible and to speculate wider is unfair —I think the final word must be Brooks's own. "And even after I came back to life and sailed out clear and free I remained conscious at moments of an abyss beside me. I seemed to catch out of the tail of my eye a cold black draughty void, with a feeling that I stood on the brink of it in peril of my reason."

On emerging from the abyss, Brooks forswore allegory. But he did not forgo his intention to write an account — as he had promised Bradford in 1925 shortly before his collapse, when the book on Emerson was "flowing like distilled honey" — of the "triumphantly successful literary life." Returning to the state of equipoise he set out, again tendentiously, to replace the life of Emerson with the whole "American pageant of genius." Having presented Emerson's life by way of stylized paraphrases of Emerson's own words, having found comfort in the state of anonymity which this style conferred, he embarked on a major effort of literary history, *Makers and Finders* (1936–55), which would "show the interaction of American letters and life," would connect "the literary present with the past," and would revive "the special kind of memory that fertilizes the living mind and gives it the sense of a base on which to build."

Reading *The Flowering of New England* and *New England: Indian Summer*, the first two volumes in *Makers and Finders*, René Wellek in 1942 mourned the disappearance of the old trenchancy of Brooks's mind, its replacement with a "belletristic skill of patching together quotations, drawing little miniatures, retelling anecdotes and describing costumes and faces." Still harsher criticism was uniform among a wide group of academic intellectuals which had been roused by Brooks's first books. "All my reading of American literature has been done during the era of Van Wyck Brooks and Parrington," F. O. Matthiessen said, but Brooks's new method of composition robs history of its clash and struggle and so dilutes the character of leading persons that it becomes hard to tell one man from another. However severe, these critics struggled to be just to the man who had revitalized their study of American themes. But even as they admired the very considerable merits of scholarship exhibited in these volumes, they condemned him for initiating that attitude toward history which today has apparently become stock-in-trade among our historians of a usable past. Brooks's nineteenth-century

New England, F. W. Dupee remarked, is presented as an "idyll of single-hearted effort." What was found unfit for this "fairy-tale" was disposed of.

The heart of the matter, as others have perceived, involves the interplay of proportion and distortion in Brooks's art. Although all writers must find external forms for internal states, must make their way through a labyrinth of motives, only a few are able to achieve an immersion in and conversion of but not subversion by their deepest wants. Brooks's myth-making embodied his inner life in vastly larger measure than it represented the exterior world, but until 1925 he contrived to transform the urgencies of private need into a prescription for society as a whole. Discovering in personal perplexity the key to a national dilemma, he defined some central confusions in American life and found for himself a short-lived relief from neurosis. In the early thirties, however, he wrote history with his eye on that cold black drafty void out of which he had so lately emerged. Our minds are darkest Africas, he told Granville Hicks in 1936, and he was at that moment exploring his own jungle trying to discover what he believed. Or, as he was to say in his sketch of Helen Keller, "She might have taken as her motto Theodore Roethke's line, 'I learn by going where I have to go.' "

Roethke's line could serve as his motto, surely, but could not justify the results of his explorations. Brooks himself maintained, in the books to which we turn now, those written during the last three decades of his life, that his early work had undervalued the American experience and that his later work merely restored balanced judgment to American studies. This position he staked out in the five volumes of history, the sketches of John Sloan (1955), Helen Keller (1956), and William Dean Howells (1959), the account of American expatriates in Italy, *Dream of Arcadia* (1958), as well as in the imposing array of works in self-explanation and self-justification: *Opinions of Oliver Allston* (1941), *The Writer in America* (1953), *From a Writer's Notebook* (1958), the three volumes of autobiography published intermittently from 1954 to 1961.

Makers and Finders, the chief ornament of Brooks's second career, is both a splendid achievement and a pernicious work. "Our greatest sustained work of literary scholarship," Malcolm Cowley has said, it has also been responsible for that view of the past which claims that authentic American literature avoids extremes, is neither highbrow nor lowbrow, but draws its inspiration from a will to resolve antithesis, banish contradiction. This view leads to the celebration of a style of literary culture, middlebrow, in which contrarieties are denied and, under the guise of consensus, radical conflict is ignored or suppressed. Above all it is a view which rests not on the history of ideas but on an illusion, a fable. And fables, as Descartes said in the *Discourse on Method*, "make one imagine many events possible which in reality are not so, and even the most accurate of histories, if they do not exactly misrepresent or exaggerate the value of things in order to tender them more worthy of being read, at least omit in them all the circumstances which are barest and least notable." Those persons who hope to regulate their conduct by examples derived from such a source are "liable to fall into the extravagances of the knights-errant of Romance, and form projects beyond their power of performance."

Makers and Finders memorializes Brooks's decision to transform himself into a knight-errant of this order. Determined to avoid Mark Twain's situation or James's fate, he divorced himself from the immediate concerns of his day and turned his curiosity on the practices of earlier centuries. He expatriated himself not to England but to Old New England, that golden land where no base circumstance undermined the conduct of life.

The key to Brooks's failure as a historian is contained in a remark addressed to Cowley (October 1939): "For there is an American grain, and I wish to live with it, and I will not live against it knowingly." Adopting William Carlos Williams's phrase, he decided that this figure of speech, taken literally, would enable him to discover exactly what was "organic" in the American past. Whatever else must be said of this doctrine it can be seriously faulted as an example of what the medievalist Johan Huizinga called historical anthropomorphism and defined as "the tendency to attribute to an abstract notion behavior and attitudes implying human consciousness." This tendency, Huizinga noted, leads all too smoothly to another, to a reliance on the resources of figurative speech — metaphor, personification, allegory. Whenever "historical presentation is fraught with passion, whether political, social, religious," figurative language shades into myth and dispatches all hope of science. And if "beneath the metaphors the claim somehow remains that the figure of speech is still to be taken philosophically and scientifically," then indeed is anthropomorphism a subversive act of the mind.

Although Huizinga in this essay ("Historical Conceptualization," 1934) doubtless intended these reflections to bear on the problem of writing history in that day of ideology, fascist and communist, his thought illumines the problem of Brooks's ideology, too, the ideology of the American grain. Brooks, who was himself alert to the dangers of his position, wrote into the *Opinions of Oliver Allston* a crucial chapter, "A Philosophical Interlude," designed to circumvent judgments of this kind. As figures of authority he chose a heterodox group of system makers — Croce, Thoreau, William James, Spengler — and drew from each what it suited him to have. Croce it was who led him to understand that America was "idealistic in its grain and essence" and that "the American mind was saturated with a sense of 'that which has to be,' — again in Croce's words, as opposed to 'that which is.'" If this view was considered unscientific, as Brooks anticipated his critics saying, so much the worse for science which is after all a discipline of thought not a guarantor of wisdom. Besides, he could make no "headway with abstract thinking, and, feeling that life was short, he abandoned himself to his tastes. To justify himself again, he copied out a passage from Thoreau's *Journals* (Vol. V): 'It is essential that a man confine himself to pursuits . . . which lie next to and conduce to his life, which do not go against the grain, either of his will or his imagination. . . . Dwell as near as possible to the channel in which your life flows.' "

Thoreau's view is unexceptionable. But nothing he said could justify Brooks's conviction that a peculiar socialismus of art and politics was apple pie but that "the communist mind runs counter to the American grain." This assertion occurs in the chapter on socialism in *Oliver Allston* where Brooks commended Williams for his fine phrase, then repeated the sentence from his letter to Cowley, and propelled himself headlong into the task of devising a whole new vocabulary of terms generated by the talismanic word, *grain*, itself. Thus reified, endowed with independent and objective life, the word conferred on Brooks's criticism the authority of pure American speech.

Expanding its range to include an infinitude of reference, he went to the language of psychotherapy for his formula of praise and blame. Having introduced Hart's language into the study of Mark Twain's life, he now concentrated his fire on the "Elioteers." To be always in reaction was "juvenile or adolescent" — were not, therefore, Eliot and Pound and Joyce infantile, sick, immature? "Were they not really unequal to life," these naysayers? Had not these very influential men of letters "lost a sense of the distinction between primary literature and coterie literature — was it not time to make this distinction clear?" Like primary instinct, "primary literature somehow follows the biological grain," he said, defining the exact "centre of his thought." Primary literature "favours what psychologists call the 'life-drive.'" The only value of coterie literature was its shock value which, like "insulin treatment for schizophrenia," restores the mind to its primitive state, a state of readiness for the fresh start. This treatment, coterie literature, is hardly necessary in America where the primary virtues of courage, justice, mercy, honor, and love represent the "tap-root" of art and "the sum of literary wisdom." To live in harmony with the American grain, in short, was to ally oneself with the forces of eros and set oneself in resolute opposition to the forces of thanatos, to the vanguard, coterie writers, "children sucking their thumbs," who incarnate "the 'death-drive' more than the 'life-drive.'"

His opinions helped to confirm an opposition to modern literature in that new audience which read *The Flowering of New England* and *New England: Indian Summer* and presented Van Wyck Brooks with its highest awards. No longer addressing himself to the Young Generation of literary men, Brooks became a hero of middle-aged and middlebrow culture — became, as the *Partisan Review* said, a pilgrim to Philistia. All too comfortably, his former colleagues felt, Brooks slipped into the role of spokesman for a public to which modernist literary forms were impenetrable. All too easily, many former allies thought, he assumed the role of laureate of American chauvinism.

Mary Colum, whose essay in 1924 had described Brooks as a pathfinder, a contributor of transforming ideas, spoke for nearly all his former colleagues when she told him in a letter two decades later that nothing he wrote about modern art showed that he knew what he was talking about.

There was in truth nothing in modern writing that Brooks cared anything for. What he did care about was to flush and dispel once and for all the issue of expatriation. He confessed that in his youth he had been "morbid" about this matter, that he had been "drawn to Europe over-much," that "many years had passed before he had learned to love his country," before he had realized that "he must cling to America to preserve his personality from disintegration" — and these extraordinary confessions explain the reasons for the conversion of Van Wyck Brooks and signify which motives underlay his fable. Along with the first two, the remaining three books in the series — *The World of Washington Irving* (1944), *The Times of Melville and Whitman* (1947), *The Confident Years* (1952) — result of nearly twenty years of independent research, supported only now and then by a grant-in-aid, form a national archives of forgotten documents, misplaced books, lost lives. Reading everything he could find lest anything of the least interest be neglected, Brooks restored to general view enormous numbers of hitherto ghostly figures. And if it were possible to set aside the fable, to take these five books as a movable feast of the American imagination, *Makers and Finders* would represent an absolute triumph of humane learning. If Brooks had had no larger aim than to revive a sort of racial memory among American readers and writers, there would be universal agreement to Cowley's view: these books caused "a revolutionary change in our judgment of the American past" and a "radical change in our vision of the future."

But it is impossible to set aside either the ideology of the American grain or the allegory of a usable past. How, for example, can we square Brooks's remark in a letter of 1933 — "I wish we could have in America the guild-life that writers have in England" — with the remark, made exactly two decades later in the essay "Makers and Finders" (*The Writer in America*) in which Brooks set down his final thoughts on his study of American history: "It seemed to me that . . . our writers formed a guild, that they had even worked for a common end." Presumably it was twenty years' research into the usable past which had led him to a major discovery. A reader making his way through the five volumes, however, is nonplussed trying to retrace the ground of Brooks's discoveries, trying to learn where Brooks had located this guild-life of American writers. Apart from a modest measure of support for this notion as applied to Boston during its heyday, the whole drift of evidence contradicts Brooks's point. Here are some examples taken nearly at random from *The Times of Melville and Whitman*: For nineteen years in New York, Melville was "all but forgotten as a man of letters." And Whitman — "to the end of his life the great magazines excluded him." After the first "flurry of interest on the part of Emerson and the dead Thoreau, he had for years only a handful of readers." Undoubtedly Whitman was "warped" by this treatment, Brooks says. Mark Twain, too, was warped by his conviction that American writers were merely "manacled servants of the public" — as if Walt Whitman "had never existed or Emerson or the free Thoreau or Cooper." Again, speaking of the main patterns of literary life in the seventies and eighties, when a few writers fled America, Brooks quotes Charles Godfrey Leland, whom in an earlier volume he had treated as a man with deep intellectual and emotional ties to his native Philadelphia: "I have nothing to keep me here. There is nothing to engage my ambitions."

Despite contentions made after the fact, Brooks was unable to prove that nineteenth-century American writers had indeed formed a guild. And in time he substituted another theme, the replacement of rural life with urban life. "More and more, as the eighties advanced and the cities grew larger and larger, the old life of the farm receded in the national mind." It was to this theme that Brooks committed himself without reserve. Deciding that the "immemorial rural life" had formed "the American point of view," he wove arabesques of history which were intended to show how a once "homogeneous people, living close to the soil, intensely religious, unconscious, unexpressed in art and letters, with a strong sense of home and fatherland" was uprooted and dispersed.

Determined at any cost to display the consistency of these ideas,

Brooks engaged in exactly the kind of struggle he had recognized in Symonds, that "congested poet" who, upon recovery from breakdown, had assumed the "fretful activity" of a *vulgariseur* and had set down with great labor large works of scholarship which tried to do what "only poetry can do." I do not know, in 1934 he told M. A. De Wolfe Howe, "how to use my thousands of notes," but it was increasingly clear to him that he could not "think in the expository form." As he proceeded from book to book his vision clarified itself: he would re-create the dream of paradise. And there his fancy fled in order to preserve his mind against disintegration, against any relapse of despair. No matter how far he ranged, this aim remained constant. Facts could not dislodge it though certain non-facts could be introduced to support it — the posthumous papers of Constance Rourke, for example (which he edited), or the phenomenal fact of Helen Keller's life.

Perhaps the most succinct way to crystallize the meaning of Brooks's double career is to note that the first half of his life was spent in demonstrating the ulcerous effects of America on the human spirit and that the second half was spent in an effort to prove that *America*, in its root meaning, signified the very spirit of health. Thus in 1956, publishing his sketch of Helen Keller, he sought to do justice to the biography of this marvelous woman and simultaneously to sanctify, by way of this inspirational tale, the whole design of his natural history of the American spirit. Was ever the physical life of man or woman more radically disfigured than Miss Keller's? Was ever the contour and lineament of moral health given more vivid configuration? She was "one of the world's wonders" — like Niagara Falls! He thought of Miss Keller when he read in Arthur Koestler's *The Age of Longing* that American women were too busy playing bridge to be cut out for the part of martyrs and saints. (Gladys Billings, Brooks's second wife — he had remarried in 1946, following Eleanor Brooks's death — was one of Henry Adams's "nieces," a figure out of Henry James.) Clearly Koestler had missed the point of America, had not got the point of James's *The Portrait of a Lady*, of Isabel Archer whom Miss Keller resembled in her "fixed determination to regard the world as a place of brightness, of free expansion, of irresistible action." Brooks repeated James's words in order to contend that Miss Keller's decision — "life was worth living only if one moved in the realm of light" — must be taken both as a personal victory and an American conquest, a triumph of private will and of national buoyancy, vitality. Didact to the end, he was convinced that the spirit's health was confirmed by those powers of "affirmative vision" inherent within the unconscious American "collective literary mind" which, as revealed in *Makers and Finders*, enables us to revere, promote, maintain, renew our "dream of Utopia."

Two years before his death in 1963, admitting that he was known mainly as the author of *America's Coming-of-Age* and *The Ordeal of Mark Twain*, he confessed that his chief hope for some kind of relative permanence was in his historical series. We are tempted to ratify this hope. But when we draw together the main lines of belief on which his claims rest — when we realize that one way to take these five volumes, according to Morton and Lucia White's *The Intellectual and the City* (1962), is as "the most striking example of anti-urbanism" in contemporary popular thought — we cherish the brilliance but mourn the uses to which it has been put.

At the point of origin in American civilization, we can now say in paraphrase of his final position on this whole matter, a primary literature develops out of one of the two primary instincts of the unconscious, the life-drive. Serving as the source of high-mindedness in politics, it brought American national experience to fruition, united high art and heroic action, joined the cities and the plains during a century of national life. Then, in manifestation of cyclic laws governing all organisms, in conjunction with the decline of rural life, the death-drive acquired authority. And it in turn generated that coterie literature which accompanied the rise of great urban centers. Made of greed, fruit of thanatos, these deracinated modern cities brought catastrophe to birth out of the world's body. The last pages of the final volume, *The Confident Years*, present recent American history as a battleground between the forces of urban and the forces of rural life, a vision of apocalypse in which the "life-affirmers" engage in a battle of the books with the "life-deniers." Wherever one "looked, in literature or in life, one found the two contrasting types," fighting it out as Brooks fought it out in unceasing battle with Eliot and the Elioteers. "So deeply engrained in the American mind" is life-affirmation, however, that the outcome was never in serious question. Because life-affirmation expresses the ineradicable will of the American spirit, it must eventually bring into being a new primary literature which will save the world from destroying itself.

Is it fair to say of all this, as he himself said of Symonds's achievement, that it was mere "high fantasy"? Had he composed book after book in praise of roots in order to devise for himself an utterly fanciful sanctuary? Is the figure of speech which he chose to describe Amiel and James an apt figure of self-description too: did he surround himself, spiderlike, in a shelter spun from his own body? Had he labored to transform the ideas of expatriation and escape and flight into so sticky and labyrinthine a version of the American pastoral myth that only the most determined and powerful of Hindus could have found him out?

None of these is a fair question and all propose answers which are probably less true than false but are just true enough to record the fact that Brooks's unconscious life played a more intrusive and persuasive role in deciding the course of his career than was good for Brooks or for the history of ideas in our time. No essay in the psychology of motive, however, can deprive Brooks of his role as a leader of the new radicalism in American letters. And I am at a loss to understand why Christopher Lasch's good book on this subject, *The New Radicalism in America* (1965), takes up Bourne but utterly disregards Brooks. This lapse is the more startling in that Mr. Lasch's account of the radical tradition, very little modified, might stand as a virtual biography of Brooks's mind. At the outset, in 1900, reformers sought to see society from the ground up "or at least from the inside out," Mr. Lasch says. Eventually this new class of intellectuals came to distrust the intellect, "to forsake the role of criticism and to identify themselves with what they imagined to be the laws of historical necessity and the working out of the popular will." Of this movement and process Brooks is indisputably the prime example.

Before he renounced the role of a radical critic, he imposed his stamp on two generations of reformist literary men, on Mumford, Waldo Frank, Matthew Josephson, Granville Hicks, Newton Arvin — above all on F. O. Matthiessen whose *American Renaissance* undertook to augment the Brooksian study of myth with the techniques of formal, textual analysis. In this way, Matthiessen believed, American criticism might achieve the repossession of "all the resources of the hidden past in a timeless and heroic present." As Matthiessen took up the subject where Brooks left off, so too others carried forward certain main themes of Brooks's thought which today receive cachet of the most flattering kind in that these are no longer recorded as Brooks's ideas at all but seem to express perennial wisdom. Reading a series of axioms on American literature in the *Times Literary Supplement* (July 20, 1967), we realize that the writer is unaware that he has reproduced a configuration of ideas which goes back fifty years to those first books in which Brooks examined our "impulse toward literary cosmopolitanism" and explored the "springs and sources of art and the right environment for its creation." It is this impulse "which has been of enormous importance in shaping the character of modern literature. Indeed it has been of the greatest importance for western literature generally, since the very idea of modernism seems to have its roots in this cosmopolitan, expatriate spirit." This matter of expatriation and cosmopolitanism has been of presiding importance in modern writing not because some leading American writers have been expatriates but because Brooks, obsessed by the problems of rootedness and deracination, their effect on the creative life in Europe and America, undertook to disclose the genesis of literature and discover the right ambience for its creation.

This vast realm was once his private preserve. At the point when he turned his mind toward other problems, his friends tried to recall him to himself. "Do not, we beg you," Edmund Wilson addressed him in 1924, "lose too much the sense of that wonder," that excitement of the artist "enchanted by the spectacle of life." It was both good advice and bad. And in any event it came too late. For Brooks was already disabled by some critical side effects of a state of mind which the English writer Tony Tanner in *The Reign of Wonder* (1965) has found to be enlivening and debilitating in classic American literature. Mr. Tanner talks round Brooks but frames the general issue in ways which correlate his life with the lives of those great men of the nineteenth century, Emerson and Whitman and Mark Twain, who loom so large in Brooks's imagination. Like them, he was "too suspicious of analytical intellect, too disinclined to develop a complex reaction to society, too much given to extreme reactions, too hungry for metaphysics" to avoid what Brooks himself had recognized as an American malady, the malady of the Idea.

Surely it is time to install Brooks among his predecessors and peers, those American romantics who have traditionally yearned to experience and to portray the "wholeness of the universe." It is time, too, to save him from entombment in the American Academy of Arts and Letters and from enshrinement as Bishop of Bridgewater, Connecticut. For if it is just the effigy of a former oracle that is preserved, then the legend of Van Wyck Brooks will in the end turn out to be simply routine and we too will have assisted at this waste of history. But because no man ever wanted less for himself, as Bernard Smith remarked thirty years ago, and more for his fellowmen, the time has come to restore Brooks to the highest place among the most eminent of twentieth-century literary intellectuals in America, those celebrants of conscience in whom the idea of America served both as a cause of malady and as a genesis of motive.

MERLE E. BROWN

KENNETH BURKE

During a career of writing beginning in the early 1920s, Kenneth Burke has worked in so many forms and on so many subjects that he may deserve to be acclaimed as the universal man of modern, mass democracy. He has written poems, short stories, a novella, a novel, essays of literary criticism, reviews of all kinds of books, and a chronicle of musical events; he has addressed audiences of all sorts, not only students and professors of literature, but also psychologists, sociologists, theologians, and even the radicals of the Communist-inspired American Writers' Congress; and he has ranged, in his writing, over a variety of subjects appropriate to audiences of such diverse composition. Such breadth of activity might well have left both his followers and his critics far behind him, silent in awe. Instead, Burke's writing has provoked outspoken responses, both in praise and in blame. Indeed, Kenneth Burke is probably the most controversial literary figure of the past fifty years in America. He is said to have the finest speculative mind of our time; he is adjudged an irresponsible sophist. Leaving a lecture by Burke, one may hear "A superb system!" from one side and "Sheer chaos!" from the other. From a single, exasperated idolater of Burke, one hears him decried as "mad" and lauded as a "genius," even in one and the same sentence.

Burke's spirit is capacious enough to evoke and, perhaps, deserve such diversity of response; but the intensity of the response, both as idolatry and as antagonism, is surprising. Burke believes, above all else, in ingratiation, and his manner is indeed ingratiating. Yet one recalls that the antihero of his novel, John Neal, said that "one sneers by the modifying of a snarl; one smiles by the modifying of a sneer." Burke's own ingratiating ways may stem from an essential combativeness.

In any case, the intensity of the commentaries on Burke has not promoted a judicious understanding of his work. To organize one's praise, as Stanley Edgar Hyman has done, around Burke's claim that "the main ideal of criticism, as I conceive it, is to use all that there is to use" is like praising a genius for his weaknesses. For the common criticism of the literati is that they know just enough to make use of everything, but so little as to ensure that they invariably misuse it. To praise Burke as a system builder, as William Rueckert does, is more reasonable, but if one takes "system building" in its ordinary sense and looks for its presence in Burke's work, he will be disappointed. In comparison with the great system builders, Aristotle, Aquinas, Hegel, Croce, and Cassirer, there is little of the system builder in Kenneth Burke. His structures are like Croce's description of the structure of *The Divine Comedy*: an arbitrary framework around which Dante weaves the garlands that are his true love. If one sees justice in Francis Fergusson's complaint that Burke is overly rationalistic, he must also agree with Sidney Hook that Burke often connects his ideas by random association.

Burke's critics, indeed, come closer to what he is truly doing than do his disciples. They err only in condemning what he is doing on the grounds that he is not doing something else, the thing they happen to value most highly. Both Austin Warren and John Crowe Ransom have chastised Burke for his sophistry, for his slippery use of language to confound all conviction and straight thinking. Tracing his progress in the thirties, Warren says that Burke began by undermining dogmatists by means of organized doubt, but then went so far as to doubt his doubt and to sympathize even with the dogmatists. For Warren this "sceptic's progress" is headed toward total collapse, and he urges Burke to recover a faith in reason. Burke is, in truth, a sophist, but not in the sense used by Warren and Ransom.

The sophist they are thinking of has been observed, criticized, and superseded by Socrates, whereas Burke is a sophist who has considered the rational criticism of sophistry and would go even beyond that criticism.

If there is a title peculiarly fitting to Burke in all his work, it is one dear to Burke himself, the title of rhetorician. Burke is a rhetorician in a double sense: whatever he considers, he considers it rhetorically as an instance of rhetoric. Rhetoric, as I am thinking of it, is the use of words to evoke a specific emotion or state of mind. Whatever Burke studies, this is what he finds it to be, whether it is open propaganda, the Constitution of the United States, psychoanalysis, philosophy, or even pure poetry. Dialectics itself he defines as a kind of rhetoric; it is "all enterprises that cure us by means of words." Pure poetry differs from other forms of rhetoric only in the sense that the state of mind it evokes is an end in itself, whereas ordinary rhetoric evokes a state of mind which is to lead to practical consequences.

The objective of Burke's own rhetoric is a consistent one: to evoke a state of oneness among men. If he can convince us that we are all rhetoricians, that we are all using words combatively for our own purposes, he will have purified our warlike natures by evoking in us a feeling of our final oneness. We are all, he would say, fighting to overcome an original divisiveness which we inherit with the neurological structure of our bodies. Once convinced of this, once convinced that we are all trying to swallow up and possess the souls of all by means of our symbols, would we not become more tolerant of each other and accept that detached view of ourselves which characterizes the Neo-Stoicism to which Burke himself subscribes? We would continue to fight with words, but, once aware that it is man's fate and delight always to fight with words, would we not, with this sense of our ultimate oneness, fight a little less viciously, with at least a modicum of good humor, with a touch of that sense of the comic which is Burke's measure of the stature of man, that laughing animal? In any case, this is Burke's objective, and to it he will sacrifice all else. This, I think, explains his persistent neglect of the differences that separate the subjects he treats and his emphasis upon that which unites them. It explains, too, why Burke so often arouses the flames of contention in his readers. After all, here is a man trying to swallow up all our souls, trying to possess them, by convincing us that we are all dedicated to using words for the purpose of swallowing each other up. Can anyone endure such engulfment, an ultimate identification which slights and belittles the distinctive aspects of his own use of words? Can we permit the man with the biggest maw of all to have his way? Such feelings explain why this man of peace, or, rather, this man who fights to purify war, stirs up such impure controversies wherever he goes.

The impressiveness of Burke's general objective is enhanced by the fact that his writing is always occasional. He has a keen sense for the peculiar form of divisiveness which he would employ his strategies to overcome. If there is any single situation which he consistently works against, it is that division separating specialists from the masses. The 1920s in America, when the direction of Burke's career was being set, were dominated by this particular division. The country was a melting pot of the masses; and their melted-down life seemed a dreary routine dominated by a technological culture. In consequence, many men of the mind sought to dissociate themselves from this routine by cultivating their specialized talents.

In his recollections of the twenties, in *The Days of the Phoenix*, Van Wyck Brooks laments the shift, which he felt to be going on everywhere, from an elevating form of literature, of importance to all human beings, to a highly specialized literature which merely renders subjects, as an end in itself. Joel Spingarn's "The American Critic" (in the 1931 edition of his *Creative Criticism*) is just the sort of thing Brooks opposes. Spingarn pleads for the repudiation of scientific techniques in criticism, usable even by the vulgar, and for a return to that richly spiritual, traditional form of literary studies then flourishing in Italy. Against such aristocratic divisiveness, men of serious mind sought to bridge the widening gap between the precious and the common. *The Waste Land* itself, often read as Eliot's act of snobbish withdrawal, instead presents a world of spiritual poverty which, even in its deadliness, is seen as a condition appropriate for spiritual rebirth. The sophisticated poet, who scorns the meaningless routine of mass culture, at the same time senses in it a need to die in order to be reborn, a need very like his own. Hart Crane's *The Bridge* is a poetic effort to redeem a technically adept but directionless society by means of a poetic vision which would unite the poetic seer even with the wop washerwoman who rides home with him on the subway. A little later, Wallace Stevens will strive, in his "The Man with the Blue Guitar," to unite the masses of men, those "mechanical beetles never quite warm," with the exceptional poet, again by means of poetic insight. And John Dewey, in his *Art as Experience*, will attempt to prove, philosophically, that the most common forms of experience and the most exquisite and intricate form of aesthetic experience are ultimately the same.

With a similar purpose, Burke's most persistent rhetorical strategies are used to overcome this divisiveness. He claims that in his time the language of poetry, of feeling, and the language of science, of information, have been separated. Poetry, he feels, is the language of pieties, of shared beliefs and conventions. The language of science, in contrast, is a methodology of doubt; it has not only been separated from the communal language of feeling but has undermined it so that most men live without a sense of social purpose. To withdraw from such an arid culture, to live a rich, isolated, aesthetic life, this is anathema to Burke as to Van Wyck Brooks, Crane, Stevens, and Dewey. In contrast to most of the New Critics, Burke would accept the science and technology of his environment and would strive to redeem it with a poetic rhetoric. That, indeed, is what is going on in most of his books. They are full of technological jargon and thus tend to offend the purists in style, the antiscientific literary critics. At the same time, the scientific jargon is being used in a most unscientific way; it is being used as part of a poetic rhetoric. As a result, it must offend the rigorous scientist as much as it offends the literary specialist. Though both are offended, Burke's real purpose is to ingratiate and unify them all. The trouble, it would seem, is that Burke's unifications are verbal and rhetorical, whereas the divisions are deeper and involve whole men, each with his own distinctive sense of the world and his place within it.

The basic problem in Burke's writing may be seen most easily in the ambiguous nature of his tolerance. Without a doubt, he is an extraordinarily tolerant man. But tolerance takes different forms. It may be what I should call dialectical, the tolerance of one who is concerned with differences among men, of one who strives to understand another person in all his individuality and to imagine that person's mode of thought and action as it is in itself, and then, and only then, to discover, even with all these differences, a fundamental unity between that person and others. Such tolerance involves endless struggle to harmonize the rich diversity among men and their underlying unity. On the other hand, there is a form of tolerance which is characteristically American and which is of a rhetorical nature. It involves the acceptance of others by means of an indifference to, or neglect of, their differences, of all the opaquenesses and knobby protrusions that make it difficult to swallow their souls into one's own. Such tolerance ignores individuality, at best attends to specific attributes, and, for the most part, concentrates upon generic sameness. Rhetorical tolerance lends itself to blurring all in a common grayness, a oneness achieved at the expense of that individuality which, finally, makes life worth living. Now Burke's tolerance tends fatally toward the second, the rhetorical kind. At times he resists the tendency, but most of the time he does not. In fact, his tolerance itself is often technological; he sends the human subjects he considers down a mass-production line with no more sense of their differences than one has between two cars of the same make. He achieves a sense of unity, but it is unearned because the very distinctions which make the unity difficult to achieve are being ignored. Thus, in his efforts to poeticize, to unify in feeling, the dominantly technological mode of our culture, he often succumbs to that which he would master.

Having said this, one must add that dialectical tolerance is extremely difficult and may inevitably be limited to small groups of people. How many other persons can the man of most astute thought and sensitive discrimination understand with sympathy? Not, one expects, very many. Burke, of course, is trying to comprehend everything, to be tolerant of all, even of those aloof, aristocratic New Critics. Such a comprehensive enterprise, such an enormous wish on his part, puts genuine, dialectical tolerance out of the question, except for the few occasions on which he writes of close friends. And, to be sure, the rhetorical nature of Burke's tolerance encourages in him a forbidding manner of thought, abstractive and classificatory. Even so, Burke's thought deserves close attention and analysis. No matter how much one emphasizes the sanctity of the individual person, even if one believes that the community itself depends, finally, on the constructive efforts of individual persons, he must recognize that he lives in a mass culture, a non-community. To follow Burke's efforts to encompass this nonpersonal non-community is a rewarding curative for the pain of living in it.

Austin Warren quotes Burke as saying that he abandoned his studies, as a college student at Columbia, "because he feared that he was acquiring a taste for study, research, scholarship, when what he inmostly desired was to learn to write and to write." Burke's passion "to learn to write and to write" is a last characteristic of his work to be considered before we turn to his individual writings. He is not merely a rhetorician, but a rhetorician who writes rather than speaks. For an academic dialectician, faced daily with a need to listen attentively and to gear his speech to that which he has heard, Burke's passion for writing is most disturbing. For Burke writes as though he has not been listening attentively. An attentive listener learns to hear words as part of an integrated action; he develops a capacity to capture the driving passion and the underlying idea of another and to bridge that speech with his own rephrasing of it, in words that combine the otherness of what is heard with his own sense of things. The translation essential to all intelligent hearing is never a mere substitution of a language of one's own for what is heard. It is rather a bridging, an act of transcending, which contains and perpetuates the voice of the other along with one's own. This gives a traditional coloring to the writing of such a listener. He does not simply lacerate what he hears in order to have his own say; he learns from that which he would pass beyond and carries much of it along with him, so that whatever novelty he achieves springs out of the tradition he carries with him. Further, learning to hear others is coincident with learning to hear oneself. Thus, the dialectician writes in such a way as to suggest that he is listening to himself and evaluating what he says as he says it; his writing seems composed by two personae, one expressive, the other attentive. Finally, as a result of these qualities, it is usually quite simple to determine the precise nature of the audience to whom the dialectician speaks. He has a sense of the critical response of those whom he addresses, and, indeed, he incorporates into his own writing many of the qualities of those for whom he writes. Ordinarily, in fact, his writing is antirhetorical. He is not trying to evoke a response from passive listeners who must remain outside his speech. Rather he encourages them to take an active part in it. He has no hidden weapons, no strategies to catch others unawares. All is open, because the very movement of thought is what he would share, with maximum freedom.

Burke does not write as though he belongs to a dialectical community of this sort. He does not seem to hear those about whom he writes. His subjects themselves are treated as so many pieces of writing which one can abstract from and rearrange according to one's own needs. His translations leave what he is presumably translating far behind, so that, by and large, in reading him one feels no need to read also that about which he writes. In fact, usually, if one knows the subject, his knowledge is an impediment. This characteristic makes Burke's work seem quite untraditional; his translations do not provide a bridge between what he would explain and himself; all such bridges are burned, as he writes and writes, without listening. It is this quality which makes Burke appear to be an autodidact. All of us must, finally, teach ourselves; but, even as educated by ourselves, we would tend to carry along a polyphony of other voices, of other personae, from whom we have learned and whose thoughts we have modified. Burke's work, in contrast, is single-voiced; as complex as it is, it is monotonal. Nor does Burke listen very carefully to himself. One has no sense in his work of the constant revision that accompanies dialectical writing. His contradictions, themselves, are never troublesome, because there is never an overarching, attentive persona to be troubled by the need to connect what is being said with what has been said. Finally, as one reads Burke, he is caught up again and again by the question: To whom could he possibly be writing? For his audience is never included actively in his writing; it is never specified with precision. It is, one supposes, everybody and nobody: everybody as a mass willing to forget their distinctions; nobody in the sense that no one, of serious mind, is willing to forget either his own individuality or that of others, since only because of such individuality does life have the purpose and richness that give it value. In a world of nonpersonal, noncommunal masses, however, Burke's manner is most appropriate. If he can evoke a sense of oneness without listening to others or to himself and without addressing anyone in particular, then he may have achieved a worthwhile objective in the world as it really is, in the given world, in the world we are all part of, rather than in that precious world made with thought and passion by men who have an underlying, intellectual, communal purpose.

The three principles which allow for a certain brevity even in the treatment of so prolific a writer as Burke are these: there is more sameness than development in his career; his books are not themselves significant units of thought; and he thinks, always, in patterns of associational revery. It is inaccurate to say that Burke began by writing poetry, then developed a theory of poetry, and, finally, turned his theory of poetry into a philosophy of life. He has always written verse, as his recently published *Collected Poems* indicates. The novella "The Anaesthetic Revelation of Herone Liddell," published in 1957, shows no falling off in quality from the short stories of *The White Oxen*, published in 1924. His theory of poetry was already fixed in the mid-twenties, in the essay "Psychology and Form." Even in the twenties, much that he said about poetry was also implicit in his general comments on life, as evidenced by his reviews for the *Dial*. His ultimate purpose as a writer was not, one must grant, clearly articulated until the mid-thirties, but its seeds are present in his earlier work.

Although his career as a whole is integral, his books are not. Each has its arbitrary framework and an emotional coloring of its own, but what he actually and vitally does within any one book might, with almost equal appropriateness, have appeared in another. What he is actually and vitally doing, wherever one looks, is to bring the most diverse subjects together by means of associational revery or what he himself calls "qualitative form." His books are full of elaborate afterthoughts, in footnotes and appendixes. But the books themselves are series of afterthoughts. Hobbesian fancy, in contradistinction to judgment, is invariably his mode. He seeks out likenesses and scorns differences. He writes by metaphor and analogy, identifying the most diverse of things. The diversity of the things identified is rarely specified; the reader must provide his own conventional sense of the differences involved. The identifications themselves, though the element emphasized, are never presented with intellectual precision; they are rather an emotion of oneness, an evoked surprise that the things one thought of as basically different may be felt to be the same. If the reader hesitates, if he analyzes a claimed identification, if he criticizes the thought instead of the rhetorical effectiveness, he will forfeit the delight which is Burke's aim and waste his own astuteness. There is little point to a sentence-by-sentence or association-by-association criticism of Burke's thought. He is rarely right or wrong; most of his statements are conspicuously too general to be called in question. From many perspectives, his words are flawed, but they work for his purpose, they evoke the delighted sense of oneness in the reader who gives himself up, passively and uncritically, to their movement. It is academic and perverse to ask more of Burke, just because one asks something else of himself. The rhetoric is extraordinary, and, if its effectiveness has dwindled in recent years, one wonders if it is not because too many of his critics have asked him to be other than he is or because his disciples have praised him for something he is not.

Burke was born in 1897, in Pittsburgh, went to Ohio State and Columbia for his academic training, and began his career as a serious writer around 1920. The essential qualities of this career may be glimpsed as early as 1932, by which time Burke's first collection of essays, *Counter-Statement*, and his novel, *Towards a Better Life*, had been published. The basic mode of his thought, connecting the diverse as identical, is foreshadowed in his enthusiastic review of Spengler's *The Decline of the West* for the *Dial* in 1926. What he likes in Spengler is his bringing together of various aspects of the most diverse cultures with a clash of identity, as in the phrase "puritan Arabs." What he dislikes is Spengler's notion that a critic in the winter of one culture cannot truly communicate with the spring of either his own culture or that of another. Differences matter for Burke mainly as the material for another ringing identification. In *Counter-Statement* he shows a similar enthusiasm for Rémy de

Gourmont's notion of the dissociation of ideas. Gourmont believed that divorce is the law of the intellect. Given two conventionally linked ideas, he analyzed them to show that they were held together by nothing essential. This method, like Spengler's, Burke felt to have an important future, especially in criticism. Its future, in Burke's writing, is a simple reversal. Surrounded by divisiveness, by specialists locked in the prisons of their own pursuits, he was to take ideas conventionally dissociated and clash them together as one. Indeed, in a later commentary on Gourmont, he claims that, though Gourmont said he was merely divorcing paired ideas, he was surreptitiously marrying other ideas at the very same time. This, of course, is what one expects of Burke: to show that even opposites, even Gourmont and Kenneth Burke, are really the same.

Burke's theory of poetry was quite fully developed in his "Psychology and Form," which was first published in 1925 in the *Dial* and then included in *Counter-Statement.* Poetry, needless to say, is rhetoric. Poetic form is eloquence and eloquence is psychology, that is, the arousal of emotion. This point, which is extended in other essays in *Counter-Statement*, entails that the poet, who is wide awake, selects a mood or emotion and then decides on certain technical devices by which he evokes the emotion in his audience. To be effective he must know the appetites and emotions of his audience, for his success depends on their being ripe for the evocation of his chosen emotion. He is the isolated magician and manipulates and hypnotizes the audience by his devices, by ringing the bells of their responses, by "saying the right thing," given their emotional makeup. The audience itself is utterly passive; it is his job to make them dream. The psychology of the audience, not of the hero of the work, is what gives it poetic form. One goes to poetry to be aroused, not to acquire information. This distinction between informative and evocative works is not characteristic of Burke. Later he will insist that even works dedicated to knowledge, works of a scientific cast, are basically rhetorical, are means of establishing an identification, say, among members of a school. Nonetheless, even in the early essay, the emphasis is on identification. Shakespeare himself is seen to be a manipulator, one who played the various stops of his audience. The porter scene in *Macbeth* is not in itself important. At that point in the play Shakespeare needed "grotesque buffoonery" to follow a scene of "grotesque seriousness." The skin, the shell, the individual texture of the scene does not concern Burke. He views the scene as simply one of any number of ways in which Shakespeare could do the essential, that is, evoke a particular emotion which he was interested in at that point because he knew it was what the audience needed. A happy bonus of this claim about Shakespeare is that he is seen as doing exactly the same thing Burke himself does in the short stories of *The White Oxen*. Those stories, at least those that work, like "Mrs. Maecenas," are calculatingly composed for their effect upon the reader.

Even the practical criticism of this period is full of anticipations of his later work. His concern for the individualizing traits of a work is subordinated to a general emotion or state of mind which he feels to be its true form. Thus, in a fine essay on Gide and Mann, having suggested that they work in opposite ways, he then surprises and delights us with the claim that they are in truth doing the same thing: "Irony, novelty, experimentalism, vacillation, the cult of conflict — are not these men trying to make us at home in indecision, are they not trying to humanize the state of doubt?" As Burke praises Gide and Mann for their efforts to shake us loose from our own rhetorical postures and to make us doubt our ultimate rightness, one recognizes that he is praising them for what will become central to his own career: the belief that a person ought to be detached from the heat of his own efforts and merged, with all, in a basic state of doubt and indecision.

If any work might represent not a paper death and rebirth of Burke the writer but a genuine transformation, it is his novel. It is, no doubt, written mainly for its effects, being a series of letters in which the only character, John Neal, is given the chance to take on the postures of lamentation, rejoicing, beseechment, admonition, moralizing, and invective. There is no plot, action, character, or scene in the usual sense of those words. The language is pure artifice, inflexible and unrelated to the events only vaguely glimpsed through the fog of its *rondeur*. There is no drama in the novel, unless it is the rhetorical drama between author and audience. All these characteristics are typical of Burke, early, middle, and late.

As Austin Warren points out, however, Burke seems more sympathetic toward his orator Neal than his preface would indicate. In fact, Neal seems to be that part of Burke's character which he would abandon as he moves toward a better life. Neal is enclosed in his own language. He records conversations with the woman he loves, and he writes directly at times to the man who wins her love. But those others are not living characters with feelings and voices of their own. Toward the end, in fact, Neal talks to others who are only projections of himself and who reply to him in his own voice. He has lost all sense of an outer world and is utterly locked within himself. Even so, he continues to write with the same well-rounded, periodic sentences and to dissect things as keenly as before. The verbalizer and analyst lives on, as Warren noted, after the man has died. Should one not infer, then, from Neal's despairing wish that he might have lived twice, and "smiled the second time," that Burke does live twice, once as the eloquent, serious, self-absorbed writer, and thereafter as a comedian? In *Counter-Statement* self-absorbed writers like Flaubert, Pater, and Gourmont find more favor with Burke than ever again. Has he not broken through his monadistic narcissism in preparation for a new interest in society, history, and the outer world? Does he not, after this novel, exhibit a humor and detachment which free him to take others as seriously as he takes himself? As a man he no doubt has always had these qualities. On rare occasions, when the subject is a close friend, he has them even in his writing. By and large, however, his writing does not exhibit them, at any period. He may range over the whole universe of thought, but is always locked in a style that bars entrance to all others, though bits and pieces of others filter through when they are serviceable. A certain solitariness, overwhelming in Neal's letters, colors almost all Burke's writing and gives it a poignancy not to be found in less serious and more facile writers of encyclopedic scope. Thus, though Burke himself, at a later time, looked back upon the novel as a *rite de passage*, it is not, in my opinion, any such emancipation. Neal, one grants, does not laugh very heartily at himself, while the later Burke is full of laughter. But even Neal is doing quite a lot of bitter laughing at others, as he exposes their pretenses. Further, at one point he explains that he is not interested in individual character, but in motives, and that "motives may be common to very different people." That is a clear and simple explanation of why so little individual character appears in any of Burke's writing. *A Grammar of Motives*, *A Rhetoric of Motives*, motives are always Burke's concern, and he thinks of them as common, as shared by people of the most diverse character.

If there is any change in Burke's career at this time, it is something like the reverse of the change undergone by Shakespeare's Richard II. Until deposed, Richard views the whole of England as though it were moved and motivated by his own whims and imaginings. After the deposition, when in prison, he recognizes that the world of his imaginings is a prison and that those outside this prison do not move according to his tune. Through 1932, Burke is aware that his world is not the world, that his interests are special and exclusive and that much experience goes on outside their range. Thereafter, though his purpose and mode of thought remain much the same, he finds that he can range everywhere by means of them and he writes as if nothing human is alien to the range of his mind.

That this actually does happen, and how it happens, may be discerned in a speech Burke gave to the American Writers' Congress in 1935. "Revolutionary Symbolism in America" is a subtle argument to the effect that the Communists should change their basic symbol from the *Worker* to the *People*. In the process of developing this point, Burke explains his conception of "the complete propagandist," and this conception is a key to all his later writings. He says that "the complete propagandist" should show interest in as many fields as he can and ally his attitudes with everything that is broadest and fullest in the world of his time. "Much explicit propaganda must be done, but that is mainly the work of the pamphleteer and political organizer. In the purely imaginative field, the writer's best contribution to the revolutionary cause is *implicit*. If he shows a keen interest in every manifestation of our cultural development, and at the same time gives a clear indication as to where his sympathies lie, this seems to me the most effective long-pull contribution to propaganda he can make. For he thus indirectly links his cause with the kinds of intellectual and emotional engrossment that are generally admired. He speaks in behalf of his cause . . . by the sorts of things he associates with it." Being wrathful and full of condemnation, Burke continues, may be justified, but the complete propagandist's "specific job as a propagandist requires him primarily to wheedle or cajole, to practice the arts of ingratiation. As a propagandizer, it is not his work to convince the convinced, but to plead with the unconvinced, which requires him to use *their* vocabulary, *their* values, *their* symbols, insofar as this is possible."

The similarity between this advice and Burke's own practice hereafter is too obvious to need emphasis. He would win his way by the sorts of things he associates with, and he associates himself with everything that has prestige in his culture — philosophies of history, the New Criticism, Freudianism, anthropology, sociology, psychology, linguistics, and theology, among other things. Further, he uses the words, values, and symbols of these fields always for an ulterior, rhetorical purpose. This may sound, indeed may be, insidious. I am not, however, suggesting that Burke's own purpose is identical with that of the Communist party or that of any other specific revolutionary movement. He is, to be sure, opposed to a competitive society and in favor of a cooperative one; but he works for this without demanding, at least most of the time, a fundamental upheaval in our economic or political structure. The important point is that by this time Burke is quite aware that he is always doing the same thing, whether he is writing of poetry, politics, philosophy, or religion. Unlike universal men of traditional cultures, like Benedetto Croce, for example, Burke does not try to write of history as a historian, logic as a logician, politics as a political scientist, language as a linguist, poetry as a literary critic, and religion as a theologian. He takes them all in his rhetorical stride, easing his way further by treating them all as forms of rhetoric themselves.

A consideration of the modes of thought and writing in his major books from 1935 on will support and explain these claims; afterwards, it should be possible to treat, with some economy, Burke's elaborate ideas about literary criticism and his multifarious essays in practical criticism. His three books published between 1935 and 1941 are consistent developments of his loosely framed program for the complete propagandist. The basic method, during this period, is denominated "perspective by incongruity." Burke himself describes this as verbal "atom cracking." "A word by custom in one category is wrenched loose and applied to another." Though this sounds more like dissociation than identification, its actual effect is to blur differences and accentuate oneness. For example, Burke affirms that Rockefeller's economic empire and Milton's epic are both "a symbolic replica" of the man's personal character. "In both cases the men 'socialized' their specific patterns of interest by the manipulation of objective materials in a way whereby the internal and the external were . . . fused." A dour critic might reply: yes, and both Rockefeller and Milton had two legs and both had eyes but could not see. But why bother to entertain oneself when Burke is so entertaining? High finance, he will tell us, is a most spiritual aspect of life. Why? It is very abstract, and so are angels. Sputter one may, but it is a jovial notion that Wallace Stevens was doing identical things as insurance executive and as poet. It is a momentary, but heartwarming joke. No one, least of all Burke, denies all the differences. He simply ignores them.

Another road into the heart of the manner of these books is Burke's modification of I. A. Richards's concept of poetry as pseudo-statement. Richards's notion is that statements are scientific and refer to external objects, whereas pseudo-statements are evocative of attitudes. This idea is undoubtedly the source of Burke's earlier distinction between informative and evocative literature. In this later period he expands the notion of pseudo-statements, with delightful abandon, much further than Richards intended. First, he rips it off the page: "A man can extract courage from a poem by reading that he is captain of his soul; he can reënforce this same statement mimetically by walking down the street as vigorously as though he were the captain of his soul." Poetry and life then are identical as rhetoric? Nay, more. Science itself is the same thing. "Yet, what is any hypothesis, erected upon a set of brute facts, but a rationalization?" Indeed, "any explanation is an attempt at socialization, and socialization is a strategy; hence, in science as in introspection, the assigning of motives is a matter of appeal." Burke will qualify these marvelous identifications by distinguishing "I am a bird" as pseudo-statement from "I am an aviator" as statement. But then he will turn about and insist that both are truly statements, because both come to terms with recalcitrant material, that of the first verbal, that of the second physical. Furthermore, though he does insist that attempts to be ingratiating may be more or less accurate, he admits that the only basis for distinguishing the more from the less accurate would be the view of "an infinite, omniscient mind," and, needless to say, that is out of our reach. Thus, even though one might debunk Richards's *Principles* by calling it a mass of pseudo-statements, he would need to add that it might as accurately be called pure statement. If reason is, finally, rationalization, it is just as accurate to say that rationalization is reason. All depends on the interests of the speaker. Burke is not a debunker, for what he lowers with one phrase, he raises with the next. He is a leveler. That is the basis of his appeal.

A limit to the sweep of these identifications might seem to be reached with Burke's distinction between the poet and the critic, at least in *Permanence and Change* (1935) and *Attitudes toward History* (1937). Burke claims that poetry is pious; that a poet can work hypnotically only in a homogeneous society, in which he may use agreed-upon labels to say the right thing and ring the bells of his audience's responses. From the Renaissance through 1900, during what Burke calls the era of da Vinci, all was called in doubt, impiously, by the endless questioning of all values. Obviously, one does not "hypnotize a man by raising a problem." This, then, was the era of criticism. The scientist treats the universe not as *being created*, but as *having been created*, and then analyzes and classifies it; so the literary critic analyzes the magic of Aeschylus and the religion of Sophocles by reducing them to a poetics, a class system of genres and rhetorical devices. Looking back on such epochal distinctions, Burke says that he was being too much a historicist during the thirties. Even during this early period, however, Burke did not rest content with the distinction between a period of poetry and a period of criticism. He will poetize his own criticism of criticism so that it is fundamentally identical with poetry. His perspectives by incongruity, indeed, carry him even further, for in the process of poetically criticizing criticism he identifies even the criticism criticized with both plain poetry and critical poetry. For example (and this is not, in the rhetorical world we are considering, a digression), Burke poetizes the practice of psychoanalysis in the following manner. A pious patient (a poet) approaches the analyst for help. The analyst cures him by impiously and rationally misnaming his distress. The cure Burke calls, with his impious piety, a secular conversion. Though Burke is criticizing psychoanalysis, he is not debunking it. It is the casting out of devils by *misnaming* them, and that is exactly what Burke says he himself is doing by means of his perspectives by incongruity. The rational effort to cure a pious man is a piously impious act. By misnaming psychoanalysis as a means for secular conversion, Burke is himself curing it of its aloof specialness. His impious piety is devoted to redeeming the piously impious curers of the pious. One may laugh at all this — and be cured, as Burke would wish.

For a moment one might have thought that Burke, like Matthew Arnold before him, had decided that he could not write poetry because he lived in a heterogeneous society riddled by doubt, and thus must turn to criticism. It soon becomes apparent, however, that Burke's criticism is just another form of poetry. Burke discovers that even his heterogeneous society is dominated by a piety, by a response of doubt, by a doubt of everything, even of the sanctity of lay conversions by psychoanalysis. With here a clang, there a clang, Burke proceeds to reduce and identify specialty after specialty and profession after profession until his reader experiences the cathartic rejuvenation of that delightful state of oneness detached from any and all specialties. Doubt itself becomes a kind of faith; skepticism becomes mysticism; science and criticism and analysis become poetic ecstasy. To top all else, Burke adds that statistics, as an attempt to extract a generalization common to all situations, also has a mystical cast to it.

Burke has his own name for the position he is advocating during this period. He calls it a "dialectical biologism," a new school merging naturalism, idealism, and dialectical materialism, all leading to a "somewhat Spinozistic conception of substance." What could be more comforting, for one and all? Nothing is omitted.

Before 1941 or so Burke's identifications are quite rowdy, as my last reference indicates. He brings together the most complex things with blithe abandon and our amusement is shocking. One arrives at his identification of poetry and criticism disruptively, only after puzzling out seeming contradictions like that between poetry as pious and metaphor as impious. In *The Philosophy of Literary Form* (1941), even though the identifications with which the work abounds are as unusual and striking as ever, they are affirmed almost as if beyond question, as if it would be unmannerly to be surprised by them. The astounding identification of poetry and criticism is here affirmed parenthetically, as the obvious sort of thing any decent reader must grant his author. One's situation and his motive, his motive and his burden of guilt, the burden and the unburdening, even the situation and the strategy to encompass it, all these are identified casually, so that one hardly sees them slip by. The machine for identifying the diverse almost seems to run by itself, as though Burke no longer simply enjoys its outrageousness, but has even come to believe in it.

Since 1941 Burke has published four major works, *A Grammar of Motives* (1945), *A Rhetoric of Motives* (1950), *The Rhetoric of Religion* (1961), and *Language as Symbolic Action* (1966). Because these books exhibit a more learned, even a more scientific, façade than his previous ones, it is important to keep in mind that for Burke science itself is but a form of rhetoric. Of the scientist he says: "One acts; in the course of acting, one organizes the opposition to one's act (or, in the course of asserting, one causes a multitude of counter-assertions to come running from all directions, like outlaws in the antique woods converging upon the place where a horn had sounded); and insofar as one can encompass such opposition, seeing the situation in terms of it, one has dialectically arrived thus roundabout at knowledge." This master of outlaws, the scientist even when at work in his laboratory, is just another version of the "complete propagandist." In these later books the opposition which Burke would encompass is indeed formidable. What is the magic with which he would tame these speaking beasts, these philosophers, men of action, poets, and even New Critics? Tasso's Rinaldo exorcized the wicked spirits from the "antica selva" only after climbing the Mount of Olives and receiving an influx of divine grace. The influx of ingratiation which assists Burke in his new trial and conquest is implicit in what becomes his favorite phrase, *in terms of*. That obnoxious cliché has genuine meaning in Burke's later works. What it implies, simply and consistently, is that whatever he considers, even if it is the most arduous philosophical argument, is viewed as no other than a set of words, a terminology.

This strategy is a very keen one, especially as used in *A Grammar of Motives*: to reduce all philosophy to the manipulation of terms. Burke accomplishes this reduction by means of his own terminology, a pentad made of the words *scene*, *act*, *agent*, *agency*, and *purpose*. He reduces all philosophy to five species, and each species is placed under the sign of one of his terms: materialism under scene, idealism under agent, mysticism under purpose, realism under act, and pragmatism under agency. All philosophies are the same in the sense that, though each features only one of the five terms, all try to account for the other four terms in the rhetorical juggling of their nomenclatures. Burke uses his terms in a purely rhetorical way, although he calls his pentad dramatistic. He does not attempt to define and delimit the meanings of his terms, but uses them as having whatever traditional meanings dictionaries record for them, varying his use of those meanings according to his occasion and interest. Although he refers to the relationships among the five terms as "ratios," he never analyzes these ratios, but considers them rather vaguely as forms of "overlapping." Further, although he admits that each type of philosophy tends to account for other terms besides its featured one, Burke's interest is to claim that realism, under the sign of *act*, accounts for all five terms more effectively than the other types do. Thus, in his consideration of two forms of realism, that of Aquinas and that of Marx, he shows how they can account for all five terms. There is no question of arguing for his preference; he simply devotes more space to the expansiveness of what he prefers than to that of the others.

The differences among the types of philosophy are spurious, so that, if a reader attends to them, he will become entangled in fruitless quarreling with Burke. The quarreling will be fruitless because it mistakes appearance for reality. The reality of *A Grammar of Motives* is the marvelously facile technique with which Burke reduces all philosophical thought to the sameness of terminological manipulation. No introductory textbook of philosophy has ever reduced its subject matter to a series of formulas half so effectively as Burke does in this book.

Arduous conceptual thought and the juggling of terms, in truth, have little in common. A serious philosopher works out his thought as an action quite distinct from the act of giving that thought a verbal shape. The act of thought is fundamentally nonrhetorical, is only minimally a verbal presentation. While he is thinking, a philosopher no doubt will, some more and some less, use notations, various forms of shorthand, to record the movement of his thought. Only thereafter will he strive to formulate his thought in words. Even this second act, however, is not primarily rhetorical. Its purpose is to assist others in their efforts to understand the original movement of thought which logically and, usually, even chronologically precedes the philosopher's verbal articulation. It is these distinctions, within the labor of philosophy itself and between it and other forms of labor, like poetry and rhetoric, which Burke studiously ignores. It is by means of this cunning ignorance that Burke is able to sweep across the centuries of philosophy with minimal thought himself and with maximal rhetorical efficacy.

Philosophers use even common words in special ways. If a philosopher would succeed in sharing his thoughts, the very act of his mind, with his readers, he must define his words scrupulously so that they cannot be taken in their conventional designations. The very last thing he can do, even if he is a common-language philosopher, is simply give himself up to the words he uses, and allow all their ambiguous, and often contradictory, meanings to function equally. Burke, however, does exactly that, giving himself up to his key words with abandon; further, he insists that the philosophers he uses for illustration must and actually do give themselves up to their words in the same fashion. As a result, if *A Grammar of Motives* were read as serious philosophy, it would no doubt provoke a riot (as it almost does, even in the review of that most gracious philosopher Abraham Kaplan). Read properly, the book should not provoke a riot, but should be a riotous experience, occurring under the sign of comedy. A few examples of what is going on should suffice. When Hobbes uses the word *action* in a precisely defined way, he is doing exactly what his job requires of him. Burke says, however, that Hobbes's usage is improper. Hobbes is a materialist; he reduces human action to motion; thus he cannot use the word *action* at all without contradicting his philosophy. Why not? The argument is absurd unless one recognizes that for Burke all writers, even the philosopher, are merely functions of their words, and their words are full of all the meanings that they have acquired over the centuries.

In another passage, which might be mistaken for philosophical thought, Burke discusses the Kantian (never Kant's) universal, "the object." He says, "the surprising thing . . . is that you can't distinguish it from *no object at all.*" "I realized this when . . . the attempt to represent the appearance of an object in general, in order to show how it was related eventually to an unseen thing-in-itself, led to the embarrassing discovery that such an object in general would be as impossible to represent as would the unseen thing-in-itself that by definition lies beyond the realm of sense relationships." Did Kant think "the object" could be represented? That is beside the point. Not the thought of Kant, but Burkean association is the intended source of our entertainment. Burke's delight is in being able to say that Kantian terms are "all about nothing." He then proceeds: "If, then, you would talk profoundly and intelligently about the conditions of the possibility of the knowledge of nothing, what *do* you have that you can talk about? You have the knower." Can that have been the movement of Kant's thought? Even Burke could not claim that, or even that it is the movement of any thought at all, since he has already pointed out that the Kantian agent, the knower, has been universalized and thus is as much "nothing" as the "object" is. The "object" and the "knower" are equally as available or unavailable for "talk about nothing." Does this confusion rob Burke's book of its value? Not at all. His purpose here is not thought, but placement. He is placing Kant, as idealist, under the sign of the agent and has accomplished his purpose. What he is doing is consistently like this: he brings together, as identical, idealism, technology, applied science, knowledge, the problem of knowledge, the epistemological problem, and a psychologistic emphasis, all falling "under the head of agent." A chain of identifications like this defies analysis, but is a fanciful delight.

The philosophy of *A Grammar of Motives*, if it can be said to have one, is not at all a philosophy of action; it is rather a curious kind of panverbalism which may be summed up in this climactic assertion: "The great departures in human thought can be eventually reduced to a moment where the thinker treats as *op*posite, key terms formerly considered *ap*posite, or *v.v.*" That Burke's preference for *action* in the discussion of that most common element of human experience, motives as he conceives of them, is of a verbalistic nature is unmistakably clear. He affirms himself that his preference for *act* over the other terms of his pentad is, at bottom, a preference for verbs over nouns. Verbs are preferable because they are most abstract, because it is harder to represent or visualize a verb like *running* or *putting* than a noun like *tree* or *bush*. The more abstract a word is, the more it lends itself to summing things up; and, of course, Burke's very concern for motives is primarily a concern for summing things up, for "lumping the lot."

The *bête noire* of *A Grammar of Motives* is all philosophy placed under the sign of agency, all pragmatism and especially the operationalism of P. W. Bridgman. Burke opposes this kind of philosophy because it tends to impose "one doctrine of motives," a doctrine of agency or means, "upon a world composed of many different motivational situations." This is a form of fanaticism, fanaticism itself being one of the two alternatives which Burke recognizes to his own efforts. The other alternative he calls dissipation: "By dissipation I mean the isolationist tendency to surrender, as one finds the issues of world adjustment so complex that he turns to the satisfactions nearest at hand." Even here, the stated alternatives collapse under the force of Burke's zest for identification. To reduce all human experience to a matter of terms, especially to reduce philosophy to mere terms, to terms which are so clearly only its means, its instruments, its agency, is surely a form of technological fanaticism of the first order. It is also a form of isolationist dissipation, as the passage on Kant, discussed above, manifests. To reduce Kant's thought to a set of terms is palpably, for a writer of Burke's dedication, to turn "to the satisfactions nearest at hand." Burkean panverbalism is not in opposition to his conception of operationalism, but identical with it.

One of the major mergers going on in both the *Grammar* and the *Rhetoric* is the merger of classification and dialectics. These forms of thought are strictly incompatible, as both R. G. Collingwood and A. J. M. Milne have amply demonstrated. Classification does not attend to individuals as such, but only to particular attributes which they exhibit and which it abstracts from them. All the books on this shelf have the attribute of being bound in paper; they belong to the abstract universal of paperbound books. The individual books are what is real, but they function, in a classificatory system, only as what exhibits the particular instances of a universal, being paperbound. Further, the specific forms of a generic attribute are mutually exclusive. Each of the books on these shelves is either paperbound or clothbound; it cannot be both. Finally, the higher the level of classificatory abstraction, the larger the class which possesses an attribute, the less determinate that attribute will be. The bigger an abstraction, the less it reveals about any individual thing. The primary concern of dialectics, in contrast, is to synthesize the universal and the individual in what is called a concrete universal. Dialectics is not abstractive; it works toward the individualization of a normative universal like rational activity or rhetorical activity. It attempts to show that an individual action, in all the richness of its individuality, is a realization of a universal form. Furthermore, unlike the species of a genus, the subforms within a universal form of activity are not mutually exclusive in dialectical thought. Ethical activity, for instance, is more than utilitarian or self-expressive activity, but it includes those inferior activities within itself as subforms essential to its own nature.

Now the common form of Burke's thought is classificatory. He begins, not with individuals, but with particular attributes, and works his way upward. But he merges this, almost at once, with a blurring and fusing of attributes which, in a classificatory system, would rightly be mutually exclusive. Thus, he arrives at the pinnacle of a ladder of thought with a universal which is invariably abstract (like his word *act*). The sharply distinguished attributes characteristic of a classificatory pyramid and the purity and cleanness both of its master abstractions and the hierarchies subsumed beneath them have been dissolved by Burke's pseudodialectics into a muddled conglomeration of free-floating attributes that slide in and out of each other, after the manner of random association. Such equivocal merging would ruin both classifier and dialectician. But it works with brilliant efficacy, especially in *A Rhetoric of Motives*, as Burke merges everything he touches into his major terms of Identification, Hierarchy, and Mystery. Indeed, Burke is at his best and purest in the *Rhetoric*, sweeping together, in swirl after swirl, the most diverse writers conceivable. Of all his books, this is no doubt the most vigorous and brilliant. In confusions of massive proportions, he brings together the pair Bentham-Richards and the pair Cicero-Longinus, and Marx and Carlyle, Mannheim and Plato, Castiglione and La Rochefoucauld, and the crime mysteries of Hollywood with a society of specialists serving one another. When he arrives, near the end, at his hymn to Pure Persuasion, to beseechment for itself alone, as pure, abstract form, one feels, as never before, the almost charismatic power of his ingratiating triumph over clarity of thought and diversity of action.

In *The Rhetoric of Religion*, in contrast, the fires of his genius burn low. Herone Liddell, transparent mask for Burke himself in his novella of 1957, has a hernia operation which provokes much troubled talk about a castration complex. A sense of sterility pervades the writing of *The Rhetoric of Religion*. In a long analysis of Augustine's *Confessions*, Burke reduces the passionate imagining and remembering and speculating of that beautifully whole man to the driest form of crafty rhetoric, the very thing Augustine most despised, after his conversion. Of course, Burke's deep purpose here is to identify the crafty rhetoric of the pagan and the candid passion of the convert and to show that they are, at bottom, the same. Words that bulge with feeling and words moved coldly as mere counters cannot be distinguished at this level of technical analysis. One may write as though castrated and sterile, but it is really the same as writing with passionate exuberance.

The purpose of Burke's analysis of the first three chapters of Genesis, in the same book, is to show that they are merely a narrative version of principles of order. The original sin, for example, is merely a narrative version of the principle of guilt. Burke is, to be sure, working with an important idea, the truth that temporal succession, that narrative development both in myth and history, is as much the construct of the human mind as logical thought is. This truth, however, does not lead to an identification of logical development and temporal development any more readily than if logic was man-made but history objectively present, there simply to be observed. But Burke drives the identification home, this time for the salutary purpose of helping theologians, with a penchant for demythologizing the Bible on their own, to feel themselves to be utterly at one with the most abstract and rational of thinkers.

Aristotle gives this example of a sophistical enthymeme: women with child are pale; this woman is pale; therefore this woman is with child. One might delight himself by reducing all Burke's writing to variations on this sophistical device. The essence of being a writer is the use of words; philosophers use words; therefore philosophy is essentially the use of words. The use of words involves ingratiation; poets use words; therefore the essence of poetry is ingratiation. Words are the signs of things; things often point to, evoke in us, words; therefore things are the signs of words. But as one toys with Burke's means, he should not lose sight of their end, which is the purifying of war, the evocation of an emotion of oneness, of all with all, in a state of pious doubt, of detachment from the causes in which men most fervently believe. If the end of Burke's Neo-Stoicism is a good, then his means are surely not the worst that might be used. Pacification may also be achieved by means of our great bombs. Burke's enthymemes are preferable, even if less efficient. Whether Burke's end, however, is the ultimate good for which one would sacrifice all else is another question.

No perspective upon poetry and criticism could be further from that of the New Critics than Burke's is. However, because Burke, as the complete propagandist, uses the values, vocabulary, and symbols most fashionable in his age, the surface of his writing sparkles with terms linking him to critics like Cleanth Brooks and R. P. Blackmur. Contributory to the confusion caused by this ingratiating device is the fact that Burke earnestly strives to be at one with even those who differ most from him. Thus, even though what matters most for Burke differs markedly from the central concerns of the New Critics, it must be recognized that an emphasis different from mine, an emphasis, say, on the surface of Burke's language, could lead to conclusions the opposite of those I propose.

For Burke, poetry is invariably a form of rhetoric. Because everything is rhetoric, this means that there is nothing special about poetry. It also means, in line with the enthymemic tendency of Burke's thought, that if poetry is rhetoric, then rhetoric is poetry. For the New Critics, no distinction is more important than that between poetry and rhetoric. Poetry is disinterested; its language is polysignificant; poetic form is individual and unique, never specific or generic; the driving force of a poem is always embodied in the poem itself as a basic feeling or shaping attitude; the poem is organic, composed of words that are interactive rather than acting upon a passive audience; and the audience of a poem are active partners who do not merely suffer the experience of the poem, but re-create that experience with an effort similar to the creative act of the poet. Rhetoric, in contrast, is interested; the rhetorician has a purpose, a principle, a state of mind, with which he begins; his piece of writing is a strategy for evoking this principle or mood or state in his audience; the writing itself is a set of devices used to achieve this end, so that its words are outer-directed rather than internally interactive; the audience is there to be worked upon, it is exposed to receive whatever the rhetorician would inject into it. As a consequence of this distinction, when a New Critic criticizes poetry, he attends to the poem above all else; as for the poet, he is important mainly as the shaping, active spirit within the poem. Although the critic is willing to consider biographical, social, and political aspects of the poet's life, since they may enter into the action of the poem, he invariably treats them as subordinate to, as transformed by, the shaping action of the poem. If the New Critic descends to analyze a piece of rhetorical writing, as he only rarely does, he treats it as a set of devices the value of which is extrinsic, in the purpose of the writer and in the effect desired. Rhetorical form he treats as generic rather than individual; given a purpose, a desired effect, the rhetorician is viewed as using one type of form, one set of devices, rather than another. Individual elements are incidental and could be replaced, without loss of value, just so long as the substitutes belong to the same type and thus would work for the same effect.

Burke does not share this distinction between poetry and rhetoric. More important, though he does not share it, neither does he oppose it; that is, he simply ignores the distinction, never arguing against it and merely assuming its nonexistence. As early, for example, as *The Philosophy of Literary Form*, he says that poetry is basically a strategy to encompass a situation. If a New Critic were to use these terms, he would argue that in poetry all strategies and situations are internal to the poetic action and that this action itself cannot be treated as a strategy to come to terms with some specific situation outside the poem. Rhetorical strategies, in contrast, are, precisely, means and devices to come to terms with an outer situation which can be analyzed and understood only if one studies not the rhetoric alone, but also its historical context. When referring to poetry, Burke blurs the distinction between outer and inner situation and seems unaware of any difference between strategies within a poem and the over-all work as either a strategy or a poetic action. Indeed, he never shows interest in any work as an individual, poetic whole. He may connect a strategy in a poem to something situational either within the poem or outside the poem. Or he may treat a strategy within a poem as though it were the strategy of the whole poem and then connect it with some outer situation.

Because the New Critical conception of poetry accentuates the individual form of a poem, the New Critics, like Croce, give little attention to genres, and they refuse to set up a critical methodology which can be used on any and all poems. The form of a poem determines the method of criticism appropriate to it; since each genuine poem has its own form, it calls for a criticism that is distinctively linked to it and it alone. Having no interest in individual form, Burke elaborates a critical methodology, with the tracing of clusters of words and images and the listing of the elements in a work according to such generalizations as "what goes with what," "what versus what," and "from what to what." He does this, he says, so that he "will not be called idiosyncratic or intuitive." His reason, however, is less servile and more serious than that. He is always concerned with reducing the work to a motive. His lists assist him in breaking down the realized poetic action so that he can move off to some psychological archetype, some general motive. This motive, Burke feels, is often of a physical nature, some uneasiness concerning urination or defecation or sexual orgasm. The poet writes in order to socialize his uneasiness, to make it respectable by evoking the same uneasiness in his audience. Or the motive may be to make the audience delight in technique itself, to satisfy them by arousing an expectation and then fulfilling it. (This is what Burke means by "Pure Poetry.") Or the poet's motive may be of a political nature, to wheedle the audience into accepting the status quo or to harangue them into working for a revolution. Or, indeed, all these motives may be working at once. Whatever the motive, in any case, as Burke sees it the poem is doing something for author and audience. Because the poem is always a means, the critic is bent upon reducing it, whether to an author's anxiety over his drug addiction or to the types of devices of which the elements of the poem are merely instances or to some specific effect to be realized in an audience.

Although this theory seems consistent and consistently at odds with the New Criticism, in *Language as Symbolic Action* Burke becomes quite explicit about the fact that he has never recognized any real difference between the New Critics and himself. His desire for identification, as always, is a deeper consistency than that of any particular theory he may espouse. As his essay "Formalist Criticism: Its Principles and Limits" shows, Burke knows that Brooks, Blackmur, and Wellek recognize no such identification; but he thrives on trying to convince the unconvinced. His strategy is to adopt the terms central to the criticism of Cleanth Brooks, terms like Form, Unity, and Internal Consistency, but to ignore the ideas that lie behind Brooks's use of the terms. He ignores the fact that for Brooks these terms are both descriptive and normative; and the fact that Brooks's notion of Form is individual, not generic as it is for him; and the fact that for Brooks Form is a synthesis of form (as used by rhetorical critics of the past and by Burke) and content; and the fact that Brooks conceives of poetic unity, not as some abstract principle, as simply one of many ingredients in a work, but as a unique sense of existence that unfolds in the evolvement of the poem and that synthesizes all its parts, from the slightest details to its most general traits, into a unique totality. The terms, but not the meanings, of the New Critics are what he adopts.

Such strategic ignorance permits Burke to use the terms in his own way, just as if he were using them as Brooks uses them. All internal criticism, he claims, is poetics, is the study of various devices used in a poem. Form, as he uses it, is a matter of audience expectancy: it may be progressive, repetitive, or conventional. Internal consistency is unrelated to the individual totality of a poem; it is but one principle at work in any poem and may exist side by side with perversions and deviations from it. Unity itself is just one more principle or device in a poem; and an inferior work may "be better unified than a superior one, simply because it did not encounter such great problems of control." Each of these terms is emptied of its poetic meaning and reduced to its meaning as a rhetorical device. Burke's next strategic move is to claim that it is not enough to attend merely to the poetics of a poem, that one ought to consider its personal and social aspects too. Of course, the New Critics do attend to those aspects of a poem, but because their conception of poetic form is integrative and individual, they attend to them as internal to the poem. Since for Burke form and unity are abstract devices, he must go outside them, outside formalism and poetics, in order to find anything personal or social that has relevance to the poem. Because of this and because he has reduced poetic formalism to rhetorical formalism, he can now say that the New Critics would be unduly narrow if they neglected all but matters of form. Since, furthermore, the New Critics do not limit themselves to formal matters, if such matters are defined rhetorically, but also consider personal and social elements, though always as working within the poem, Burke can then say, with what must be keen pleasure, that the New Critics are not at all the formalists they claim to be. They attend to matters extrinsic to form, just as Burke does. That they do not go sifting about the private diaries or intimate letters of a poet, as Burke does, to find things of personal importance, but find them working effectively within the poem, is another distinction which Burke studiously ignores. He concludes, in a state of mock bepuzzlement: since the New Critics practice both extrinsic and intrinsic criticism, just as Burke himself does, how can they criticize and condemn his procedures?

The subjects of the best of Burke's practical criticism which is consistent with his idea that all writing is rhetorical are, reasonably enough, of an overtly rhetorical nature. Emerson, Nietzsche, Marx, and Veblen, among others whom Burke considers, form strategies to encompass actual, historical situations. There is no need to fancy some hidden motive or to imagine a nonexistent audience in order to make the claim that writing such as theirs is truly rhetorical. The relations between situation and strategy, in their writings, are clear, close, and significant. Burke's essay on the Constitution of the United States, as the "representative anecdote" of the *Grammar*, is an impressive analysis of the difficulties which arise when the historical situation to which the Constitution is being applied differs from that which it was originally framed to counter. "War, Response, and Contradiction," the finest essay in *The Philosophy of Literary Form*, is a study of an argument between Archibald MacLeish and Malcolm Cowley concerning the kind of book which ought to be written, in the 1930s, about World War I. He agrees with Cowley that it is less important to tell things as they were than to tell things in such a way as to help prevent the outbreak of another war. But he opposes Cowley in agreeing with MacLeish that to write of World War I as it was, as a human war with its horrible aspects, is more effective propaganda than to write of it as though it were an unmitigated horror story. The value of the essay is limited by the fact that what appears to be Burke's subtlest thinking is all to be found in MacLeish's own essay, though in a less emphatic form. Nonetheless, Burke's rhetorical balancing of the mediocre arguments of his friend, Malcolm Cowley, and the brilliant arguments of MacLeish is a masterpiece of delicacy.

When Burke's subject matter is genuine poetry, his practice is less effective, so long as he remains faithful to his general theory and methodology. Much of this criticism is typological, the subsumption of a poem under some class term. "It is a beauteous evening, calm and free," for example, is described in the *Grammar* as featuring the ratio between scene (the evening) and agent (Dear Child! dear Girl!). To make his point, Burke ignores the speaking voice of Wordsworth himself, the poetic action which is an intricate linking of the poet's ecstatic response to evening and his awareness that the "dear Girl" appears untouched by the scene. A similar blindness vitiates his effort to subsume "Composed upon Westminster Bridge" under the lyrical genre, in contrast to the dramatic. Burke is so concerned to show that, as a lyric, the sonnet is static, is lacking in all action, that he ignores the dramatic action of the lines themselves, the subtle development of the poet's thoughts and feelings as he observes London in the early morning light.

Burke's best known criticism — where the influence of Freud is most obvious — is the reduction of poems to some burden of guilt. In *The Philosophy of Literary Form*, he strives so to exhibit the clusters in Coleridge's poetry linking Sara, his wife, with a marriage problem, and that, in turn, with Coleridge's political interests in Pantisocracy, and that, again, with snakes and the poet's drug addiction, that he wholly misses the hilarious, poetic movement of "The Eolian Harp." In that poem, Coleridge sits, on an evening, with his wife and expatiates on the cosmic oneness suggested by what they can see in the surrounding scene. At the end of the poem, in response to a rebuke from Sara, Coleridge shamefacedly apologizes for his exuberance. For Burke, this is simply the raising of the marriage problem, whereupon he goes sailing off into other skies; whereas, in the poem itself, it is the delightful realization that the poet's philosophizing about cosmic oneness was in truth a rather scholarly and involuted form of making love to the woman beside him. Sara sees through the subterfuge, Coleridge confesses to her insight, though again in a most abstract form, and the poem concludes on a playfully pious note of solemnity. Burke's most famous essay, his analysis of the "Ode on a Grecian Urn," which is to be found in both *A Grammar of Motives* and *Perspectives by Incongruity*, is weakened by a similar distractedness on Burke's part. He is so occupied with the idea that the poem is a symbolic action, a symbol of the alternating chill and fever of Keats's sickness, and with the various shifts from scene to act, and with some big identifications, like that between the theme of the second stanza and the Wagnerian *Liebestod* and Shakespeare's *The Phoenix and the Turtle* and a letter from Keats to Fanny Brawne, that he is insensitive to the style and movement of the poem itself. Throughout the poem Keats is bringing together his response to the beauty of the urn and his questioning of the significance of its beauty in relation to the actual world. Burke guts the questioning by calling it merely rhetorical; as a result, he cannot make contextual sense of Keats's identification of truth and beauty. He says that making contextual sense of a poem is just a game. He must be doing more serious things, like reducing "Beauty is Truth" to "Poetry is Science," or, as he later does, like transposing some letters and changing others, in a Joycean manner, so that the phrase becomes "Body is Turd."

The trouble with scatological reduction, an instrument more and more frequently used in Burke's later criticism, is that our language for secret and shameful aspects of bodily experience, at least those parts of that language which Burke draws upon, is extremely crude and undeveloped. Using such language has a momentary shock value, but this is canceled out by the fact that it reduces the delicacy and intricacy and subtlety of a poem to its crudest possible analogues.

Another major area of Burke's criticism is his treatment of Shakespearean drama as social and political persuasion. This criticism depends largely upon Burke's fanciful and unhistorical notions about the nature of Shakespeare's audience. His analysis of *Julius Caesar*, in "Antony on Behalf of the Play," hinges on his identification of the audience of the play with the Roman mob inside the play. When Antony persuades the mob to be loyal to him as the "Caesar principle," he is really persuading the audience to be loyal to Queen Elizabeth. In the scene before Antony's speech, Shakespeare makes it clear to his audience, but not to the mob, that Antony is irreconcilably opposed to Brutus and the other assassins. As a result, the audience could not be passively swayed by Antony's rhetoric as the Roman mob is. Burke, however, has too much faith in rhetoric and too little in Shakespeare's audience to be affected by this complication.

In a more elaborate analysis, of *Othello* (published in *Perspectives by Incongruity*), Burke's treatment of Othello and Iago as two halves of one motive and of all the characters as rhetorical topics, as means used to advance the rhetorical act of persuasion that is the play, depends upon a neglect of the central value of individual, human character for Shakespeare and, so far as we can tell, for his audience. The weakest of his Shakespearean studies, that of *Antony and Cleopatra* (in *Language as Symbolic Action*) is based upon the phrase "The Ostentation of our love" as "an excellent formula for the sweeping poetic devices whereby, in this play, the naked physiology of sex is so grandly adorned." The movement of the play, for Burke, is this: the audience is deceived by the showiness of Antony and Cleopatra; at the end, when Cleopatra dies as a common woman, the audience is undeceived and recognizes that the ostentation was a sham. In fact, Cleopatra is both common and great from the beginning to the end of the play. Burke gets at his point, of affirming that the greatness of her love is a mere semblance for the raw bodiliness of sex, only by adopting the cold, brutal stance of Octavius Caesar and by viewing the whole play from that point of view. Nowhere else is he led so far astray by his belief in Shakespeare as a cold manipulator.

Burke's weakest essays of criticism are those in which he is mainly compiling lists. These essays, the one on Whitman and the one on Joyce's "The Dead," to name only two, are merely preparatory; in them we move "in and about the workshop." Burke is apt to intersperse asides like "Where are we now?" as though he really does not know, and he may conclude by saying, "Frankly, I don't know what all this adds up to." Their quality is summed up by Burke's claim, in the essay on "The Dead," that a critic can never discuss the quality of a work and that all must go to the story itself for that.

Burke's finest criticism is to be found in three essays in which he abandons his rhetorical schemes, and even the idea that what he is reading is rhetoric, and strives to capture the peculiar aesthetic quality of the poems he discusses. These are essays on the poetry of his friends Marianne Moore, Theodore Roethke, and William Carlos Williams. Even in these essays, in which Burke seeks out the tentativeness and contractility of Miss Moore's poetry and explores the *tactus eruditus* of Williams and the vegetal radicalism of Roethke, the basic mode of thought is associational revery. But the subjects of his revery are objects of love, not objects to be dismembered and swallowed; they are objects the beauty of which he would exhibit as it is in itself, not objects to be distorted for hortatory purposes. Of the essays on Roethke and Williams, he says: "my memory of voice and manner is imperious in ways that I have not been able to indicate." He has, nonetheless, indicated enough of their voice and manner, and of that of Marianne Moore, to reveal the fundamental weakness, by contrast, of his other criticism. Of these three writers, whom he knew as persons, he has virtually nothing to say concerning secret burdens of guilt or scatological underpinnings. There is too much respect for their actuality to permit any such destructive maneuvers.

Although these essays are uncharacteristic of Burke, they do exhibit a talent which is characteristic of most of his writing — that is, his marvelous facility with language and that freedom with which he puts words together in the most unconventional and undisciplined ways. At last, in these essays, he finds a purpose worthy of his agile talent. Given objects of genuine love, Burke was prepared, as few critics have been, to do justice to those objects. Not his verbal techniques, but the absence of an ultimately significant purpose is the limitation in so much of his writing. Once guided by such a purpose, once gripped by the living manner and voice of a poet, qualities which are present in all great poetry but which Burke could hear only when he knew the makers of the poetry in person, he could articulate his love of poetry with rare insight and precision and delicacy. Three choice essays, for all that mountain of labor? It would be enough. But, of course, there is much more. Though it may be of lesser value, being rhetorical rather than poetic, it is of immense importance for a mass culture, as possibly the finest effort of our time to make unified sense of the multifarious world as it is, as it is given to us to endure.

NATHAN A. SCOTT, JR.

REINHOLD NIEBUHR

"MAN has always been his most vexing problem. How shall he think of himself?" These are the opening lines of the Gifford Lectures which Reinhold Niebuhr delivered at the University of Edinburgh in the spring and autumn of 1939, and they identify the theme that unified all his thought and writing, even as early as the 1920s, when he first appeared on the national scene as the young pastor of a Detroit congregation of the Evangelical Synod who was projecting a critique of both religion and modern culture more radical than anything that had yet emerged from liberal Protestantism. What is the proper estimate of man? This was Niebuhr's fundamental question. As he said in his Gifford Lectures, "The obvious fact is that man is a child of nature, subject to its vicissitudes, compelled by its necessities, driven by its impulses, and confined within the brevity of the years which nature permits its varied organic forms, allowing them some, but not too much, latitude. The other less obvious fact is that man is a spirit who stands outside of nature, life, himself, his reason and the world." He stands, in other words, at a point of juncture between nature and spirit: he is subject to all the brutal contingencies of nature and history; and yet, in the incalculable reaches of his freedom, he has the capacity to stand outside the forces of nature and to subdue them to his purposes. And not only does man's radical freedom permit him to transcend the necessities of nature and every concretion of historical circumstance: he can also transcend himself, making himself the object of his own knowledge, of his own judgment and forgiveness — and deception. When the full human truth is collapsed into some simplistic formula that over-stresses either man's uniqueness and dignity or his affinity with the world of nature and his misery, then the consequence, inevitably, is some fatuity which is irrelevant to the real complexity of things. This was the fundamental insight at the core of Reinhold Niebuhr's entire thought, and it provided the controlling principle of the theological work and the brilliant forays into social and political criticism that made him a figure of commanding importance in American intellectual life from the late 1920s until the time of his death in 1971.

In an autobiographical essay published in 1956, Niebuhr spoke of the central interest of his life as having been "the defense and justification of the Christian faith in a secular age, particularly among what Schleiermacher called Christianity's 'intellectual despisers.' " And this was indeed the principal focus of his career. But, unlike Schleiermacher at the beginning of the nineteenth century, Niebuhr did not approach the characteristic intellectual expressions of his age from the premise that *anima humana naturaliter Christiana*; and thus he did not understand his task to be one of identifying what is already proximately Christian in the major secular philosophies of the modern period with which the Christian faith finds itself in contention: the field of "apologetics" did not, in other words, in its traditional form, provide the basic emphasis of his thought and writing. Like his distinguished European colleagues in theology, Emil Brunner and Karl Barth, his deepest conviction was that the Christian estimate of man is truer and profounder than any of its secular alternatives, whether classical or modern; and his chief concern, therefore, was to accomplish such a transvaluation of modern secularity as might disarm his contemporaries into a fresh apprehension of the cogency and relevance to their condition of the analysis of the human quandary implicit in Biblical faith.

But Niebuhr has also wanted to keep a lively awareness of "the falsehoods and corruptions which may use a final truth as their instrument in actual history." The genuinely prophetic cast of his mind always kept him alert to the necessity of bringing "the judgment of Christ to bear as rigorously on the household of faith as on the secular and the pagan world, even as the prophets of Israel were as severe in mediating the divine judgment upon Israel as upon Babylon." In this connection, he was particularly critical of two recurrent temptations in the history of the Church — the one to establish as an absolute some special status quo in the social or economic order (in the name of the eternal verities of faith); and the other to take up an obscurantist attitude toward the intellectual disciplines of culture.

Indeed, it was his stringently iconoclastic stance — vis-à-vis at once Schleiermacher's "cultured despisers of religion" and his "religious despisers of culture" — that conditioned Niebuhr toward a way of doing theology that was essentially polemical. And it was this penchant for polemic that kept him from producing the kind of serenely architectonic system of theology that was possible for a Protestant thinker like Paul Tillich or such a Catholic theologian as Lionel Thornton. The whole texture and drive of his thought were "dialogical"; for him, Christianity wins the deepest kind of self-knowledge only as it risks the rough-and-tumble of radical encounter with its chief competitors. And, in his own work, he never had any great predilection for the stricter forms of systematic theology.

It is just his tendency to conceive the work of Christian theology in polemical terms that makes it exceedingly difficult for his interpreters to specify the genre that most accurately describes the rich and enormous body of his published work. Was he primarily a specialist in the application of theological perspectives to the issues of social ethics? Is he properly viewed in the terms in which he was regarded by men like Walter Lippmann and Hans Morgenthau and George Kennan and by many secular intellectuals, as one whose principal role was that of practical strategist and theoretical interpreter of politics? Or do others, such as Arthur Schlesinger, Jr., and Charles Frankel and Will Herberg, reach a better vantage point in more spaciously conceiving his role as that of philosopher of history? These are undoubtedly all views that are arguable and that are indeed partially validated by the leadership that Niebuhr gave to such organizations as the Congress for Cultural Freedom, the Americans for Democratic Action, the Liberal party in New York State; by the profound impact of his political thinking on the State Department's Policy Planning Staff in the 1940s; by the volumes of social and political criticism that he contributed to such organs of the national intelligence as the *Atlantic Monthly*, *Harper's*, the *Yale Review*, the *Sewanee Review*, the *Virginia Quarterly Review*, *Partisan Review*, the *American Scholar*, the *Nation*, the *New Republic*, the *New Leader*, and the *Reporter*; by his editorship of the fortnightly paper *Christianity and Crisis*; and by many of his books — notably *Moral Man and Immoral Society* (1932), *Christianity and Power Politics* (1940), *The Nature and Destiny of Man* (the two volumes of his Gifford Lectures, published in 1941 and 1943), *The Children of Light and the Children of Darkness* (1944), *Faith and History* (1949), *The Irony of American History* (1952), *Christian Realism and Political Problems* (1953), and *The Structure of Nations and Empires* (1959).

But, delving beneath all the rich multiplicity of theme that his thought presents, the interpreter of Niebuhr has finally to reckon with that in his work which gives body and substance to everything else, and this is the analysis of the fundamental constitution of *humanitas* — of the mysterious heights and depths of *human being* — that forms his whole sense of reality. He stands in that great line of Christian thinkers — stretching from Augustine to Pascal and from Kierkegaard to Berdyaev — whose principal preoccupation is with anthropology, with the doctrine of man. And his eminence in American cultural life is in large part a consequence of the brilliance and passion with which he rendered the intricate tableau of man's historical existence. It is he, indeed, more than anyone else who (in the period of his lifetime) reinstated for the intellectual community in the United States a sense of the peculiar kind of toughness and grandeur that are possible for the Christian vision. And there is perhaps no other American thinker of the recent past (excepting Paul Tillich, as a German *émigré*) whose work is so capable of competing for our attention with great European systematicians like Jaspers and Heidegger or with those — such as Faulkner and Camus and Sartre and Auden — who have expressed the most vital poetic vision of our period.

Though Niebuhr's thought moves most deeply within the dimension of theological anthropology, it was always hammered out in the process of his responding to whatever presented itself as problematic in the social and political environment of his time. In this connection, one feels that his first great formative experience occurred during the years in Detroit (1915–28) when, as a young parson, the blighting effect upon human life of modern industrialism, as it was manifest in the vast automobile manufactory of Henry Ford, began to focalize for him the crisis of the person in an advanced technocratic civilization. After his birth in Wright City, Missouri, in the summer of 1892, as the third son and fourth child of the Reverend Gustav Niebuhr and his wife Lydia, his boyhood was spent first in St. Charles, Missouri, and then in Lincoln, Illinois, the places where his father had the major part of his career as a pastor of the Evangelical Synod (a small Lutheran denomination which merged with a Calvinist communion in 1934 to form the Evangelical and Reformed Church, this in turn merging with the Congregationalists in 1956 to form the United Church of Christ). And then, after four years at Elmhurst College (in Elmhurst, Illinois) and three at Eden Theological Seminary in Missouri, he had two years in the Divinity School of Yale University, which awarded him the M.A. degree in the spring of 1915. So, in taking up his work that autumn as the minister of the Bethel Evangelical Church in Detroit, he was having his first encounter with life in a large industrial metropolis. And here it was, in Detroit — in the years following World War I, when the motor car industry was in the flush of its first great boom — that Niebuhr, as he confronted the Ford system, began to discover the real costs, in the worker's dehumanization, of this delightful new machine with which the world had fallen in love. The Ford administration was, to be sure, loudly trumpeting their magnanimity in having instituted a five-day week and in paying a minimum wage of five dollars a day. But they said nothing of the nervous tensions that were exacted of their workers through the cunning innovations of their efficiency experts; nor did they acknowledge the long annual periods of unemployment for which no compensation was provided out of the company's reserves of a quarter of a billion dollars. As Niebuhr later remarked, "Ford was celebrated throughout the world as a great humanitarian and undoubtedly regarded himself as one." But he himself, as a working parson in Detroit, knew young men so broken by their labor in the automobile foundries that they had to spend the better part of their weekends in bed. And he had directly observed the appalling conditions of work in the factories. After visiting one of them he recorded his impressions in his diary (*Leaves from the Notebook of a Tamed Cynic*, 1929): "The heat was terrific. The men seemed weary. Here manual labor is a drudgery and toil is slavery. The men cannot possibly find any satisfaction in their work. They simply work to make a living. Their sweat and their dull pain are part of the price paid for the fine cars we all run. . . . We all want the things which the factory produces and none of us is sensitive enough to care how much in human values the efficiency of the modern factory costs."

On Niebuhr's reckoning, the claims of the Ford people to produce a cheap car of good quality were to be granted; but, increasingly in the 1920s, he came to feel that the production of this little tin lizzie entailed a rape of human personality so brutal as to make a mockery of the moral pretensions of the Ford establishment. It is not therefore surprising that his first book, *Does Civilization Need Religion?* (1927), was a direct consequence of the reflections on the predicament of the person in a technocratic society that were induced by his Detroit experience. It is pervasively imbued with alarm at the threat of depersonalization that is posed by the fundamental structures of life in an industrial civilization. The question raised in the title of the book is answered affirmatively because "the social imagination which religion, at its best, develops upon the basis of its high evaluation of personality" makes for a profound "reverence for human personality." It was a time, he felt, when the main task of social reconstruction needed to involve resistance against the tendency of a technocratic culture to make men mere functions of economic process — and in such a time, he argued, the reverence for man that is fostered by the religious imagination must be acknowledged as indispensable.

But Niebuhr was already beginning to question the relevance to the modern situation of the particular forms of the religious imagination represented by liberal Protestantism. Its social idealism — as expressed in the tradition of men like Washington Gladden, Francis Peabody, Lyman Abbott, Shailer Mathews, and Walter Rauschenbusch — had, to be sure, voiced an authentic protest against much of the moral crudity of laissez-faire capitalism, but its overreadiness to identify the shape of its own meliorism with the Kingdom of God betrayed a "psychology of defeat" and a pathetic abrogation of the distinctive office of religion in the cultural order. For "a religion which is perfectly at home in the world has no counsel for it which the world could not gain by an easier method." When, for the sake of impressing the world with its "mundane interests," religion so secularizes itself as to become merely "a kind of harmless adornment of the moral life," then it is nothing more than a dispensable excrescence. Already in the late 1920s, Niebuhr had begun to feel that something like this kind of failure had resulted from that whole impulse in liberal Protestantism that had found its characteristic expression in the Social Gospel movement. This was a style of Christian thought that prided itself on "its bright and happy worldliness," and, in permitting its commitment to any kind of transcendent religious position to be dissipated in eagerness to transform "the natural and social environment of personality," it was by way of degenerating into merely another kind of "culture-religion" and of losing its capacity for genuinely radical criticism. "Whenever religion feels completely at home in the world," said Niebuhr, "it is the salt which has lost its savor." Yet, though his book of 1927 anticipated his later and more stringent critique of theological liberalism, it was itself, fundamentally, an expression of the ethos of the liberal movement in American Protestantism — most notably perhaps in the persistence with which it took "religion" (or something called "high religion") as its main premise, Christianity being implicitly regarded as merely one expression of the *homo religiosus*.

A year after the appearance of this first book Niebuhr resigned his Detroit pastorate and went to New York City to join the faculty of Union Theological Seminary, where he was to remain until his retirement in 1960. But his removal from a parochial ministry to an academic post was in no way accompanied by any withdrawal from the arena of social action and political debate; indeed, if there was any shift in this phase of his life, it was toward a deepening of involvement. In 1929, he was serving with Paul Douglas (then a professor at the University of Chicago, and later to become a member of the United States Senate) and John Dewey on the Executive Committee of the League for Independent Political Action; he was still active in the Fellowship of Reconciliation, the leading pacifist organization on the American scene; and, in 1930, he was founding the Fellowship of Socialist Christians and running for Congress as the candidate of the Socialist party in the Morningside Heights community of New York City. And, despite all these and other activities in public life, his restless pen was fast becoming one of the most prolific in American intellectual life.

Throughout the early years in New York Niebuhr was steadily moving toward a more radical political orientation and a more conservative theological position. These were of course years — the early 1930s — of economic stoppages and social breakdown: everywhere, despite the nation's enormous productive capacity, there was grinding poverty. And the wintry bleakness that had settled down not only on the American scene but on the larger part of the Western world brought to men the sense of being somehow utterly unprotected before the irrational hazards of life in a technological culture. It was indeed a time that found its aptest description in Yeats's lines in "The Second Coming":

> Things fall apart; the centre cannot hold;
> Mere anarchy is loosed upon the world,
> The blood-dimmed tide is loosed, and everywhere
> The ceremony of innocence is drowned;
> The best lack all conviction, while the worst
> Are full of passionate intensity.

As Niebuhr contemplated the shambles, he became deeply convinced that modern liberalism, whether in its secular or in its religious version, could not be expected to provide any relevant guidance for social and political reconstruction. The secular tradition of Locke and Jefferson and Stuart Mill and John Dewey appeared to him to be very largely the ideological expression of the characteristic utopianism of bourgeois mentality, with its faith that "the egoism of individuals is being progressively checked by the development of rationality . . . and that nothing but the continuance of this process is necessary to establish social harmony. . . ." In accordance with such a faith, social injustice is believed to have its main roots in ignorance — which must itself gradually yield before the extension of enlightenment through education and before the power of moral suasion. But to suppose that justice is guaranteed by the characters of individuals rather than social systems and, in the ordering of society, to pin one's faith on the extension of scientific intelligence is to be blinded to the living actualities of politics. For, wherever there is injustice in society, there is some significant disproportion of power, and whichever group it is that constitutes the agency of exploitation can be dislodged only when power is raised against it. By the early 1930s Niebuhr had become convinced that no realistic recognition of this fact could be expected from secular idealists whose mild Pelagianism was for him most perfectly instanced in the social philosophy of John Dewey.

Nor could he find Protestant liberalism to be any less bankrupt; in fact, by now he had come to regard it as involving little more than a reinterpretation of the Christian faith in accordance with the system of secular values descending from the Enlightenment. In its identification of the Kingdom of God with that ideal society which secular idealists expected to develop through an evolutionary process, in its belief that man's natural egoism was being progressively checked through "the growth of a religiously inspired goodwill," in its simple confidence in the possibility of politically incarnating the absolute imperatives of the Gospel, in its radiant optimism about the moral plasticity of human nature, in its incorrigible habit of supposing that "if only" men would take the Sermon on the Mount seriously, then all human tensions would become easily manageable — in all this Niebuhr discerned what he took to be proof of the spiritual dependence of Christian liberals upon the secular piety of bourgeois idealism. So, in the face of the social debris of 1930, he found the Social Gospel, with its naive preachments about the "service motive," to be as incompetent and irrelevant as secular rationalism.

It was out of this profound exasperation with "the liberal culture of modernity" that his famous book of 1932 was written, *Moral Man and Immoral Society*. And its explosive effect in American theological circles has been unequaled by the impact of any other single book of the last half-century. As the English theologian Alan Richardson recalls, it seemed, "especially to those of the older generation, to be the outpouring of a cynical and perverse spirit, very far removed from the benevolent and sanguine serenity which was held to be the hallmark of a truly Christian mind." Indeed, far from laying the ground for any kind of theological reconstruction, it seemed to many of his Christian readers that Niebuhr was destroying the very possibility of a Christian philosophy, for, as Dr. Richardson says, "their dearest assumptions concerning man's perfectibility, his kinship with the divine, his natural goodness, were [being] . . . demolished with ruthless iconoclasm." But Niebuhr felt that Christianity could not be relevantly related to the malaise of modern society until it achieved an understanding of the problem of power more sophisticated than that of either secular or religious moralism. And it was toward such a sober realism that his book was poised.

To those who proposed education and scientific intelligence as the sufficient solvent of social disorder, Niebuhr wanted to say — and chiefly to John Dewey — that "while it is possible for intelligence to increase the range of benevolent impulse . . . there are definite limits in the capacity of ordinary mortals . . . to grant to others what they claim for themselves." Men simply are not as careful of the interests of their fellows as they are of their own. And the inability of reason, however highly developed, to overcome this natural sluggishness of the moral imagination makes nonsense, he declared, of the whole theory of the "cultural lag" for which the social science of the period had a great fondness — the notion that the achievement of social and political harmony waits only upon the development of "experimental procedures" in the common life commensurate with the experimentalism of the physical sciences. No, said Niebuhr, the natural egoism of social collectives is such that a tolerable justice can be achieved only by guaranteeing to each group enough power to counterbalance that of other groups by which it might be exploited. In short, his contention was that the ordering of society is a matter of *politics*, not of pedagogy.

And against the moralism of liberal Christianity, Niebuhr asserted that the ethic of *agape* represents "a final and absolute possibility which is, in some respects, equally distant from all political programs because all of them involve elements of coercion and resistance which are foreign to a commonwealth of pure brotherhood and love." The relevant norm, in other words, for political decision and social policy is not love but justice, not the uncoerced self-oblation of the Kingdom of God but the kind of mutuality that envisages a decent balance between the claims and counterclaims of the contending factions which constitute a dynamic society. To attempt to derive proximate social and political judgments from the absolute ethic of the Sermon on the Mount is merely to indulge in a sentimental perfectionism that obscures the concrete possibilities of social reformation — which never move beyond an uneasy armistice between the demands of love and the demands of competing power blocs.

The problem, then, to which *Moral Man and Immoral Society* addressed itself was the problem of power. Its most basic contention was that, though to some extent "it may be possible . . . to establish just relations between individuals . . . purely by moral and rational suasion and accommodation," in "inter-group relations this is practically an impossibility. The relations between groups must therefore always be predominantly political rather than ethical: that is, they will be determined by the proportion of power which each group possesses at least as much as by any rational and moral appraisal of the comparative needs and claims of each group." Instead of sentimental dreaming about the "beloved community" of Protestant liberal idealism, the course of responsibility, then, requires strict attention to the most judicious ways in which force may be deployed toward the end of securing a just distribution of power within the commonalty.

It was precisely his growing sense of the impossibility ever of discarding the tactics of force in the relations between nations and social classes that increasingly led Niebuhr in the early 1930s to doubt the cogency of pacifism. His book of 1932 makes it clear that, by this time, he had reached the point of having virtually to abandon his earlier commitment to the pacifist position. For, instead of making their witness simply as a way of disavowing the moral ambiguity inherent in all the more tentative norms of relative justice, American pacifists were in the habit of claiming the gospel of nonviolence (Christ-*cum*-Gandhi) to be a viable alternative at the level of *political* strategy. And though in 1932 Niebuhr was still somewhat uncertain about the possibility of validating international war, it had become apparent to him, at least in terms of the class struggle, that the more conventional forms of pacifism were but another indication of the political incompetence of Christian liberalism, of its penchant for the purity of ideals and its distaste for the practical requirements of social strategy in a morally ambiguous world. The trouble with pacifists, he had come to feel (as he was to say a few years later to the Canadian Richard Roberts), was that they supposed they could live in history without sinning; their moral fastidiousness was too great to permit them to pit self-interest against self-interest as a way of achieving justice; and, in thus abdicating from the messiness of politics, they were in effect preparing to submit "to any demands, however unjust, and . . . to any claims, however inordinate." Men like the missionaries Kirby Page and E. Stanley Jones and the editor of the *Christian Century*, Charles Clayton Morrison, were calling this the "way of Jesus" or the "way of the Cross," but, for Reinhold Niebuhr, it was simply a way of contracting out of history.

In *Reflections on the End of an Era*, the book which appeared two years after *Moral Man and Immoral Society*, Niebuhr continued to argue the importance of developing a political theory which would be radical "not only in the realistic nature of its analysis but in its willingness to challenge the injustices of a given social system by setting power against power until a more balanced equilibrium of power is achieved." At this stage in his development, his reaction against the optimistic moralism of liberal Christianity was leading him toward Marxism, for here at least was a system into which there was built some sense of the recalcitrances of history, of the duplicitousness of which man is capable, and some realistic understanding of the dynamics of power in human affairs. The Marxist analysis of "the logic" of modern history struck him as essentially sound: he liked its apocalyptic melodramatism, its imagination of judgment and disaster, which more closely approximated, he felt, the spirit of Hebrew prophecy than liberalism, either secular or religious; and he, too, had begun to feel that capitalism was doomed.

Though Niebuhr on occasion chose to refer to himself in the early 1930s as a "Christian Marxist," it would in fact be erroneous to regard Marxism as having had any greater importance for him than as a kind of armory that furnished additional resources of rhetoric for the critique of liberalism. His impatience with what he took to be the bumbling of the New Deal in the first eight years of the Roosevelt administration did, to be sure, confirm his misgivings during this period about the capacity of capitalism to effect any deep reform of itself — so that, in this way, he was open to Marxist pessimism about bourgeois society. It is also true that it was not until the end of the decade that the issues of foreign policy led him to see the dangerous irrelevance of the Socialist party's isolationism; it was only then that Roosevelt's crafty expedience began to represent for him, instead of mere lack of principle, precisely the kind of realistic exercise of power that he had always regarded as the hallmark of political sagacity. Many years elapsed, in other words, before Niebuhr came round to acknowledging that the kind of mixed economy and pragmatic political program that had been elaborated under the New Deal may have been "a better answer to the problems of justice in a technical age than its critics of either right or left had assumed."

But, for all the captiousness with which he evaluated public policy in the first two terms of the Roosevelt administration, he was never in any sense a doctrinaire Marxist. Arthur Schlesinger, Jr., has brilliantly reviewed this aspect of Niebuhr's thought, reminding us of the anxiety he was expressing throughout the decade about the tendency of Communist Messianism to breed a reckless fanaticism and, through the socialization of economic power, to create an inordinate political tyranny. The Moscow trials of 1938 and the Hitler-Stalin pact of '39 were, of course, for him, as for many others, an unambiguous disclosure of the corruption at the very center of the Communist movement. And, thereafter, the virulence of Stalinism was nowhere (on either the European or the American scene) more trenchantly exposed than in his voluminous political and theological writings.

So it is not incorrect to say that Niebuhr never had any serious illusions about Marxism. Yet its rhetoric and certain of its insights (its organic view of society, its theory of class conflict and social ideology, its definition of the problem of social injustice in terms of economic inequality) did for a time sharpen his polemic against liberalism, particularly at the point of its illusions about the possibility of simply translating ethical ideals into political actuality. It is this phase of his thought that is perhaps most apparent in *Reflections on the End of an Era*.

But, then, the very ruthlessness of Niebuhr's deflation of moralism as a style of social and political thought made it necessary that he should himself eventually attempt to restate in a constructive way the relation of ethics to politics. This was the task that he began to undertake in his book of 1935, *An Interpretation of Christian Ethics* — and particularly in the famous chapter of that book that is called "The Relevance of an Impossible Ethical Ideal." Here it was that Niebuhr's campaign against the "free-floating imperatives" — the phrase is Donald Meyer's — of Social Gospel idealism began to issue in a recovery of the doctrine of original sin, and his analysis of social and political reality thus moved into the more fundamental dimension of theological anthropology. Indeed, it would not be oversimplifying his development to say that by the mid-1930s he had truly become for the first time a theologian, his thought being now fecundated by the more emphatically distinctive insights of the Christian faith.

The essential question that is tackled in *An Interpretation of Christian Ethics* is how one moves from the ethic of *agape*, with its radical perfectionism, to viable norms of ethical discrimination in the historical order. Niebuhr's contention was that the bankruptcy of both conventional orthodoxy and liberal Christianity is nowhere more in evidence than in the extent to which this problem, from both perspectives, ceases to be a real problem. For orthodoxy, in prematurely identifying the radical imperatives of faith with the myths of a prescientific age and with "canonical moral codes" of the past, abdicates from any genuine effort to make its heritage relevant to contemporary experience. Liberalism, on the other hand, in its anxiety "to prove . . . that it does not share the anachronistic ethics or believe the incredible myths of orthodox religion," has so completely adjusted what is radical in the Christian faith to "the characteristic credos and prejudices of modernity" that all the tension between "the transcendent impossibilities of the Christian ethic of love" and the immanent possibilities of the historical process has disappeared.

Niebuhr wanted very much to insist that the normative element in

Christian ethical thought is radically perfectionist and transcendent. For the *agape* of the Cross, in its sacrificial heedlessness and universalism, represents a degree of moral rigorism that surpasses any simple historical possibility: it makes no concessions even to the most "natural" self-regarding impulses and distances itself from every form of self-assertion, even from "the necessary prudent defenses of the self, required because of the egoism of others." The ethic of *agape* is, in short, an utterly unprudential rigorism which is impossible of fulfillment by the natural man in the immediate situations of historical existence.

Yet, as Niebuhr consistently maintained after the appearance of his book of 1935, *agape* is the only adequate final norm of human life, because no other does full justice to the dimension of depth in which the human spirit is set. It does not, to be sure, "deal at all with the immediate moral problem of every human life — the problem of arranging some kind of armistice between various contending factions and forces. It has nothing to say about the relativities of politics and economics, nor of the necessary balances of power which exist and must exist in even the most intimate social relationships." But, then, it is the nature of man, through his radical freedom, perpetually to transcend all the cohesions that make up his communal life: he is not bound by any of them. He is, of course, "imbedded in the passing flux" of nature and history and is "the prisoner of the partial perspectives of a limited time and place." But the fact that, through reason and memory and imagination, he can surmount himself and his world indeterminately means that his life cannot find its true ground in any of the proximate norms that emerge out of historical experience, and that he is therefore driven by the inner dynamism of his nature toward a transcendent norm.

This was for Niebuhr the mark of the unique dignity of man, that, though mortal and "imbedded in the flux of finitude," he stands, by reason of his radical freedom, under ideal possibilities. But it is precisely his situation on this frontier between the temporal and the eternal, between the realm of nature and the realm of spirit, that makes possible at once everything that is noble and everything that is ignoble in the human drama. Man is always trying to "translate his finite existence into a more permanent and absolute form of existence. Ideally men seek to subject their arbitrary and contingent existence under the dominion of absolute reality. But practically they always mix the finite with the eternal and claim for themselves, their nation, their culture, or their class the center of existence. This is the root of all imperialism in man and explains why the restricted predatory impulses of the animal world are transmuted into the boundless imperial ambitions of human life." Thus it is that "devotion to every transcendent value is corrupted by the effort to insert the interests of the self into that value. The organizing center of life and history must transcend life and history, since everything which appears in time and history is too partial and incomplete to be its center. But man is destined, both by the imperfection of his knowledge and by his desire to overcome his finiteness, to make absolute claims for his partial and finite values. He tries, in short, to make himself God." And this is the root and the nature of sin.

The seat of the trouble, in other words, is not finitude itself, but finitude pretending to be something more than finite. *An Interpretation of Christian Ethics* suggests that it is just its illumination of this profound pathos of human spirituality that constitutes the genius of the classical Christian doctrine of "original sin." Niebuhr had little patience, however, with the tendency of traditional orthodoxy so to historicize the myth of the Fall as to convert the doctrine of "original sin" into a doctrine of "inherited corruption." "If original sin is an inherited corruption, its inheritance destroys the freedom and therefore the responsibility which is basic to the conception of sin. The orthodox doctrine is therefore self-destructive." And sin is "original" only in the sense of its being pervasively and perennially characteristic of human existence.

Now this incorrigible tendency of the human creature always to claim more for himself than he ought to claim, always to mingle idealizing pretensions with his most ideal aspirations, and to accentuate "his natural will-to-live into an imperial will-to-power by the very protest which his yearning for the eternal tempts him to make against his finiteness" — this deep crookedness and duplicity of the human heart is not something that can be broken by simple rational suasion or by moralistic exhortations to "follow in His steps." The self-emptying love that is incarnate in the New Testament picture of

Jesus as the Christ does, indeed, surpass the limit of man's moral possibilities, and to confront it is to be reduced to despair. But it is precisely out of such despair that there arises "the godly sorrow which worketh repentance." And it is just here, Niebuhr suggested, that we may discern "the relevance of an impossible ethical ideal." The law of love is, to be sure, an impossibility; yet it cannot be "relegated simply to the world of transcendence," for always "it offers immediate possibilities of a higher good in every given situation," and it is for this reason that it proves itself to be the true pinnacle of the moral imagination. A perfectionist ethic presents us, in other words, with a final norm that transcends the range of possible achievement; but, though it is never fully realized in either intention or action, it makes possible the kind of searching criticism of both intention and action that provides the impetus for the highest moral creativity.

So to conceive the relation of the sacrificial heedlessness of *agape* to the various modes of calculated mutuality that make up the realm of proximate norms and achievement is not, however, wholly to dispel the suspicion that Niebuhr's ethical thought arouses, that it does in some degree involve a very abstract kind of Kantian formalism. Though he made frequent use of such general principles of morality as equality and justice and freedom, he never proposed any systematic definition of precisely how it is that such "middle axioms" bring the "possibilities of a higher good" disclosed by the absolute norm of *agape* into immediate relation to the concrete issues of moral perplexity. He tended to see the ethical situation as one in which an absolute norm always makes possible a critical perspective on whatever systems of reciprocity men devise for the conduct of life. But never did he manage fully to rescue from the realm of the problematical the precise nature of the assistance that the unprudential rigorism of a perfectionist ethic offers men living in a world in which it is perilous ever to forswear prudence. It does, to be sure, offer a vision of higher "possibilities," but this hardly provides a workable canon of ethical discrimination.

The whole shape and direction of his argument in the book of 1935 (which was originally presented as the Rauschenbusch Memorial Lectures in the Colgate-Rochester Divinity School) made it clear that Niebuhr's social and political analysis and his debate with "the liberal culture of modernity" were gradually deepening into a fundamental restatement of Christian theology. In its theological richness, it was his book of 1937, *Beyond Tragedy*, that made this maturing process unmistakably manifest, for here it began to be evident that his tutelage under the Fathers and the Reformers — and particularly under Augustine — was making for a brilliant recovery of the great themes of classical Christianity.

Beyond Tragedy — like the moving book that appeared in 1946, *Discerning the Signs of the Times* — is a collection of "sermonic essays" which grew out of sermons that had been preached in college and university chapels. Both books put us in mind of what a pity it is that so few of Niebuhr's sermons reached the printed page — and these in a form representing such a systematization of the original deliverances that they have very nearly ceased to be examples of the sermon as a genre of rhetoric and have become theological essays. For he was one of the great Christian preachers of the modern period, his only peer on the American scene perhaps having been the Presbyterian George Buttrick (sometime dean of the Chapel of Harvard University). But his immense popularity in the great churches and university chapels of the land was never won by way of reliance, even in the slightest degree, on the vague hyperbole and tawdry homiletical devices of the conventional sorcerer of the pulpit. Those who faced his lucid and mercurial brilliance from the pew will surely agree that their deepest impression was that of an enormously shrewd and worldly intelligence whose overriding interest centered in the special kind of illumination that is cast by the Christian faith on the major perplexities of modern man. The general impression (as T. S. Eliot said of Pascal) was of a man "highly passionate and ardent, but passionate only through a powerful and regulated intellect" — who was speaking "to those who doubt[ed], but who [had] the mind to conceive, and the sensibility to feel, the disorder, the futility, the meaninglessness, the mystery of life and suffering, and who [could] only find peace through a satisfaction of the whole being."

The basic analysis of the human situation in *Beyond Tragedy* moves very much along the same line that is taken in *An Interpretation of Christian Ethics*: "Man is mortal. That is his fate. Man pretends not to be mortal. That is his sin. Man is a creature of time and place, whose perspectives and insights are invariably conditioned by his immediate circumstances. But man is not merely the prisoner of time and place. . . . He is not content to be merely American man, or Chinese man, or bourgeois man, or man of the twentieth century. He wants to be man. . . . His memory spans the ages in order that he may transcend his age. His restless mind seeks to comprehend the meaning of all cultures so that he may not be caught within the limitations of his own." Without all this "man could not come to his full estate. But it is also inevitable that these towers should be Towers of Babel, that they should pretend to reach higher than their real height; and should claim a finality which they cannot possess." In the ever wider and wider spheres of reality which he is capable of envisaging, man "knows that he ought to act so as to assume only his rightful place in the harmony of the whole. But his actual action is always informed by the ambition to make himself the centre of the whole." Thus it is that "guilt and creativity are inextricably interwoven" in human existence. Yet "Christianity does not regard the inevitability of guilt in all human creativity as inherent in the nature of human life. Sin emerges, indeed, out of freedom and is possible only because man is free; but it is done in freedom, and therefore man . . . bears responsibility for it," rather than creation or existence as such. The testimony that creation as such is essentially good is, in short, a basic affirmation of the Christian faith, for its trust is in "a good God who created a good world, though the world is not now good."

But the fact that that which contaminates the world with the poisons of sin arises out of man's freedom means that the hope of the fulfillment of life must be a hope that envisages a fulfillment beyond the possibilities of historical existence. "The possibilities of the fulfilment of this life transcend our experience not because the soul is immortal and the body is mortal but because this human life, soul and body, is both immersed in flux and above it, and because it involves itself in sin in this unique position from which there is no escape by its own powers. The fulfilment of life beyond the possibilities of this existence is a justified hope, because of our human situation, that is, because a life which knows the flux in which it stands cannot be completely a part of that flux. On the other hand this hope is not one which fulfils itself by man's own powers." God, therefore, "must complete what remains incomplete in human existence."

Yet "the Kingdom of God must still enter the world by way of the crucifixion." Though love is the law of life, "when it enters the world of relative justice and balanced egotism it is destroyed in it. The suffering servant dies on the cross." The paradox at the heart of the Christian faith arises out of the assertion that, nevertheless, in this apparently tragic fact we may discern man's deliverance from his woe. For He who dies upon the Cross, though He is God incarnate, also represents the essential nature of man, the "second Adam," as St. Paul says; and the crucifixion of the second Adam by the first Adam, in proving that human nature has deviated from its own inner law, proves also that sin is not an essential part of human nature as such. It does, to be sure, prove that "sin is so much a part of existence that sinlessness cannot maintain itself in it." But it also establishes that "sin is not a necessary and inherent characteristic of life. Evil is not a part of God, nor yet a part of essential man. This Saviour is a revelation of the goodness of God and the essential goodness of man, *i.e.*, the second Adam. He is indeed defeated in history but in that very defeat proves that he cannot be ultimately defeated. That is, he reveals that it is God's nature to swallow up evil in Himself and destroy it. Life in its deepest essence is not only good but capable of destroying the evil which has been produced in it. Life is thus not at war with itself. Its energy is not in conflict with its order. Hence the Saviour truly says: 'Weep not for me.' "

Now what in part makes this book of 1937 so notable a milestone in the development of Niebuhr's thought and in twentieth-century theology is the radicalism with which it carries forward the proposal that had been made in *An Interpretation of Christian Ethics*, regarding the necessity of interpreting Christian dogma in "mythical" terms. In the earlier book he had expressed his impatience with the tendency of traditional orthodoxy so to literalize the mythical element in religious discourse as to annul what is truly dialectical in the Christian apprehension of time and eternity. The real genius of myth as a mode of thought is, as he argued there, that "it points to the timeless in time, to the ideal in the actual, but does not lift the temporal to the category of the eternal (as pantheism does), nor deny the significant glimpses of the eternal and the ideal in the temporal (as dualism does)." But traditional orthodoxy, in developing the Biblical view of reality into a rigid supernaturalist scheme of two discrete levels of being, simply achieves an obscurantist petrifaction of apprehensions whose dynamic and dialectical character ought to be preserved. So an ancillary theme in the argument of *Beyond Tragedy* concerns "the necessary and perennially valid contribution of myth to the biblical world view."

We are, for example, says Niebuhr, "deceivers yet true, when we say that God created the world," for this is not to account for the origin of the world in some particular and dateable moment of cosmic history; but in no other way can the mythical imagination of religious faith express its sense of the transcendent majesty of God and of the utter dependence upon Him of everything that exists. "We are deceivers, yet true, when we say that man fell into evil," for the Garden of Eden is to be found on no one's map, and the Fall is locatable on no historical calendar; but, though the myth of the Fall designates no single historical occurrence, it does in a way speak profoundly of that which is presupposed in every human action. "We are deceivers, yet true, when we affirm that God became man to redeem the world from sin. The idea of eternity entering time is intellectually absurd." Nevertheless, when Christianity speaks of God's Word having been made flesh, it is asserting that "God's word is relevant to human life"; it is declaring "that an event in history can be of such a character as to reveal the character of history itself; that without such a revelation the character of history cannot be known." And so too are we "deceivers, yet true, when we insist that the Christ who died on the cross will come again in power and glory, that he will judge the quick and the dead and will establish his Kingdom"; but in this way Christianity speaks of its belief that the human enterprise will not end tragically, and it declares that "the ground of our hope lies not in human capacity but in divine power and mercy. . . ."

This, then, is the reading of the Christian faith that Niebuhr offered in *Beyond Tragedy*. And by the late 1930s it was becoming apparent not only on the American scene but also in British and European circles that here was a gifted new presence in modern theology who had already found the authority of his own brilliant and commanding voice. At the great conference in Oxford in 1937, where the world leadership of the rapidly burgeoning ecumenical movement in non-Roman Christianity was gathered in an impressive convocation, he was a striking figure. The greeting that was uttered by William Temple (then Archbishop of York, later of Canterbury) on this occasion of their first meeting — "At last I've met the troubler of my peace" — doubtless expressed what was being felt by many of Christendom's most distinguished theologians. The word was fast getting round that Reinhold Niebuhr, along with Karl Barth and Emil Brunner and Paul Tillich, was one of the most formidable strategists of "Neo-Orthodoxy" — though the term *Neo-Orthodoxy* was one with which he himself was not happy, and this piece of journalistic jargon was later to be rejected by many others, as a clumsy counter that in many ways distorted the actual situation in the theology of the period.

It came as no great surprise to Niebuhr's colleagues in the theological community when he was invited to the University of Edinburgh as the Gifford lecturer for the spring and autumn of 1939, an old and famous post whose only previous American incumbents had been William James, Josiah Royce, William Ernest Hocking, and John Dewey. It was in the following year that his volume *Christianity and Power Politics* appeared, a book made notable in part by the powerful critique of Christian pacifism that it presented, as the clouds of war began to hover ominously over the international horizon. But this work was quickly overshadowed by the Gifford Lectures on *The Nature and Destiny of Man*, the first volume of which, when it was published in 1941, brought the general recognition that this was Niebuhr's masterpiece.

The design of this central achievement of his career is so grandly conceived and, in its execution, is architecturally so intricate that it is impossible to produce any simple compression of the argument that gathers up and does justice to its innumerable themes. Nor is it possible in a brief essay to convey any vivid impression of that special richness of texture in the Gifford Lectures which is a result of the author's seeming to carry in his head the whole of Western intellectual tradition and to have a constantly simultaneous vision of all its myriad strands. In so curtailed an exposition as this must be, one must simply take the risk of settling upon the particular angle that affords the best view of the entire structure and, having done this, proceed then to indicate something of what is entailed in this perspective on the whole. When such rigorous concision is imposed, it would seem that the Gifford Lectures will be most fruitfully regarded as involving one of the profoundest and most original essays of the modern period in the phenomenology of selfhood. The two volumes of *The Nature and Destiny of Man* have, of course, many other dimensions: they present many startlingly fresh and acute interpretations of various phases of theological and philosophic tradition, and of movements in general intellectual and cultural history (Hellenism, Renaissance humanism, romanticism, Marxism, etc.); and Niebuhr's own constructive theological position is extended toward a formal theory of history, a systematic Christology, and a remarkably brilliant restatement of the eschatological motifs in the Christian faith. But the decisive fulcrum is the inquiry into the nature of selfhood.

The guiding premise of Niebuhr's anthropology is grounded in a vision of human existence as composed, in its most essential character, of ambiguity. Man is, on the one hand, a creature of nature who is "unable to choose anything beyond the bounds set by the creation in which he stands": he needs air to breathe and space in which to abide; he cannot survive without the nourishment of warmth and food; yet, however abundant may be that nourishment, his life is but of short duration — and, as Pascal says, he is "engulfed in the infinite immensity of spaces . . . which know [him] not." But, though frail and subject to the contingencies of nature and history, he stands above "the structures and coherences of the world," being able to order them and reorder them toward ends of his own choosing. And not only can he make the structures of nature and history the object of his own thought and the instruments of his creativity; he can also make himself the object of his thought, and even the self which thus surmounts itself — and this on into indeterminate degrees of self-transcendence.

Man is, for Niebuhr, "both free and bound, both limited and limitless." It is the necessity of recognizing this essentially ambiguous character of the human situation that provides him with the basic requirement of adequacy in terms of which he evaluates the various accounts of man's estate that are furnished by the history of culture. He finds the trouble with most of the great alternatives to the Christian faith — whether in classical rationalism or Renaissance humanism, in modern naturalism or in idealistic and romanticist philosophies — to lie in their tendency to collapse this fundamental antinomousness of human existence into some formula which either overstresses man's "dignity" and understresses his "wretchedness" or overstresses his limitation and fails sufficiently to appreciate his radical freedom. But the genius of what he calls "Biblical faith" does for him become most apparent precisely in the kind of dialectic that it maintains between its doctrine of man as creature and its doctrine of man as *imago Dei*. The contention that he argues, with great learning and rhetorical power, in book after book — but most persuasively perhaps in *The Nature and Destiny of Man* — is that "the Christian view of man is [most] sharply distinguished from all alternative views" just in the clarity with which it perceives that man belongs to *both* realms, to the realm of nature *and* to the realm of spirit.

It is, in Niebuhr's view, precisely this duality of emphasis that permits Christianity to give so profound an account of the origin and nature of sin. Its alertness to the human position as a point of juncture between nature and spirit gives it an especially acute perspective on the psychological environment in which sin becomes possible. This environing *possibility* of sin — which is "the inevitable concomitant of the paradox of freedom and finiteness in which man is involved" — Niebuhr defines as anxiety. For it is this — namely, anxiousness — which is the psychological consequence of man's being "both free and bound, both limited and limitless." And it is the analysis of anxiety in its relation to freedom and sin — with its subtle echoes, occasionally, of the similar analysis conducted in Kierkegaard's *The Concept of Dread* — that constitutes one of the most brilliantly original contributions in the first volume of the Gifford Lectures.

"Man is anxious not only because his life is limited and dependent and yet not so limited that he does not know of his limitations. He is also anxious because he does not know the limits of his possibilities. He can do nothing and regard it perfectly done, because higher possibilities are revealed in each achievement. All human actions stand under seemingly limitless possibilities. There are, of course, limits but it is difficult to gauge them from any immediate perspective. There is therefore no limit of achievement in any sphere of activity in which human history can rest with equanimity." The human condition is like that of "the sailor, climbing the mast (to use a simile), with the abyss of the waves beneath him and the 'crow's nest' above him. He is anxious about both the end toward which he strives and the abyss of nothingness into which he may fall." It is this suspension betwixt finiteness and freedom that gives rise to that sense of vertigo that induces man's profoundest dispeace. Anxiety is not itself sin; it is only the precondition of sin and the "source of temptation," to make oneself the basis of one's security or to escape from the anguish of freedom by immersing oneself in some natural vitality. But though anxiety, once conceived, tends to bring forth pride and sensuality, it does not, as the precondition of sin, make sin logically necessary: sin is committed in freedom and "can therefore not be attributed to a defect in [man's] essence. It can only be understood as a self-contradiction, made possible by the fact of his freedom but not following necessarily from it." That, says Niebuhr, is "the doctrine of original sin, stripped of literalistic illusions" — that, though sin does not necessarily follow from our human nature as such, it is nevertheless so pervasive in every moment of human existence that it seems therefore, in Kierkegaard's phrase, to "posit itself."

But, now, though human life, even in its most saintly expressions, nowhere seems to be uninfected by sin, the historical drama is by no means an affair of sheer moral anarchy. It is the Christian faith that in Christ the true meaning of history has been disclosed, that in the *agape* of the Cross the final norm of man's life has been revealed. Which means — since this norm, though disclosed, remains unfulfilled — that the actuality of man's historical existence is set within an "interim" between the First and the Second Coming of Christ; and it is to the exposition of the doctrine of history as interim that the second volume of the Gifford Lectures is very largely devoted. Here, in the interim, "sin is overcome in principle but not in fact," and thus love has "to live in history as suffering love because the power of sin makes a simple triumph of love impossible." History is not without meaning, but it presents no decisive fulfillments of its own meaning, for every realization of good is stained by the improbities of sin. Thus the New Testament hope of the *parousia*, of the suffering Messiah's coming again with "power and great glory," though it requires "demythologization," yet "embodies the very genius of the Christian idea of the historical. On the one hand it implies that eternity will fulfil and not annul the richness and variety which the temporal process has elaborated. On the other it implies that the condition of finiteness and freedom, which lies at the basis of historical existence, is a problem for which there is no solution by any human power." In short, the Christian faith reaches its ultimate pinnacle in the belief that "only the infinite pity of God is equal to the infinite pathos of human life": this is the robust confidence that lies at the heart of Niebuhr's entire thought. So one feels that the old Scotswoman had laid hold of the crux of things when, after listening to his lectures at the University of Edinburgh, she told him: "I dinna understand a word ye said, but somehow I ken ye were making God great."

The numerous books that Niebuhr produced after the appearance of the two volumes of *The Nature and Destiny of Man* all represent special applications of the structure of thought that, in its main outlines, was completed by the Gifford Lectures. In 1944 his lectures on the West Foundation at Stanford University were published under the title *The Children of Light and the Children of Darkness*, and the best concise statement of Niebuhr's stratagem here is given in the book's subtitle — "A Vindication of Democracy and a Critique of Its Traditional Defence." His central thesis in this work finds perhaps its aptest summation in the famous sentence in his preface which says: "Man's capacity for justice makes democracy possible; but man's inclination to injustice makes democracy necessary." The book is in part poised against those who, in underestimating — whether in the secular terms, say, of Hobbes or in the religious terms of Luther — man's capacity for justice, invariably tend toward some form of political absolutism. But its fiercer polemic is reserved for "the children of light," for the sentimentality of the conventional liberal democrats who "are usually foolish" because their "too consistent optimism in regard to man's ability and inclination to grant justice to his fellows obscures the perils of chaos which perennially confront every society, including a free society. . . . When this optimism is not qualified to accord with the real and complex facts of human nature and history, there is always a danger that sentimentality will give way to despair and that a too consistent optimism will alternate with a too consistent pessimism." And the unillusioned profundity with which the fortunes and misfortunes of post-Enlightenment democratic ideology are analyzed puts one in mind of the similar analysis that Camus was to undertake a few years later in *L'homme révolté*.

The book on democracy also looks forward to the book of 1952, *The Irony of American History*, in which Niebuhr undertook a closer specification of the predicament of democratic society in terms of the American experience. Here, again, it is "the children of light" who are dealt with most critically. For theirs, he suggests, is the legacy that makes it most difficult today for America to address itself with sobriety to the troubled scene of international politics; that is to say, both New England Puritanism on the one hand and Jeffersonian-Virginian Deism on the other have bequeathed us a spiritual heritage that induces a sense of America as God's new "Israel," as a "separated" people through whom mankind makes a new beginning. But the conviction of innocence that is thereby deeply wrought into the nation's sense of its identity ill equips it for the exercise of power in its present position of supremacy in the world community. And the American situation is rendered particularly ironical by the fact that what we face in our chief foe (Russian communism) is very largely an intensification of many of our most characteristic values and illusions — our materialism, our preoccupation with technics, our "innocence" and self-righteousness, and our supposition that we are the masters of historical destiny. Indeed, the refutation of our forefathers' hopes that is offered by the reality of our present situation makes irony, in Niebuhr's view, the definitive category for the interpretation of American history; and we are saved, he suggests, only by the triumph of practice over dogma, only by "the ironic triumph of the wisdom of common sense over the foolishness of [our] wise men."

After the close of World War II, the rapid and terrifying intensification of Cold War politics, under the threatening specter of the big mushroom, increasingly prompted Niebuhr to explore the relevance of an eschatological faith in a period of frustration and disappointment, when "the moral and spiritual resources to achieve a just and stable society in global terms are not yet available." In the volume of "sermonic essays" called *Discerning the Signs of the Times*, which appeared in 1946, he undertook to speak of the special kind of sanity which may be the fruit of such a faith in this late, bad time.

It is, he said, an "age between the ages," when " 'one age is dead and the other is powerless to be born.' The age of absolute national sovereignty is over; but the age of international order under political instruments, powerful enough to regulate the relations of nations and to compose their competing desires, is not yet born." We are therefore a people who must learn how to live with the problem of frustration. And, in a time when contemporary history offers us nothing but "calculated risks" and disappointed hopes, we must also learn "to do our duty without allowing it to be defined by either our hopes or our fears." For "we do not know how soon and to what degree mankind will succeed in establishing a tolerable world order. Very possibly we will hover for some centuries between success and failure, in such a way that optimists and pessimists will be able to assess our achievements, or lack of them, with an equal degree of plausibility. In such a situation it is important to be more concerned with our duties than with the prospect of success in fulfilling them." But when we make the meaning of our life dependent wholly upon what we hope to accomplish tomorrow or the day after tomorrow, and when that achievement fails to be the perfect fulfillment of our highest hopes, our last state is apt to be worse than the first, the confusion of cynicism and despair having succeeded the confusion of optimism and illusion.

So, amidst the hell of global insecurity in which we live today, we shall perform our duties with the greater steadiness if we have something of the faith expressed by Saint Paul when he declared: "Whether we live, we live unto the Lord; and whether we die, we die unto the Lord: whether we live therefore, or die, we are the Lord's." It is in "this final nonchalance about life and death, which includes some sense of serenity about the life and death of civilizations, that we shall find the strength for doing what we ought to do, though we know not what the day or the hour may bring forth." In a period "when our hopes so far exceed our grasp that we can not count on historic fulfillments to give completion to our life," the radicalism of an eschatological faith "may beguile a few from their immediate tasks." But those who are sober will find their steps fixed and stablished by the knowledge that "if in this life only we have hope in Christ, we are of all men most miserable." Such a peace as this "will offend both rationalists and moralists till the end of history. . . . But it alone does justice to the infinite complexities and contradictions of human existence. Within this peace all of life's creative urges may be expressed and enlarged. There is therefore no simple calm in it. It is as tumultuous as the ocean, and yet as serene as the ocean's depths, which bear the tumults and storms of the surface." And it is the only peace that will permit us to steer a steady course through the uncharted waters of life, in the difficult period to which history has committed us.

Discerning the Signs of the Times was followed, in 1949, by *Faith and History*, which more rigorously systematized many of the themes in the Gifford Lectures into a formal philosophy of history. And, thereafter, most of Niebuhr's writing — *The Irony of American History* (1952); *Christian Realism and Political Problems* (1953); *Pious and Secular America* (1958); *The Structure of Nations and Empires* (1959); *Man's Nature and His Communities* (1965) — was concerned with the issues of politics, either in the dimension of history or formal theory or of concrete public policy. One feels that the hazards of life in the late years of the century increasingly brought him to something like the position expressed by Lionel Trilling in *The Liberal Imagination*, that our present "fate, for better or worse, is political." So he wanted, increasingly, to force into the definition of politics so rich and complicated a conception of humanity as might enable our politics to be not merely a politics of survival but also a politics for the redemption and renewal of human life.

In one significant book of this period, however, he resumed and further developed that aspect of his thought which I have spoken of as entailing a phenomenology of selfhood. Though *The Self and the Dramas of History* (1955) may bring to focus issues on which it was natural for Niebuhr to be meditating during his long and desperate illness in the early 1950s, his having been able to produce so intricately reasoned and brilliant a book after a series of small strokes provides an interesting measure, in human terms, of the man's resilience and genius. This work, in defining human selfhood in terms of man's capacity for "dialogue," reveals how deeply he was influenced by the Jewish existentialist Martin Buber; in a manner recalling Buber's classic *I and Thou*, he, too, regards the life of man as a fundamentally "dialogic life," since human being is, for him, always being-in-relationship. But, whereas Buber sometimes appeared to view the form of the I-Thou relation as essentially monadical, Niebuhr insisted on the large degree to which the I-Thou reality is influenced by "the dramas of history"; and it was from this perspective that he analyzed the three dimensions of the dialogue in which man is constantly engaged — with himself, with his neighbors, and with God. "Man is primarily a historical creature," says Niebuhr — which means, in his view, that the self is at once determined by the necessities of nature and is yet able "to transcend not only the processes of nature but the operations of its own reason, and to stand, as it were, above the structures and coherences of the world." The self is not only patient of natural process: it is also free enough of it to create culture, though it "is not simply a creator of this new dimension, for it is also a creature of the web of events, in the creation of which it participates." Human existence is, in other words, "a compound of freedom and necessity" — which is to say that each aspect of man's "dialogic life" is historical. And the central contention of Niebuhr's book of 1955 is that the *historical* character of dialogic life is more truly and profoundly described by the poetic-dramatic categories of Biblical personalism than by classical rationalism (with its concern to submit the self to structures of ontology) or philosophic idealism (which, as in Hegel, absorbs the rough angularity of the existing self into universal mind) or romanticism (which ascribes to the realm of the organic "what is clearly a compound of nature and spirit") or modern psychology (whether in its behavioristic or Freudian versions).

Now, with the full stretch of Niebuhr's thought in view, the significance of his role in American intellectual life asks, finally, for some definition. And though his career may still be so much a part of the immediacy of the contemporary scene as to make remote the possibility of an adequately measured assessment, at least it can be said (as Arthur Schlesinger, Jr., has remarked) that here was a thinker of enormous power who succeeded in restating the great themes of Christian theology "with such irresistible relevance to contemporary experience that even those who have no decisive faith in the supernatural find their own reading of experience and history given new and significant dimensions." He is perhaps the one American ever to have established his claim on that modern theological pantheon which includes such Europeans as Friedrich Schleiermacher and Albrecht Ritschl and Sören Kierkegaard and in which such distinguished figures of the recent past as Paul Tillich and Rudolf Bultmann and Karl Barth will also ultimately find their place. And — excepting possibly Kierkegaard (whose posthumous reputation is a development of our own period) and Paul Tillich, whose influence has been widely felt — there is no other Christian theologian of the modern period whose work has exerted so profound an impact upon secular intellectual life. This is perhaps most immediately measurable in the field of political thought, where, as Hans Morgenthau says, he is our "greatest living political philosopher, perhaps the only creative political philosopher [in American thought] since Calhoun." This is a judgment which Professor Morgenthau and many others are prepared to make not merely because of the immense volume of brilliant analysis of the concrete issues of modern politics that Niebuhr produced over more than forty years. In this vein, of course, his work was powerfully influential in the thinking of many of the ablest journalists and theoreticians and architects of public policy in this country. But his eminence in the realm of political thought, as Professor Morgenthau rightly suggests, is more centrally a result of the kind of awareness that he — more than any other American thinker of his time — promoted of the essentially "tragic character of the political act."

Niebuhr was occasionally charged by his colleagues in the theological community with being too much inclined, in his political thinking, toward a kind of rough-and-ready pragmatism insufficiently controlled by moral and theological principle — or by what they sometimes heavily denominated as "vision." But he knew that, though that balancing of claims and counterclaims by which justice is achieved can never provide the absolute norm of a social ethic, there is — short of disavowing our historical responsibilities — no escaping our involvement in these morally ambiguous pressures. He also knew that, however much "vision" may accord a certain slender dignity to our politics, the dynamism of history is such that the consequences of political action have a way of outrunning both the intent that prompted the act and any capacity that might have been mustered to foresee those consequences — so that, for the responsible man, there is no deliverance from the rough-and-ready expedience of pragmatic realism. In his strong sense of what he liked to call the "indeterminate possibilities" of history, he does indeed put us in mind of William James and his vision of the universe as open and dynamic; and, in his commitment, at the level of political methodology, to a radically empiricist experimentalism, he was, for all the antagonism that he expressed in his earlier years, not far removed from John Dewey. So, in terms of American cultural tradition, in his profound concern to invest Christianity with relevance for the social and political order, he is to be seen as an heir of the Social Gospel, despite his early rejection of its tendency to identify Christianity with the religion of progress; and, despite the polemical way in which he frequently faced many of its chief representatives in American philosophy, he is also to be seen as an heir of pragmatism.

Though he gave short shrift to the people who were being called in the early 1950s "the new conservatives," their fondness for quoting Edmund Burke did not blind him to the wisdom in Burke's view of politics as the art of the possible. Nor did he ever forget that, however many new possibilities for the realization of good each new development in history may bring, it also brings new hazards corresponding to these new possibilities — so that (as he said in the second volume of *The Nature and Destiny of Man*) "the new level of historic achievement offers us no emancipation from contradictions and ambiguities to which all life in history is subject." History, in other words, "is not its own redeemer. The 'long run' of it is no more redemptive in the ultimate sense than the 'short run.' " And thus it is that the choices which we make are never choices which have any chance of achieving a final settlement of the human problem: the peace of the *civitas terrena* is always an uneasy peace, and, as a consequence, in one of its dimensions, politics is, in its very nature, something essentially tragic.

But then, of course, to define Niebuhr's importance in secular intellectual life as having consisted in part in his reinstatement of a sense of what is tragic in political existence is to be reminded that here is indeed the basic emphasis not only of his political thought but of his total account of what André Malraux has taught us to speak of as *la condition humaine*. For, radical as his commitment was to the Christian faith, he never lost his fidelity to what Unamuno called "the tragic sense of life." It is doubtless in this aspect of his vision that the literary community has found its most congenial access to his work. Here, the extent and depth of his influence — though widely observed — are more difficult to measure than in the field of social and political thought. His presence as a shaping force in American literary life is something that is more often conveyed in the nuances of stress and intonation than in the form of documented reference. The late F. O. Matthiessen, for example, in his European journal of 1947, *From the Heart of Europe* (published in 1948), acknowledging Niebuhr's great influence on himself, gives a clear hint of what lay behind his own powerful critique of "the nineteenth-century belief in every man as his own Messiah" in *American Renaissance*. Or, again, one suspects that the kind of stringently critical assessment of modern liberalism that Lionel Trilling has conducted in much of his writing owes something, in part, to the current of ideas that were seminally present in Reinhold Niebuhr. And his influence can be felt not only in contemporary criticism but also in the realm of our creative literature as well — as, for example, in the trenchant reassessment of Jeffersonian liberalism in Robert Penn Warren's *Brother to Dragons* (with its likeness, in its basic ideas, to *The Children of Light and the Children of Darkness*) or in Frederick Buechner's equally trenchant reassessment of a later, Stevensonian liberalism in his fine novel of 1958, *The Return of Ansel Gibbs* (written after Buechner had had a period of study under Niebuhr at Union Seminary).

That, outside theological circles, Niebuhr's wider influence on the American cultural scene should today be felt to have been that of an eloquent spokesman for "the tragic sense of life" does, however, put us in mind of what may be the chief inadequacy in his work as a Christian theologian. And this is related to our earlier observation of what seems regularly to have been his inability, finally, to overcome the disjunction in his ethical thinking between the *agape* of Christ and the various forms of mutuality in human relations that are the aim of all concrete ethical decision in the historical order. The sacrificial love of Christ is, in Niebuhr's view, a love which transcends all considerations of reciprocity and is therefore "beyond history," since historical existence is, perennially, a matter of adjusting the claims and counterclaims which men bring to one another in all the relations of life. Now, to be sure, this absolute norm furnishes a vantage point from which complacency about any particular system of mutuality can be criticized. But he never succeeded in making clear precisely how it is that the *agape* of Christ which is "beyond history" affords a way of concretely taking account of all the quandaries which men face in attempting to build systems of reciprocity that are just and humane. The fundamental issue here is, of course, one which concerns the way in which the order of grace becomes effectually operative in history. But it is just at this point — where the logic of his task as a Christian theologian required him to indicate what is involved in the whole drama of redemption — that Niebuhr was least satisfactory. He had a genius for setting forth the kind of critical pressure that the Christian doctrine of man exerts on many of the characteristic forms of modern thought. But, as one of his critics, Paul Lehmann, has suggested, "the Cross, which is apprehended and interpreted as the *basis* of a new wisdom and power, is not adequately apprehended and interpreted as *operative* wisdom and power." Which is to say that there is no systematic specification of how it is, in the perspective of Christian faith, that God actually renews and transforms human life. And this vagueness which characterizes his rendering of the doctrine of redemption is of a piece with his failure to develop systematically the doctrines of the Holy Spirit and of the Church (which Christianity has classically regarded as that extension of the Incarnation whereby God continues the atoning work that was begun in Christ).

But, though Niebuhr's rendering of the great themes of the Christian faith was in certain respects unfinished and incomplete, he did, nevertheless, clarify with a singular power the continuing vitality of Reformation Christianity and the possibilities for cogent interpretation of modern experience that are still resident in its basic message. Perhaps no other native American thinker of this century has invested a Christian position with such relevance to the political and general intellectual situation of his time; and, as a consequence, his career is among the most eminent in that forum of thought which has given to the nation its most creative engagements.

SELECTED BIBLIOGRAPHIES

SELECTED BIBLIOGRAPHIES

HENRY ADAMS

Works

BIOGRAPHIES

The Life of Albert Gallatin. Philadelphia: Lippincott, 1879.
John Randolph. Boston: Houghton Mifflin, 1882.
The Life of George Cabot Lodge. Boston: Houghton Mifflin, 1911.

HISTORY

History of the United States of America during the First Administration of Thomas Jefferson. 2 vols. New York: Scribner's, 1889.
History of the United States of America during the Second Administration of Thomas Jefferson. 2 vols. New York: Scribner's, 1890.
History of the United States of America during the First Administration of James Madison. 2 vols. New York: Scribner's, 1890.
History of the United States of America during the Second Administration of James Madison. 3 vols. New York: Scribner's, 1891.
Historical Essays. New York: Scribner's, 1891. (Containing "Captain John Smith," "The Bank of England Restriction," "The Declaration of Paris," "The Legal Tender Act," "The New York Gold Conspiracy," "The Session.")
Memoirs of Arii Taimai of Tahiti. Paris: Privately published, 1901.
Mont-Saint-Michel and Chartres. Boston: Houghton Mifflin, 1913.
The Degradation of the Democratic Dogma. New York: Macmillan, 1919. (Containing "The Rule of Phase Applied to History," *A Letter to American Teachers of History.*)

AUTOBIOGRAPHY

The Education of Henry Adams. Boston: Houghton Mifflin, 1918.

NOVELS

Democracy: An American Novel. (Anonymous.) Leisure Hour Series No. 112. New York: Holt, 1880.

Esther: A Novel. (Pseudonym, Frances Snow Compton.) American Novel Series No. 3. New York: Holt, 1884.

VERSE

Letters to a Niece and Prayer to the Virgin of Chartres. Boston: Houghton Mifflin, 1920.

BOOKS EDITED

Essays in Anglo-Saxon Law. Boston: Little, Brown, 1876.

The Writings of Albert Gallatin. 3 vols. Philadelphia: Lippincott, 1879.

LETTERS

Letters of Henry Adams 1858–1891, edited by Worthington C. Ford. Boston: Houghton Mifflin, 1930.

Letters of Henry Adams 1892–1918, edited by Worthington C. Ford. Boston: Houghton Mifflin, 1938.

Henry Adams and His Friends, edited (with a biographical introduction) by Harold Dean Cater. Boston: Houghton Mifflin, 1947.

Biographical and Critical Studies

Adams, James Truslow. *Henry Adams.* New York: Albert and Charles Boni, 1933.

Blackmur, Richard P. "The Novels of Henry Adams," *Sewanee Review*, 51:281–304 (Spring 1943).

Brooks, Van Wyck. *The Confident Years, 1885–1915.* New York: Dutton, 1952.

Chanler, Mrs. Winthrop. *Roman Spring.* Boston: Little, Brown, 1936.

Jordy, William H. *Henry Adams, Scientific Historian.* New Haven, Conn.: Yale University Press, 1952.

Levenson, J. C. *The Mind and Art of Henry Adams.* Boston: Houghton Mifflin, 1957.

Samuels, Ernest. *The Young Henry Adams.* Cambridge, Mass.: Harvard University Press, 1948.

———. *Henry Adams: The Middle Years.* Cambridge, Mass.: Harvard University Press, 1958.

———. *Henry Adams: The Major Phase.* Cambridge, Mass.: Harvard University Press, 1964.

Stevenson, Elizabeth. *Henry Adams.* New York: Macmillan, 1955.

WILLIAM JAMES

The most complete checklist of William James's publications is Ralph Barton Perry's *Annotated Bibliography of the Writings of William James* (New York: Longmans, Green, 1920), reprinted with additions by John J. McDermott in *The Writings of William James: A Comprehensive Edition* (New York: Random House, 1967), pp. 811–858. The books by Linschoten, Wilshire, and Wild, listed below, also contain titles of critical studies and books relating to the study of James.

Principal Works

Introduction to *The Literary Remains of the Late Henry James*, edited by William James. Boston: Houghton Mifflin, 1884.
Introduction to *The Foundations of Ethics* by John Edward Maude, edited by William James. New York: Holt, 1887.
The Principles of Psychology. 2 vols. New York: Holt, 1890.
Psychology, Briefer Course. New York: Holt, 1892.
The Will to Believe, and Other Essays in Popular Philosophy. New York and London: Longmans, Green, 1897.
Human Immortality: Two Supposed Objections to the Doctrine. Boston and New York: Houghton Mifflin, 1898.
Introduction to *The Psychology of Suggestion* by Boris Sidis. New York: Appleton, 1899.
The Varieties of Religious Experience: A Study in Human Nature. New York and London: Longmans, Green, 1902.
Introduction to *Little Book of Life after Death* by G. T. Fechner, translated by M. C. Wadsworth. Boston: Little, Brown, 1904.
Preface to *The Problems of Philosophy* by Harold Höffding, translated by G. M. Fisher. New York: Macmillan, 1906.
Pragmatism: A New Name for Some Old Ways of Thinking. New York and London: Longmans, Green, 1907.
A Pluralistic Universe. (Hibbert Lectures at Manchester College on the Present Situation in Philosophy.) London: Longmans, Green, 1909.
The Meaning of Truth: A Sequel to "Pragmatism." New York and London: Longmans, Green, 1909.
Some Problems of Philosophy: A Beginning of an Introduction to Philosophy. New York and London: Longmans, Green, 1911.
Essays in Radical Empiricism. New York and London: Longmans, Green, 1912.
Collected Essays and Reviews, edited by Ralph Barton Perry. New York and London: Longmans, Green, 1920. (Thirty-nine articles.)

Selected Editions of Works and Letters

Letters of William James, edited by Henry James. 2 vols. Boston: Atlantic Monthly Press, 1920; London: Longmans, Green, 1920.
The Philosophy of William James, selected (with an introduction) by Horace M. Kallen. New York: Modern Library, [1925].
The James Family: Including Selections from the Writings of Henry James, Senior, William, Henry & Alice James, by F. O. Matthiessen. New York: Knopf, 1948.
The Selected Letters of William James, edited (with an introduction) by Elizabeth Hardwick. New York: Farrar, Straus and Cudahy, 1961.
William James on Psychical Research, compiled and edited by Gardner Murphy and Robert O. Ballou. New York: Viking Press, 1960.
The Letters of William James and Théodore Flournoy, edited by Robert C. Le Clair. Madison: University of Wisconsin Press, 1966.
The Writings of William James: A Comprehensive Edition, edited (with an introduction) by John J. McDermott. New York: Random House, 1967. (Includes "Annotated Bibliography of the Writings of William James.")

The Moral Philosophy of William James, edited by John K. Roth. New York: Crowell, 1969.

A William James Reader, selected and edited (with an introduction) by Gay Wilson Allen. Boston: Houghton Mifflin, 1971.

Biographies

Allen, Gay Wilson. *William James, a Biography*. New York: Viking Press, 1967.

Perry, Ralph Barton. *The Thought and Character of William James*. 2 vols. Boston: Little, Brown, 1935.

Critical Studies

Allen, Gay Wilson. "Pragmatism: A New Name for Some Old Ways of Thinking," in *Landmarks in American Writing*, edited by Hennig Cohen. New York: Basic Books, 1969.

Allport, G. W. "The Productive Paradoxes of William James," *Psychological Review*, 50:95–120 (1943).

Ayer, Alfred Jules. *The Origins of Pragmatism in the Philosophy of Charles Sanders Peirce and William James*. London: Macmillan, 1968.

Boutroux, Emile. *William James*, translated from the second edition by Archibald and Barbara Henderson. London: Longmans, Green, 1912.

Capek, Millic. "The Reappearance of the Self in the Last Philosophy of William James," *Philosophical Review*, 62:526–544 (October 1953).

Chapman, Harmon M. "Realism and Phenomenology," in *The Return of Reason*, edited by John Wild. Chicago: Regnery, 1953.

Dewey, John. "The Vanishing Subject in the Psychology of William James," *Journal of Philosophy*, 37:589–599 (1940). Reprinted in *The Problems of Men*. New York: Philosophical Library, 1946.

Edie, James M. "Notes on the Philosophical Anthropology of William James," in *An Invitation to Phenomenology*. Chicago: Quadrangle Books, 1965.

Eisendrath, Craig Ralph. *The Unifying Moment: The Psychological Philosophy of William James and Alfred North Whitehead*. Cambridge, Mass.: Harvard University Press, 1971.

Flournoy, Théodore. *The Philosophy of William James*, translated by Edwin B. Holt and William James, Jr. New York: Holt, 1917.

Hook, Sidney. *The Metaphysics of Pragmatism*. Chicago: Open Court, 1927.

Kallen, H. M., editor. *In Commemoration of William James*. New York: Columbia University Press, 1942. (Contributions by H. M. Kallen, A. Metzger, D. S. Miller, E. B. Holt, John Dewey, R. B. Perry, G. S. Brett, D. C. Williams, H. W. Schneider, J. R. Kantor, Victor Lowe, Charles Morris, E. W. Lyman, and W. H. Hill.)

Linschoten, Hans. *On the Way toward a Phenomenological Psychology: The Psychology of William James*, translated from the Dutch by Amedeo Giorgi. Pittsburgh: Duquesne University Press, 1968.

Lovejoy, A. O. *The Thirteen Pragmatisms*. Baltimore: Johns Hopkins Press, 1962.

MacLeod, Robert B., editor. *William James: Unfinished Business*. Washington, D.C.:

American Psychological Association, 1969. (Based on a series of lectures and discussions at the 75th convention of the American Psychological Association.)

Morris, Lloyd R. *William James: The Message of a Modern Mind*. New York: Scribner's, 1950; New York: Greenwood Press, 1969.

Otto, Max. "The Distinctive Psychology of William James," in *William James: Man and Thinker*. Madison: University of Wisconsin Press, 1942.

Perry, Ralph Barton. *In the Spirit of William James*. New Haven, Conn.: Yale University Press, 1938; Bloomington: Indiana University Press, 1958.

Roggerone, Giuseppe Agostino. *James e la crisi della conscienza contemporanea*. Milan: Marzorati, 1967.

Roth, John K. *Freedom and the Moral Life: The Ethics of William James*. Philadelphia: Westminster Press, 1969.

Santayana, George. *William James: Philosopher and Man*, edited by C. H. Compton. New York: Scarecrow Press, 1957.

Schuetz, Alfred. "William James's Concept of the Stream of Thought Phenomenologically Interpreted," *Philosophy and Phenomenological Research*, 1:442–452 (June 1941).

Wahl, Jean. *The Pluralistic Philosophies of England and America*, translated by Fred Rothwell. London: Open Court, 1925.

Wild, John. *The Radical Empiricism of William James*. New York: Doubleday, 1969.

Wilshire, Bruce. *William James and Phenomenology: A Study of the "Principles of Psychology."* Bloomington: University of Indiana Press, 1968.

H. L. MENCKEN

Principal Works

George Bernard Shaw: His Plays. Boston: Luce, 1905.

The Philosophy of Friedrich Nietzsche. Boston: Luce, 1908.

A Book of Burlesques. New York: Lane, 1916; revised edition, New York: Knopf, 1920.

A Book of Prefaces. New York: Knopf, 1917.

In Defense of Women. New York: Goodman, 1918; revised edition (with new introduction), New York: Knopf, 1922.

The American Language. New York: Knopf, 1919; second edition revised and enlarged, 1921; third edition, revised and enlarged, 1923; fourth edition, enlarged and rewritten, 1936.

Prejudices: First Series. New York: Knopf, 1919.

Prejudices: Second Series. New York: Knopf, 1920.

Prejudices: Third Series. New York: Knopf, 1922.

Prejudices: Fourth Series. New York: Knopf, 1924.

Notes on Democracy. New York: Knopf, 1926.

Prejudices: Fifth Series. New York: Knopf, 1926.

Prejudices: Sixth Series. New York: Knopf, 1927.

Treatise on the Gods. New York, London: Knopf, 1930.

Making a President: A Footnote to the Saga of Democracy. New York: Knopf, 1932.

Treatise on Right and Wrong. New York: Knopf, 1934.

Happy Days, 1880–1892. New York: Knopf, 1940.

Newspaper Days, 1899–1906. New York: Knopf, 1941.

Heathen Days, 1890–1936. New York: Knopf, 1943.
The American Language: Supplement One. New York: Knopf, 1945.
Christmas Story. (Illustrated by Bill Crawford.) New York: Knopf, 1946.
The American Language: Supplement Two. New York: Knopf, 1948.
Minority Report: H. L. Mencken's Notebooks. New York: Knopf, 1956.

Selected Editions of Works and Letters

The American Language, abridged (with annotations and new material) by Raven I. McDavid, Jr. New York: Knopf, 1963.
A Bathtub Hoax and Other Blasts and Bravos from the Chicago Tribune, edited by Robert McHugh. New York: Knopf, 1958.
H. L. Mencken: The American Scene, a Reader, selected and edited (with an introduction and commentary) by Huntington Cairns. New York: Knopf, 1965.
H. L. Mencken on Music, selected by Louis Cheslock. New York: Knopf, 1961.
Letters of H. L. Mencken, selected and annotated by Guy J. Forgue (with a Personal Note by Hamilton Owens). New York: Knopf, 1961.
A Mencken Chrestomathy, edited and annotated by the author. New York: Knopf, 1949.
On Politics: A Carnival of Buncombe, edited by Malcolm Moos. New York: Vintage (Knopf), 1956.
Prejudices: A Selection, edited by James T. Farrell. New York: Vintage, 1958.
The Vintage Mencken, gathered by Alistair Cooke. New York: Vintage, 1955.

Bibliographies

Adler, Betty. *Man of Letters: A Census of the Correspondence of H. L. Mencken*. Baltimore: Enoch Pratt Free Library, 1969.
———, with the assistance of Jane Wilhelm. *H. L. M.: The Mencken Bibliography*. Baltimore: Johns Hopkins Press for Enoch Pratt Free Library, 1961. (Lists, so far as can be ascertained, Mencken's shorter works, newspaper and magazine contributions, and miscellaneous writings, as well as his books; also lists critical studies of Mencken and his work, including many brief studies, published and unpublished.)
Adler, Betty, ed. *Menckeniana* (a quarterly miscellany and bibliographical supplement). Baltimore: Enoch Pratt Free Library, 1962–.
Frey, Carroll. *A Bibliography of the Writings of H. L. Mencken* (with a foreword by H. L. Mencken). Philadelphia: Centaur Bookshop, 1924.
Porter, Bernard H. *H. L. Mencken, a Bibliography*. Pasadena, Calif.: Geddes Press, 1957.
Swan, Bradford F. *Making a Mencken Collection*. New Haven, Conn.: Yale University Gazette, 1950.

Critical and Biographical Studies

Angoff, Charles. *H. L. Mencken, a Portrait from Memory*. New York: Yoseloff, 1956.
Boyd, Ernest Augustus. *H. L. Mencken*. New York: McBride, 1925.
De Casseres, Benjamin. *Mencken and Shaw: The Anatomy of America's Voltaire and England's Other John Bull*. New York: Silas Newton, 1930.

Forque, Guy Jean. *H. L. Mencken, l'homme, l'oeuvre, l'influence.* Paris: Minard Lettres Modernes, 1967.
Goldberg, Isaac. *H. L. Mencken.* Girard, Kans.: Haldeman-Julius, 1920.
———. *The Man Mencken, a Biographical and Critical Survey.* New York: Simon, 1925.
H. L. Mencken. New York: Knopf, 1920. (A reprint of three articles: "Fanfare" by Burton Rascoe; "The American Critic" by Vincent O'Sullivan; "Bibliography" by F. C. Henderson.)
Kemler, Edgar. *The Irreverent Mr. Mencken.* Boston: Little, Brown, 1950.
Manchester, William. *Disturber of the Peace: The Life of H. L. Mencken* (with an introduction by Gerald W. Johnson). New York: Harper, 1951.
Mayfield, Sara. *The Constant Circle: H. L. Mencken and His Friends.* New York: Delacourt, 1968.
Nolte, William H. *H. L. Mencken, Literary Critic.* Middletown, Conn.: Wesleyan University Press, 1966.
Stenerson, Douglas C. *H. L. Mencken: Iconoclast from Baltimore.* Chicago: University of Chicago Press, 1971.
Wagner, Philip M. "Mencken Remembered," *American Scholar*, 32:256–274 (Spring 1963).

RANDOLPH BOURNE

Principal Works

BOOKS

Youth and Life. Boston: Houghton Mifflin, 1913.
The Gary Schools. Boston: Houghton Mifflin, 1916.
Towards an Enduring Peace, edited by R. S. Bourne. New York: American Association for International Conciliation, 1916.
Education and Living. New York: Century, 1917.
Untimely Papers, edited by James Oppenheim. New York: B. W. Huebsch, 1919.
History of a Literary Radical and Other Essays, edited by Van Wyck Brooks. New York: B. W. Huebsch, 1920.
The History of a Literary Radical and Other Papers, edited by Van Wyck Brooks. New York: S. A. Russell, 1956. (A slightly different collection.)

ARTICLES

Bourne wrote chiefly for the *Columbia Monthly* (January 1910–November 1913), the *Atlantic Monthly* (May 1911–June 1917), the *New Republic* (November 7, 1914–September 28, 1918), the *Dial* (December 28, 1916–December 18, 1918), *The Seven Arts* (April 1917–October 1917). Consult the volumes by Schlissel and Moreau, listed below, for detailed citations.

LETTERS AND DIARY

"Some Pre-War Letters (1912–1914)," *Twice a Year*, 2:79–102 (Spring–Summer 1939).

"Letters (1913–1914)," *Twice a Year*, 5–6:79–88 (Fall–Winter 1940, Spring–Summer 1941).
"Diary for 1901," *Twice a Year*, 5–6:89–98 (Fall–Winter 1940, Spring–Summer 1941).
"Letters (1913–1916)," *Twice a Year*, 7:76–90 (Fall–Winter 1941).
The World of Randolph Bourne, edited by Lillian Schlissel. New York: Dutton, 1965. Pp. 293–326.

Bibliographies

Filler, Louis. *Randolph Bourne*. Washington, D.C.: American Council on Public Affairs, 1943. Pp. 152–155.
Moreau, John Adam. *Randolph Bourne: Legend and Reality*. Washington, D.C.: Public Affairs Press, 1966. Pp. 210–227.
Schlissel, Lillian, editor. *The World of Randolph Bourne*. New York: Dutton, 1965. Pp. 327–333.

Critical and Testimonial Studies

Brooks, Van Wyck. "Randolph Bourne," in *Emerson and Others*. New York: Dutton, 1927.
———. "Randolph Bourne," in *Fenolossa and His Circle*. New York: Dutton, 1962.
Dahlberg, Edward. "Randolph Bourne: In the Saddle of Rosinante," in *Can These Bones Live*. Revised edition. New York: New Directions, 1960 (first edition, 1941).
———. "Randolph Bourne," in *Alms for Oblivion*. Minneapolis: University of Minnesota Press, 1964.
Filler, Louis. *Randolph Bourne*. Washington, D.C.: American Council on Public Affairs, 1943.
Lasch, Christopher. "Randolph Bourne and the Experimental Life," in *The New Radicalism in America (1889–1963): The Intellectual as a Social Type*. New York: Knopf, 1965.
Lerner, Max. "Randolph Bourne and Two Generations," *Twice a Year*, 5–6:54–78 (Fall–Winter 1940, Spring-Summer 1941). Reprinted in *Ideas for the Ice Age*. New York: Viking Press, 1941.
Madison, Charles. "Randolph Bourne: The History of a Literary Radical," in *Critics and Crusaders: A Century of American Protest*. New York: Holt, 1947.
Moreau, John Adam. *Randolph Bourne: Legend and Reality*. Washington, D.C.: Public Affairs Press, 1966.
Resek, Carl. Introduction to *War and the Intellectuals: Essays by Randolph S. Bourne, 1915–1919*. New York, Evanston, and London: Harper and Row, 1964.
Rosenfeld, Paul. "Randolph Bourne," *Dial*, 75:545–60 (December 1923). Reprinted in *Port of New York*. New York: Harcourt, Brace, 1924; Urbana: University of Illinois Press, 1961.
Schlissel, Lillian. Introduction to *The World of Randolph Bourne*. New York: Dutton, 1965.

VAN WYCK BROOKS

Principal Works

The Wine of the Puritans: A Study of Present-Day America. London: Sisley's, 1908.

The Malady of the Ideal: Senancour, Maurice de Guérin, and Amiel. London: A. C. Fifield, 1913.

John Addington Symonds: A Biographical Study. London: Mitchell Kennerley, 1914.

The World of H. G. Wells. London: Mitchell Kennerley, 1914.

America's Coming-of-Age. New York: B. W. Huebsch, 1915.

Letters and Leadership. New York: B. W. Huebsch, 1918.

The Ordeal of Mark Twain. New York: Dutton, 1920.

History of a Literary Radical and Other Essays by Randolph Bourne, edited by Van Wyck Brooks. New York: B. W. Huebsch, 1920.

The Pilgrimage of Henry James. New York: Dutton, 1925.

The American Caravan, edited by Van Wyck Brooks, Alfred Kreymborg, Lewis Mumford, and Paul Rosenfeld. New York: Macauley Company, 1927.

Emerson and Others. New York: Dutton, 1927.

Sketches in Criticism. New York: Dutton, 1932.

The Life of Emerson. New York: Dutton, 1932.

The Journal of Gamaliel Bradford, 1883–1932, edited by Van Wyck Brooks. New York: Houghton, Mifflin, 1933.

Three Essays on America. New York: Dutton, 1934.

The Flowering of New England, 1815–1865. New York: Dutton, 1936.

New England: Indian Summer, 1865–1915. New York: Dutton, 1940.

Opinions of Oliver Allston. New York: Dutton, 1941.

Roots of American Culture and Other Essays by Constance Rourke, edited by Van Wyck Brooks. New York: Harcourt, Brace, 1942.

The World of Washington Irving. New York: Dutton, 1944.

The Times of Melville and Whitman. New York: Dutton, 1947.

A Chilmark Miscellany. New York: Dutton, 1948.

The Confident Years, 1885–1915. New York: Dutton, 1952.

The Writer in America. New York: Dutton, 1953.

Scenes and Portraits: Memories of Childhood and Youth. New York: Dutton, 1954.

John Sloan: A Painter's Life. New York: Dutton, 1955.

Helen Keller: Sketch for a Portrait. New York: Dutton, 1956.

Days of the Phoenix: The Nineteen-Twenties I Remember. New York: Dutton, 1957.

Dream of Arcadia: American Writers and Artists in Italy, 1760–1915. New York: Dutton, 1958.

From a Writer's Notebook. New York: Dutton, 1958.

Howells: His Life and World. New York: Dutton, 1959.

From the Shadow of the Mountain: My Post-Meridian Years. New York: Dutton, 1961.

Fenollosa and His Circle, with Other Essays in Biography. New York: Dutton, 1962.

Introduction to *Writers at Work: The Paris Review Interviews, Second Series.* New York: Viking Press, 1963.

The Van Wyck Brooks–Lewis Mumford Letters, edited by Robert E. Spiller. New York: Dutton, 1970.

Studies in Criticism and Appreciation

Angoff, Charles. "Van Wyck Brooks and Our Critical Tradition," *Literary Review*, 7:27–35 (Autumn 1963).

Brooks, Gladys. *If Strangers Meet*. New York: Harcourt, Brace, and World, 1967.

Cargill, Oscar. "The Ordeal of Van Wyck Brooks," *College English*, 8:55–61 (November 1946).

Collins, Seward. "Criticism in America: The Origins of a Myth," *Bookman*, 71:241–256, 353–364 (June 1930).

Colum, Mary. "An American Critic: Van Wyck Brooks," *Dial*, 76:33–40 (January 1924).

Cowley, Malcolm. "Van Wyck Brooks: A Career in Retrospect," *Saturday Review*, 46:17–18, 38 (May 25, 1963).

Dupee, F. W. "The Americanism of Van Wyck Brooks," in William Phillips and Philip Rahv, editors, *The Partisan Reader*. New York: Dial Press, 1946.

Foerster, Norman. "The Literary Prophets," *Bookman*, 72:35–44 (September 1930).

Glicksberg, Charles I. "Van Wyck Brooks," *Sewanee Review*, 43:175–186 (April–June 1935).

Hyman, Stanley Edgar. "Van Wyck Brooks and Biographical Criticism," in *The Armed Vision*. New York: Knopf, 1948.

Jones, Howard M. "The Pilgrimage of Van Wyck Brooks," *Virginia Quarterly Review*, 8:439–442 (July 1932).

Kenton, Edna. "Henry James and Mr. Van Wyck Brooks," *Bookman*, 42:153–157 (October 1925).

Kohler, Dayton. "Van Wyck Brooks: Traditionally American," *College English*, 2:629–639 (April 1941).

Leary, Lewis. "Standing with Reluctant Feet," in *A Casebook on Mark Twain's Wound*. New York: Crowell, 1962.

Leavis, F. R. "The Americanness of American Literature," in *Anna Kerenina and Other Essays*. New York: Pantheon Books, 1967.

Maynard, Theodore. "Van Wyck Brooks," *Catholic World*, 140:412–421 (January 1935).

Morrison, Claudia C. "Van Wyck Brooks's Analysis of Mark Twain," in *Freud and the Critic*. Chapel Hill: University of North Carolina Press, 1968.

Munson, Gorham B. "Van Wyck Brooks: His Sphere and His Encroachments," *Dial*, 78:28–42 (January 1925).

Rosenfeld, Paul. "Van Wyck Brooks," in *Port of New York*. New York: Harcourt, Brace, 1924; Urbana: University of Illinois Press, 1961.

Smith, Bernard. "Van Wyck Brooks," in *After the Genteel Tradition*, edited by Malcolm Cowley. New York: Norton, 1937; Carbondale: Southern Illinois University Press, 1964.

Wade, John D. "The Flowering of New England," *Southern Review*, 2:807–814 (Fall 1937).

Wasserstrom, William. *The Legacy of Van Wyck Brooks*. Carbondale and Edwardsville: Southern Illinois University Press, 1971.

Wellek, René. "Van Wyck Brooks and a National Literature," *American Prefaces*, 7:292–306 (Summer 1942).

Wescott, Glenway. "Van Wyck Brooks," *New York Times Book Review*, December 13, 1964, p. 2.
Wilson, Edmund. "Imaginary Conversations: Mr. F. Scott Fitzgerald and Mr. Van Wyck Brooks," *New Republic*, 38:249–254 (April 30, 1924). Reprinted in *The Shores of Light*. New York: Farrar, Straus, and Young, 1952.

KENNETH BURKE

Works

BOOKS

The White Oxen & Other Stories. New York: Albert and Charles Boni, 1924; Berkeley: University of California Press, 1968 (paper).
Counter-Statement. New York: Harcourt, 1931; Los Altos, Calif.: Hermes, 1953; Berkeley: University of California Press, 1968 (paper).
Towards a Better Life. New York: Harcourt, 1932; Berkeley: University of California Press, 1966.
Permanence and Change. New York: New Republic, 1935; Los Altos, Calif.: Hermes, 1954; Indianapolis: Bobbs-Merrill, 1965 (paper).
Attitudes toward History. New York: New Republic, 1937; Los Altos, Calif.: Hermes, 1959; Boston: Beacon Press, 1961 (paper).
The Philosophy of Literary Form. Baton Rouge: Louisiana State University Press, 1941, 1967; New York: Random House, 1957 (paper); Berkeley: University of California Press, 1973 (paper).
A Grammar of Motives. New York: Prentice-Hall, 1945; Berkeley: University of California Press, 1969 (paper).
A Rhetoric of Motives. New York: Prentice-Hall, 1950; Berkeley: University of California Press, 1969 (paper).
Book of Moments: Poems 1915–1954. Los Altos, Calif.: Hermes, 1955.
The Rhetoric of Religion. Boston: Beacon Press, 1961; Berkeley: University of California Press, 1970 (paper).
A Grammar of Motives and A Rhetoric of Motives. Cleveland: World, 1962 (paper).
Perspectives by Incongruity, edited by Stanley Edgar Hyman, Bloomington: Indiana University Press, 1964 (paper).
Terms for Order, edited by Stanley Edgar Hyman. Bloomington: Indiana University Press, 1964 (paper).
Language as Symbolic Action. Berkeley: University of California Press, 1966.
Collected Poems: 1915–1967. Berkeley: University of California Press, 1968.
Dramatism and Development. Barre, Mass.: Barre Publications, 1972.

UNCOLLECTED WORKS

Revolutionary Symbolism in America," in *American Writers' Congress*, edited by Henry Hart. London: Martin Lawrence, 1935.
"The Relation between Literature & Science," in *The Writer in a Changing World*, edited by Henry Hart. New York: Equinox Cooperative Press, 1937.
"Policy Made Person: Whitman's Verse & Prose — Salient Traits," in *Leaves of Grass:*

One Hundred Years After, edited by M. Hindus. Stanford, Calif.: Stanford University Press, 1955.

"The Anaesthetic Revelation of Herone Liddell," *Kenyon Review*, 19:505–559 (Autumn 1957).

"Rhetoric — Old & New," in *New Rhetorics*, edited by M. Steinmann, Jr. New York: Scribner's, 1967.

"On Stress, Its Seeking," in *Why Man Takes Chances*, edited by S. Z. Klausner. Garden City, N.Y.: Doubleday, 1968.

"Towards Helhaven: Three Stages of a Vision," *Sewanee Review*, 79:11–25 (Winter 1971).

"As I Was Saying," *Michigan Quarterly Review*, 9:9–27 (Winter 1972).

Critical Studies

Bewley, Marius. "Kenneth Burke as Literary Critic," in *The Complex Fate*. London: Chatto and Windus, 1952.

Fergusson, Francis. "Kenneth Burke's *Grammar of Motives*," in *The Human Image in Dramatic Literature*. Garden City, N.Y.: Doubleday, 1957.

Frank, Armin Paul. *Kenneth Burke*. New York: Twayne, 1969.

Holland, Laura Virginia. *Counterpoint: Kenneth Burke and Aristotle's Theories of Rhetoric*. New York: Philosophical Library, 1959.

Hook, Sidney. "The Technique of Mystification," *Partisan Review*, 4:57–62 (December 1937).

Hyman, Stanley Edgar. "Kenneth Burke and the Criticism of Symbolic Action," in *The Armed Vision*. New York: Knopf, 1948.

Kaplan, Abraham. "A Review of *A Grammar of Motives*," *Journal of Aesthetics and Art Criticism*, 5:233–234 (March 1947).

Knox, George. *Critical Moments: Kenneth Burke's Categories and Critiques*. Seattle: University of Washington Press, 1957.

Lansner, Kermit. "Burke, Burke, the Lurk," *Kenyon Review*, 13:324–335 (Spring 1951).

Nemerov, Howard. "Everything, Preferably All at Once: Coming to Terms with Kenneth Burke," *Sewanee Review*, 79:189–205 (April–June 1971).

Parkes, Henry B. "Kenneth Burke," in *The Pragmatic Test*. San Francisco: Colt Press, 1941.

Ransom, John Crowe. "An Address to Kenneth Burke," *Kenyon Review*, 4:219–237 (Spring 1942).

Rosenfeld, Isaac. "Dry Watershed," *Kenyon Review*, 8:310–317 (Spring 1946).

Rueckert, William H. "Burke's Verbal Drama," *Nation*, 194:150 (February 17, 1962).

———. *Kenneth Burke and the Drama of Human Relations*. Minneapolis: University of Minnesota Press, 1963.

———, editor *Critical Responses to Kenneth Burke, 1924–1966*. Minneapolis: University of Minnesota Press, 1969. (Contains 67 reviews and essays.)

Warren, Austin. "Kenneth Burke: His Mind and Art," *Sewanee Review*, 41:225–236, 344–364 (April–June, July–September 1933).

———, "The Sceptic's Progress," *American Review*, 6:193–213 (December 1935).

Wellek, René. "Kenneth Burke and Literary Criticism," *Sewanee Review*, 79:171–188 (April–June 1971).
Williams, William Carlos. "Kenneth Burke," in *Selected Essays*. New York: Random House, 1954.

REINHOLD NIEBUHR

For the period up to 1954, the definitive checklist of Reinhold Niebuhr's writings is to be found in *Reinhold Niebuhr's Works: A Bibliography*, by D. B. Robertson (Berea, Ky.: Berea College Press, 1954). Professor Robertson's bibliography is particularly valuable as a guide to the hundreds of articles that Niebuhr contributed to American journals in the years after he published his first pieces in the *Atlantic Monthly* in 1916.

Principal Works

Does Civilization Need Religion? — A Study in the Social Resources and Limitations of Religion in Modern Life. New York: Macmillan, 1927.
Leaves from the Notebook of a Tamed Cynic. Chicago: Willett, Clark and Colby, 1929.
The Contribution of Religion to Social Work. New York: Columbia University Press, 1932.
Moral Man and Immoral Society: A Study in Ethics and Politics. New York: Scribner's, 1932.
Reflections on the End of an Era. New York: Scribner's, 1934.
An Interpretation of Christian Ethics. New York: Harper, 1935.
Beyond Tragedy: Essays on the Christian Interpretation of History. New York: Scribner's, 1937.
Christianity and Power Politics. New York: Scribner's, 1940.
The Nature and Destiny of Man: A Christian Interpretation. Vol. I, *Human Nature*. New York: Scribner's, 1941. Vol. II, *Human Destiny*. New York: Scribner's, 1943. (Since 1949, Scribner's has been making available a one-volume edition of these Gifford Lectures.)
The Children of Light and the Children of Darkness: A Vindication of Democracy and a Critique of Its Traditional Defence. New York: Scribner's, 1944.
Discerning the Signs of the Times: Sermons for Today and Tomorrow. New York: Scribner's, 1946.
Faith and History: A Comparison of Christian and Modern Views of History. New York: Scribner's, 1949.
The Irony of American History. New York: Scribner's, 1952.
Christian Realism and Political Problems. New York: Scribner's, 1953.
The Self and the Dramas of History. New York: Scribner's, 1955.
Love and Justice, edited by D. B. Robertson. Philadelphia: Westminster Press, 1957.
The Godly and the Ungodly: Essays on the Religious and Secular Dimensions of Modern Life. London: Faber and Faber, 1958.
Pious and Secular America. New York: Scribner's, 1958.
Essays in Applied Christianity, edited by D. B. Robertson. New York: Meridian Books (World), 1959.
The Structure of Nations and Empires: A Study of the Recurring Patterns and Problems of the

Political Order in Relation to the Unique Problems of the Nuclear Age. New York: Scribner's, 1959.

Reinhold Niebuhr on Politics, edited by Harry R. Davis and Robert C. Good. New York: Scribner's, 1960.

A Nation So Conceived: Reflections on the History of America from Its Early Visions to Its Present Power, with Alan Heimert. New York: Scribner's, 1963.

Man's Nature and His Communities. New York: Scribner's, 1965.

Faith and Politics: A Commentary on Religious, Social, and Political Thought in a Technological Age, edited by Ronald H. Stone. New York: Braziller, 1968.

The Democratic Experience: Past and Prospects, with Paul E. Sigmund. New York: Praeger, 1969.

Critical and Biographical Studies

Allen, E. L. *A Guide to the Thought of Reinhold Niebuhr*. London: Hodder and Stoughton, n.d.

Bingham, June. *Courage to Change: An Introduction to the Life and Thought of Reinhold Niebuhr*. New York: Scribner's, 1961.

Carnell, Edward J. *The Theology of Reinhold Niebuhr*. Grand Rapids, Mich.: W. B. Eerdmans, 1951.

Davies, D. R. *Reinhold Niebuhr: Prophet from America*. London: James Clarke, 1945.

Fackre, Gabriel J. *The Promise of Reinhold Niebuhr*. Philadelphia: Lippincott, 1970.

Hammar, George. *Christian Realism in Contemporary American Theology: A Study of Reinhold Niebuhr, W. M. Horton, and H. P. Van Dusen*. Uppsala, Sweden: A.-B. Lundequistska Bokhandeln, 1940.

Harland, Gordon. *The Thought of Reinhold Niebuhr*. New York: Oxford University Press, 1960.

Hofmann, Hans. *The Theology of Reinhold Niebuhr*, translated by Louise Pettibone Smith. New York: Scribner's, 1956.

Kegley, Charles W., and Robert W. Bretall, editors. *Reinhold Niebuhr: His Religious, Social, and Political Thought*. (Vol. II of The Library of Living Theology.) New York: Macmillan, 1956. (Includes essays by Emil Brunner, Paul Tillich, John C. Bennett, Paul Ramsey, Arthur Schlesinger, Jr., Kenneth Thompson, Richard Kroner, Daniel D. Williams, Alan Richardson, William John Wolf, Paul Lehmann, and others.)

Landon, Harold R., editor. *Reinhold Niebuhr: A Prophetic Voice in Our Time*. Greenwich, Conn.: Seabury Press, 1962. ("Essays in Tribute" by Paul Tillich, John C. Bennett, and Hans J. Morgenthau.)

Meyer, Donald B. *The Protestant Search for Political Realism, 1919–1941*. Berkeley and Los Angeles: University of California Press, 1960. See especially Chapters XIII and XIV.

Stone, Ronald H. *Reinhold Niebuhr: Prophet to Politicians*. Nashville and New York: Abingdon, 1972.

Thelen, Mary Frances. *Man as Sinner in Contemporary American Realistic Theology*. New York: King's Crown Press, 1946.

Vignaux, Georgette P. *La théologie de l'histoire chez Reinhold Niebuhr*. Neuchâtel: Delachaux & Niestlé, 1957.

ABOUT THE AUTHORS

ABOUT THE AUTHORS

LOUIS AUCHINCLOSS is the author of many novels, short stories, and works of literary criticism, including *Pioneers and Caretakers: A Study of Nine American Women Novelists.* His autobiography is titled *A Writer's Capital.*

GAY WILSON ALLEN is a professor emeritus of English at New York University. He is the author of a number of books, among them *William James, a Biography* and *The Solitary Singer: A Critical Biography of Walt Whitman*, and editor of *A William James Reader.*

PHILIP WAGNER, who succeeded H. L. Mencken as editor of the *Baltimore Evening Sun*, retired as editor of the *Sun* in 1964. He writes a syndicated newspaper column on public affairs and is the author of a number of books on wine growing.

SHERMAN PAUL is M. F. Carpenter Professor of American Literature at the University of Iowa. His books include *Emerson's Angle of Vision*, *The Shores of America: Thoreau's Inward Exploration*, *Louis Sullivan: An Architect in American Thought*, *Edmund Wilson*, *The Music of Survival*, and *Hart's Bridge.*

WILLIAM WASSERSTROM, who has written or edited seven books, chiefly on modern American and European literature, is a professor of English at Syracuse University. Among his books are *Heiress of All the Ages*, *The Time of the Dial*, and *Civil Liberties and the Arts.*

MERLE E. BROWN is a professor of English at the University of Iowa. He is the author of *Neo-Idealistic Aesthetics* and *Wallace Stevens: The Poem as Act*, and he has published numerous essays in American and Italian criticism.

NATHAN A. SCOTT, JR., is Shailer Mathews Professor of Theology and Literature in the Divinity School and the Department of English at the University of Chicago. Among his numerous books are *The Wild Prayer of Longing: Poetry and The Sacred* and *Three American Moralists: Mailer, Bellow, Trilling.*

INDEX

INDEX